D1234628

QUALITY AND EDUCATION:
Critical Linkages

Received
JAN 1997
Carrie Rich
Memorial Library

QUALITY AND EDUCATION:
Critical Linkages

Edited by Betty L. McCormick

Eye On Education
P.O. Box 388
Princeton Junction, NJ 08550
(609) 799-9188
(609) 799-3698 fax

ABOUT THE EDITOR

Betty L. McCormick, formerly at IBM, served as Director of Governor Ann Richards' National Conference on TQM and Education, and is now a consultant specializing in Total Quality Management in schools. She is the President of Critical Linkages Consulting in Austin, Texas and also serves as Director of Consulting Services for the Education Publishing Group in Boston, Massachusetts.

Copyright © 1993 Eye On Education, Inc.
All Rights Reserved.

For information about permission to reproduce selections from this book, write:
Eye On Education, Permissions Dept., Box 388, Princeton Junction, NJ 08550

Library of Congress Catalog Number: 93-71524

ISBN 1-883001-04-8

Printed in the United States of America

Printing 9 8 7 6 5 4 3 2

CONTENTS

CARRIE RICH MEMORIAL LIBRARY
CAMPBELL UNIVERSITY
BUIES CREEK, NC 27506

PREFACE

Ann W. Richards
Governor of Texas

In November of 1992, I had the privilege of hosting the national invitational conference on Total Quality Management and National Education Goals. More than 1,500 educators, parents, and leaders in business, national, state, and local government from 40 states and five countries attended.

In the past, numerous governors have held conferences on national education goals. Until this conference, however, we had never focused on a system communities could use to achieve those goals.

During the last 10 years in Texas, we've doubled state spending on our schools and virtually every school system has done the same. This is a story that can be heard in almost any part of the country. We have poured more money into a system that does not produce better quality. The lack of results has frustrated students, parents, and, especially, our teachers who have done everything they know how to do with the resources they have. To renew our schools and communities, all of us have to come together to find the solution that none of us could have thought of alone.

Total Quality Management gives us a way to turn mistakes and failures into opportunities to improve. We already have the goals we want to reach; the principles of Total Quality Management provide the framework that schools, communities, and businesses can use to form the partnership to reach those goals.

This book presents examples of how TQM is being used in schools all across the nation. Some of the people in this book were presenters at the November conference. I am grateful to them for sharing their stories with us and giving us some basic blueprints for building quality schools and quality communities.

FOREWORD

David T. Kearns

A decade ago, as CEO and Chairman of Xerox, I had the opportunity to oversee the companywide introduction of Total Quality Management: TQM, as it is now called. Although we were convinced that the future of Xerox lay with TQM, we had no idea then that the ideas embodied in TQM would find so wide an audience. In particular, we did not foresee the dramatic and obvious applications of TQM principles in the nation's schools. Luckily, others did. The fact is, TQM works in any large, complex organization. Indeed, its principles can and should be applied in any organization, large or small.

I have written about this at greater length, in *Winning the Brain Race: A Bold Plan to Make our Schools Competitive* (ICS Press, San Francisco), with my coauthor Denis P. Doyle. Our uncomplicated insight was that business and the schools need each other, not for one to serve the other, but for each to improve. Good schools are good business. It's that simple.

It is, of course, poetic justice that TQM should find such a ready acceptance in schools, for just as modern business needs the schools so too the schools need business. Not just as a partner, though partnerships are important, but as a model and a source of innovation and inspiration.

Rather than repeat what I have said elsewhere, however, let me xii   Foreword

simply say that TQM is a perfect example of a model that business can offer. But if TQM today seems so obvious and simple, it was not always so; let me revisit its history briefly.

Once upon a time TQM was a novel, even alarming, way to think about running a business. Its insistence on total quality through every step of the production process—from design to manufacturing to marketing to delivery to customer service—meant a complete transformation of the organization. Easy to say, hard to do. Hard to do because old ways and old habits die hard. They are comfortable, and, in most cases, served the organization well—once upon a time. But no longer.

Change becomes necessary when old ways no longer work. That was the case with Xerox; change was essential. Indeed, it was change or die. Xerox, one of the greatest success stories in the history of business, was hurting. We were losing market share to Japanese and domestic competitors. This in a market that Xerox had dominated totally, for decades. To recover market share—as Xerox did—demanded not only new ways of thinking and new ways of doing things but, in fact, a complete culture change. TQM was a large part of the answer.

This simple lesson should not be lost upon schools. They too have a proud history; the accomplishments of the nation's schools are legendary. There is nothing wrong with what they have done. The problem is not the past; it is the present, and, more importantly, the future. Our schools must set and meet a higher standard; they, too, must use Total Quality Management, because the whole process of schooling, from "design to delivery to marketing" must be transformed.

From the vantage point of my recent public service as Deputy Secretary of Education and my responsibility as a member of the New American Schools Development Corporation Board, I am convinced, as never before, that we must transform our schools. TQM can be and will be a large part of that transformation. This is as it should be. Those of us in the employing community—in government, in the private for-profit sector, and the not-for-profit sector—all owe our schools a great debt of gratitude. They have produced the world's greatest work force. Those of us in business are pleased to be able to repay our debt, at least in part, by offering examples of best practices that have a direct bearing on how schools are managed.

For that, in the final analysis, is what school-business interchange is all about—sharing ideas, each learning from the other, for mutual benefit.

With this book—*Quality and Education: Critical Linkages*—Betty Mc-Cormick brings together an impressive collection of essays, by both educators and educational stakeholders, about school improvement through commitment to the total quality process. Yet, as she points out in her introduction, there "are many different approaches to TQM. No one approach is right for all." Ms. McCormick's careful selection of essays provides educators and non-educators alike with the tools to identify how TQM can work—in your school, in your community, and in your state. Everyone interested in school reform and renewal will find this book rewarding reading.

INTRODUCTION

Betty L. McCormick

Educators across the country are beginning to utilize Total Quality Management (TQM) as a practical way to help restructure education, implement site-based decision making, and improve student performance. The private sector TQM journey has been motivated by the increased need to be more internationally competitive. For educators, concerns about student outcomes, increased private school competition and the general dissatisfaction with educational results are providing similar motivation. Educators are also finding that TQM provides a common language to capitalize on the unprecedented level of business involvement in educational reform.

Quality and Education: Critical Linkages is a collection of articles prepared by educators and educational stakeholders. Just as quality and education can be thought of as a critical linkage, so too can these stakeholders be thought of as critical linkages to educators in their pursuit of TQM. They represent community and state resources, in some cases untapped resources, that have much to share with their educational partners. The vision is one of an ever increasing number of educators marching arm-in-arm with these stakeholders, working together as a team to transform their schools.

The contributing authors are from all over the nation. They represent some of the best known models of TQM implementation as evidenced by their frequent appearances at conferences and in professional periodicals. If readers can use this book to replicate these models in their own community, the TQM journey can be made much easier.

The book is divided into 6 sections:

* *School leaders in TQM implementation*—Two superintendents and four principals discuss their experiences. These are educators from across the country and in urban, suburban, and rural settings.
* *Primary links*—Students, parents, a teacher, and a school board member describe their various TQM experiences. They are called primary linkages because every school administrator continually relates to these people as either workers, suppliers, or customers.
* *Secondary links*—A business partner, a consultant, a college of education Dean, a community college president, and a director of a center for Total Quality Schools reflect on their role in supporting school initiatives. They are both customers of and suppliers to schools, and are not secondary in importance, but secondary only in frequency of contact by administrators.
* *State level links*—A state superintendent and a governor's education policy adviser describe TQM initiatives that can support local efforts.
* *Other links*—

    Technology and TQM—An analysis of another critical linkage. The importance of technology in the classroom and as an information source for site-based decision making is often overlooked when implementing TQM. A national education association executive and a regional service center executive, with broad experience in both areas, bring new knowledge to this subject.

* *Appendices*—

    Directory of TQM Schools—Over 60 school districts and schools with ongoing TQM initiatives are included, in sequence by state. Many have provided information on goals, training, funding, implementation tips, and contacts.

    Selected References—K-12 Focus—Provides suggested reading material for further study.

    Author Directory—Provides names, addresses, and telephone numbers of chapter authors.

Quality and Education: Critical Linkages is intended primarily for school administrators and school board members. However, anyone in the system of education who has an interest in school restructuring and/or TQM will find it a valuable reference. As has often been said, "it takes the whole village to educate the child." Therefore, our definition of the education system includes:

♦ School administrators
♦ Students
♦ Parents
♦ Teachers
♦ Local businesses and other employers
♦ Community leaders and coalitions
♦ Community colleges
♦ Schools and colleges of education
♦ County or city political leaders
♦ State education agencies
♦ State legislatures and other policy makers
♦ Governors and education policy advisers
♦ State and national education associations.

All of these players can provide the critical linkages to a successful implementation of TQM in a school environment.
There are 3 reasons to read this book:

(1) A TQM journey does not have to be made alone. This book provides real examples of how people and/or organizational linkages can be of assistance to educators in this endeavor. No one school administrator could expect to have all these resources in their own community, but the book can be used to expand the TQM awareness of everyone in the system. It can provide the common language needed to explore the roles that each real or potential partner might be able to play in this endeavor.
(2) A key concept of TQM is benchmarking—finding the best possible example of a process or program and using that as a model to emulate. This book provides many benchmark examples. In addition to the school administrators sharing their experiences in detail, the Directory at the end of the book provides 50 additional references, by state, that can be used to establish benchmark sites.

(3) An innovative format has been used in recognition of the fact that time is precious and the traditional paragraph format is time consuming. Most of the chapters have short paragraphs and make extensive use of bulleted lists, making this book easier to scan and use as a reference. How many times have you been reading a book and wanted to go back and find a previous passage? With a conventional format it's difficult. With this format, it will be easy to refer back to key thoughts.

As represented here, there are many different approaches to TQM. No one approach is right for all. Whether help is obtained from a business partner or from a consultant, the important thing is to involve many people from all parts of the education system in making adaptations for the local environment. This is the only way to assure the real ownership and commitment which is essential to ultimate success.

Quality and Education: Critical Linkages represents the combined efforts of many people. The cooperation of the authors has been exemplary. The educators who provided information for the Directory know of the demands that will be made upon them in responding to inquiries. Their willingness to serve as benchmark sites and share their experiences is typical of those involved in TQM and very much appreciated. We have tried to include as many examples of TQM initiatives as possible, however, there are, without doubt, some educators whose efforts have been unintentionally omitted. For this we apologize and request that you write to us for inclusion in subsequent editions of *Quality and Education: Critical Linkages*.

— Part One —

FOUR LEADING SCHOOLS IN TQM IMPLEMENTATION

— 1 —

"WE EXPECT EXCELLENCE"

KENMORE-TOWN OF TONAWANDA SCHOOL DISTRICT WINNER NEW YORK STATE EXCELSIOR QUALITY AWARD

John E. Helfrich, *Superintendent of Schools*

Dorothy Vienne, *Principal, Thomas Edison Elementary*

Introduction: Superintendent Jack Helfrich is one of the rare persons who has been in his position for over a decade. This story of his implementation of continuous improvement principles started long before anyone had ever thought of TQM in schools. As you will read, his results have been spectacular and, in 1992, earned his district the first ever quality award for education. The Ken-Ton experience also confirms that continuous improvement does not happen overnight and requires a long-term commitment by everyone in the system.

IN THE BEGINNING . . .

By 1981, the Kenmore-Tonawanda Union Free School District, a system known for its excellence, had undergone the most rapid and radical reduction in size over the previous 10 years in the State of New York:

* The loss of 11,000 students in 10 years
* The closing of 16 buildings during that time
* The reduction of the staff by half—approximately 600 teachers lost their jobs
* The involuntary transfer of teachers to different buildings
* The need to focus on instruction

The Board of Education hired a new superintendent and directions were simple. Get us back on track. Focus on instruction. The order may have been simple but the task was complicated and difficult.

To get the process started the consulting group I/D/E/A, then a branch of the Charles F. Kettering Foundation in Dayton, Ohio, was called in to help conceptualize a program that refocused the staff on the teaching/learning process. They did this by:

- Convening a group that consisted of a cross section of the school community – the stakeholders
- Arriving at consensus on the fact that the district would become involved in an as yet undefined school improvement program
- Enlisting the support of the Board of Education for at least 3 years with funding, possibly as many as 5

This act in itself was rare and unusual as the Board was actually buying a pig in a poke. However, the consultants from I/D/E/A were very convincing as a result of drawing heavily from the research of John Goodlad in his 5-year study of schooling. They espoused the ideas that:

- The school building was the unit of change
- A support system was highly desirable
- A cross section of the school community needed to be involved in the process
- It would be consensus driven
- There would be training of facilitators and others
- It would be evolutionary not revolutionary

Inservice for principals was an integral part of the new and different focus as the district began to move in new directions:

- Two districtwide facilitators were appointed
- Two administrative support groups were formed so topical issues could be reviewed and discussed
- Administrative, later planning, retreats were begun where successful programs could be shared and the district vision could be discussed
- Facilitator training was begun for administrators, teachers, and some parents

Clinical supervision was selected as an alternative to formal teacher evaluation and all administrators and teacher union leaders were trained. Teachers were given a choice as to whether they wanted to be evaluated in the traditional sense or volunteer for the clinical approach. Over the course of the next 2 years, nearly 100% of the teaching staff was involved in the new process. The focus in this program was the improvement of how and what students learned vis-à-vis the teaching act.

The first step toward implementation of clinical supervision was the training of administrators and union leaders. Building administrators in turn trained building teams. All participants on the teams shared and rotated the roles of teacher, leader, and observer. The 6 steps of the program are:

* A pre-conference to discuss the lesson and desired feedback
* Teacher preparation of the lesson
* Leader and observer determination of how best to provide feedback
* Observation of the lesson
* Leader and observer discussion of their observations and how to feed back the information in a positive manner
* Team discussion of lesson with teacher including teacher reactions

Clinical supervision was one vehicle for the improvement of instruction; however, the greater focus had to be long range improvement with plans for schoolwide improvement. Perhaps the most important result of the clinical supervision was the trust and new respect shared between teachers and administrators. With this newly established foundation of trust, it was easier to begin moving in new directions.

One of the first new directions was the implementation of a teacher's union program, ER&D (Educational Research and Dissemination). This program was run entirely by teachers; individuals participated on a voluntary basis and focused on the improvement of instruction.

Thus, the fledgling program was up and running and dubbed "**Building on Excellence**" so as to recognize previous success of the schools. Each of the 13 schools in the district formed a **Planning Team** which consisted of:

* Administrators
* Teachers
* Parents
* Community members
* High school students
* Board of Education members (in some instances)
* Trained facilitators

It is important to note that support staff members and central office personnel were left out of the process at that time. This was a grave error and was corrected a year or so into the program.

GETTING THE BALL ROLLING . . .

The school planning teams worked at the task of creating a **vision statement**, a 5-year plan designed to answer the question "What is the best that we can become?" Out of this vision a 1-year bite would be taken—the annual plan—something that could be achieved in 1 year. The annual plan brought about design teams dealing with one goal or objective each. The design teams would be made up of individuals who had expertise in that very specific goal area. Each team would create its own time line, agenda, and budget necessary to implement their creations. They could also create and implement staff development activities, if they were deemed necessary.

As one might suspect, the first efforts were:

* Low risk—success oriented
* High visibility—this met the need to show success

Some examples of the start up goals were:

* discipline code development
* improved bus dismissal procedures
* site improvements
* improved faculty rooms
* increased school spirit

More important accomplishments were yet to be completed. Building teams soon sorted out the members who were serious about school improvement from those who were pursuing their own agenda, and those who understood the concept of long range vision from those who wanted a quick fix. At this point a second week of facilitator training was made available for the committed team members.

This refocused effort began to correct the results of the initial attempts and renewed energy in pursuing directions more visionary in nature. The new focus included the following:

* Support staff participation on the planning teams
* Board of Education member representation on the teams
* An invitation to the community to be team members
* The encouragement of central office personnel to be team members

The payoff was immediate. Just imagine having Board of Education members who understand how buildings operate and strive to improve. Support staff members who identify with the team's goals are real assets. The community person can offer business-school partnership opportunities and other spin-offs. As one teacher said, "I've never worked harder, but I've never been happier." Word spread that the extra effort was worth the extra work and effort because the positive results were extraordinary.

The first gain realized in every building was the esprit de corps that came through staff involvement on the planning and design teams. A broad base for staff involvement had been established. More people, more projects, and more involvement were evident everywhere.

The employment of new staff members became the next site-based decision arena. The procedure called for committees made up of stakeholders to interview applicants and arrive at consensus on the one(s) to be offered a contract. In every instance, the results of this process were approved by the Superintendent and Board of Education. This same process is utilized in the hiring of building administrators with the exception that the team sends three finalists to the Superintendent, who recommends one to the Board.

Staff Development design teams were established in every buiiding to determine how best to meet the individual school needs and concerns. The first priority was to examine student results in depth to determine instructional deficiencies. Staff development activites were then targeted to those identified deficiencies. Staff development moved from a systemwide activity to a building level process often involving building staff as presenters to better meet the specific needs of the staff.

All staff members are included in the building staff development activities. Having staff development in buildings rather than for the entire district has had the following benefits:

* Site-based directness and intimacy
* Awareness by staff that needs are being met
* Increase in self-esteem for participating colleagues
* A renewed respect for colleagues in audiences
* A greater sense of ownership of and conmitment to staff development days

Some schools hit the ground running; others worked at it with less conviction. At least some tangible efforts were under way and productive results were evident in most cases.

At this point we corrected the fact that we did not include two very important groups – the support staff and central office administrators. This was done and we immediately eliminated the have/have not syndrome. A few factors still troubled us:

+ How will we know when we succeed?
+ How do we get teams to take risks?
+ How can we better communicate what we are doing?
+ Where do districtwide goals fit in?

It was decided to work on these outcomes in our administrative support groups which met once a month to deal with organizational and developmental opportunities and concerns. Subsequently, **monitoring**, a process that would help us know when we were successful in implementing our design elements, was developed. Monitoring was begun with the involvement and training of parents and teachers, who would design instruments and methods of securing data, and was implemented in each school. Questionnaires, interviews, and other hard data were gathered in pursuing that end.

Risk taking was a little trickier as it involved a great deal of trust and assurance that there would not be a problem if a high-risk program was attempted and failed. Over the years we have moved into high-risk, low visibility areas with gusto, resulting in significant gains in areas such as reading and mathematics.

Communication continues to dog us as a concern. We utilized pyramid groups where 5 planning team members communicated with 5 other staff members about their activities and plans. Those 5 staff members communicated with 5 others each and so on until the entire staff had the message. Printed reports were also issued and newsletters and bulletins went to both staff and parents. We still are not satisfied and are refining new methods at this time.

On the matter of a districtwide vision statement and goals, the Board of Education met and generated the first draft, which was sent to all departments of the secondary schools and planning teams in the elementary schools for verification or modification. They were then returned to the Board, edited and adopted.

CELEBRATING SUCCESS . . .

We learned early on to recognize individuals and groups for their accomplishments. We had numerous coffee hours, pizza parties, and staff receptions. These celebrations worked wonders; individuals who were contributors understood that they were appreciated.

Portraits of individuals who took on leadership roles in developmental activities were placed on a **Staff Development Heroes and Heroines Wall of Fame** in the Community Room of our staff development building. In the beginning we had to augment the portraits with pictures of students; however, today we are running out of space due to the ever increasing size of the leadership group. We value this emerging leadership and strive to honor it.

Another factor came into play 2 years into the program. There was no vehicle to help us renew and create visions of the future. It was at that time that a **summer planning retreat** was developed. This concept gave us the capability of interacting with visionaries, practitioners, and others who had a message that would lead us beyond where we were.

At this point we began to focus on student outcomes by benchmarking against every kind of available norm group. This process did lead to significant improvement and has continued.

DEVELOPING PEOPLE . . .

If a system is to flourish it must attend to providing opportunities and resources that encourage personal and professional development. Our district received one of the early Teacher Center grants and grew into one of the leading teachers' centers in the state. We modified our contracts with teachers to the degree that personal and professional development is rewarded on a non-reoccurring basis. This **career step** replaced the former columns that paid individuals for graduate credits, but the individuals needed to become involved annually if they wanted the career pay. This concept has since been placed in each of our three union contracts.

As a result of broadening functions, the former Teacher Center became the Staff Development Center, providing wonderful training opportunities to all of our over 1200 employees. The Staff Development Center has a Board of Directors made up of teachers, support staff members, and administrators. They have complete autonomy over the Center's activities. Responsibilities of the Board include hiring both the director (a former science teacher) and the assistant director (a teacher's aide). In addition, the Board approves courses and the hiring of instructors. They also have the ability to approve graduate credit in place of Career Credits, receiving appeals in relation to these matters. The Center provides courses for our total employee group and is involved in the developing of leaders in the form of instructors for these courses. The district has funded the Center over and above that received from the state and is completely supportive of the operation. There is great pride in the Center and it has received national recognition for its excellence.

DEVELOPING COOPERATION . . .

As a result of the trust that has been built up over the years, we have been able to achieve agreements with our unions on an informal basis. Our last three contracts, which ran for 3 years each, were developed informally. This informal style has been used for our administrative contract and the support staff contract as well. Thus, the unusual has become the usual with our employee relations. Some of the benefits to our district that have resulted from this process are:

* The career credit program
* The devaluation of the college credits beyond the Masters degree
* The availability of elementary teachers before school so meetings and other professional endeavors can be held without interruption
* The institution of **Career Option II** – which permits teachers to apply for a project grant over the summer and receive their full-time salary for that period of time

WHAT ABOUT TQM?

When business and industry in the Buffalo area began looking at TQM and other quality issues, the schools were largely ignored. After a few months we were able to be included in various quality meetings and joined the **Total Quality Network**, which put us in touch with a number of individuals and corporations who were all working hard on quality related issues. This provided the launching pad we were looking for and, subsequently, issues related to quality were explored with the goal of implementing them in the school setting. We were happily surprised to find that many of the elements of our school improvement program fit with the principles of quality as can be seen in Figure 1.1.

When administrators heard about TQM, some had the following reaction: "How does this business oriented program fit with education?" There were nay sayers who could not see the connection between producing goods and services and educating children.

One of the first tasks that needed attending to was that of language. It appeared that quality program people in business and industry spoke in tongues. It also seemed evident to the business segment that educators used funny words that were fuzzy; thus, the job of arriving at a common vocabulary was a priority. For example, the idea of re-identifying our students and parents as customers was, and remains, a hard sell. Teachers and administrators as suppliers is also somewhat foreign. We are still working on the conceptual nuances of the language of quality and see this as an ongoing task. However, it has given us a new awareness of relationships that were forever taken for granted. Seeing a fifth grade teacher as the customer of a fourth grade teacher who supplies him or her students can create a high level of awareness that there is someone who must deal with the results of one's work and that of one's customers, the students.

The Relationship of School Improvement to Quality Issues	
Improvement Program Elements	*Quality Principles*
1. Personal — Professional Development — Career Credits	Human Resource Development — Continuous Improvement
2. Avoiding Failure	Zero Defects 6 Sigma
3. Networking With The Best School — Comparing Results	Benchmarking
4. Consensus — Shared Decisions	Quality Circles Collaborative Decisions
5. Data Driven Decisions	Management by Fact

FIGURE 1.1

Some of the key concepts of quality that relate to schools are as follows:

* Determining customer needs/expectations
* Achieving customer satisfaction
* Continuous improvement
* Expecting involvement in the decision process and accepting responsibility for achieving quality results
* Focusing on the customer
* Effective communication
* Commitment to personnel development
* Long term commitment of CEO and Board
* Valuing rewards and recognition
* Exceeding customer demands or expectations
* Benchmarking against the best

Although these items are disjointed, they can be embedded in school-based improvement programs and will improve their effectiveness. For instance, the idea of continuous improvement certainly has a place in any vision statement and should become a part of that school culture.

Another concept that enhances the educational process is that of benchmarking—comparing yourself to the best. This approach relates to the idea that what gets measured gets attention and what gets rewarded gets more attention. So identification of outcomes, measuring progress toward achieving them, and rewarding attainment can produce very powerful results.

As we develop our plans for improvement we are paying more attention to quality indicators and outcomes than ever before. We are working on becoming more precise and rigorous in defining quality outcomes, determining the requirements of our customers, and striving to exceed those expectations. There is some evidence that leads us to believe that American parents do not demand or expect enough from their children; thus, to meet those lowered expectations will produce results that are average or slightly above. We must do better than that! This insight may be the crux of our national dilemma in education.

On the other hand, there are some things that are being done in our pursuit of quality:

* Involving our stakeholders in the process
* Implementing our visionary planning process which does not get problem solving mixed-up with the vision quest

+ Developing human resources which involve all of our employees on an annual basis
+ Applying real measurement to our benchmarking processes
+ Exceeding customer expectations

It was interesting to talk to a principal recently and hear that she used an analogy of quality in trying to make a point with a teacher. It was noted that it is a good experience to have someone respond who puts the customer first when calling a business for service. The teacher was reluctant to contact a parent in the evening as it was not during school hours, but when the analogy was made it became crystal clear that customer satisfaction would compel her to make a call at the parent's convenience. It was not a big issue, but one that illustrated the use of a quality approach to improve our operation.

Another application of a quality principle is our effort to assess customer satisfaction. Each of our schools and the central office are calling 10 to 15 of our customers a week and asking three very simple questions.

+ What pleases you about our schools?
+ Is there anything that you would like to see improved?
+ How can we become more effective?

Over the course of a year, or even a semester, a great deal of information relating to customer satisfaction can be amassed. We will also have some ideas as to what common concerns there are about our individual schools and, when collated, about our district in general. It seems certain that we will be able to acquire some very valuable information about ourselves as a result of this polling.

We are in the process of installing the language of quality. It will not replace everything that we have done, but does lend itself to changing our perceptions as to what we are about as a district and how we interrelate with various groups. It will also give us new directions as we strive to become world class in all our efforts.

The idea of zero defects is also a very compelling concept. We have a much more difficult job in pursuing this goal than our counterparts in industry. Widgets do not have a mind of their own or suffer either the advantages or disadvantages of their culture and environment. However, the prevention of defects or failure is a concept worth pursuing and refining in the coming years. By getting to youngsters who are at risk in their preschool or kindergarten years, we may well be able to avoid the failure syndrome, which is most difficult to conquer in later years. We have a lot to learn in this respect, but need to capitalize on what business and industry have developed in this arena.

EXCELSIOR . . .

In 1991, Governor Mario Cuomo conceived the idea of instituting a New York Quality Award based on criteria similar to those of the Malcolm Baldrige national recognition program. However, Governor Cuomo thought it wise to include the public and private sector educational institutions, from preschool through university levels. In addition, governmental agencies would also be given a chance to pursue this recognition.

In 1992, the first awards were made and four winners were announced by the Governor. Two were private sector industries, one was a governmental agency, and one was a school district. The Kenmore-Tonawanda Union Free School District was able to demonstrate, through a written application, the rigor of a 2-day site visit from four, very well qualified, examiners, and a final review by a panel of judges, that it was worthy of being the educational recipient. The criteria used for the selection process were:

+ Leadership
+ Information and Analysis
+ Strategic Quality Planning
+ Human Resource Excellence
+ Quality Assurance of Programs and Services
+ Quality Results
+ Client/Constituent Satisfaction

Completing the application involved a writing team of 35 individuals including administrators, teachers, support staff members, and parents. The writing team was truly a mirror image of our stakeholders and was charged with the task of reducing our recent history and operation to writing. The effort was headed up by the Administrative Assistant to the Superintendent and, due to a very short time line, became an all out blitz to condense 11 years of development into a 75 page report.

It was a grueling task, but one which paid off in unanticipated ways:

+ It constituted a history of our school improvement efforts
+ It gave us cause to celebrate about some of our accomplishments
+ It focused our efforts on areas which needed to be improved

• New vistas were opened up for us to pursue in the area of Quality

Looking at the Excelsior award in relation to W. Edwards Deming's 14 points for quality improvement, gives an instant picture of how our district was judged on Quality related principles (Figure 1.2). This certainly does not imply that we were tops in any of the categories, but gives the global perspective of what is considered to be important. It is easy to see that the expectations for the Excelsior Award relate

RELATIONSHIP BETWEEN DEMING AND EXCELSIOR CRITERIA

EXCELSIOR CRITERIA

DEMING'S 14 POINTS	Leadership	Info & Analysis	Planning	Human Resources	Quality Results	Quality Assurance	Customer Satisfaction
1. Constancy of Purpose		X					
2. Adopt A New Philosophy	X						X
3. Cease Mass Inspection			X	X			X
4. End Low Bid Purchasing			X		X	X	
5. Improve Constantly	X	X	X	X	X	X	X
6. Institute Training	X		X	X		X	
7. Institute Leadership			X				
8. Drive Out Fear					X		
9. Break Down Barriers		X			X	X	X
10. Eliminate Slogans	X				X		
11. Eliminate Arbitrary Targets			X		X		
12. Increase Joy in Job					X		
13. Encourage Education				X	X		X
14. Top Management Commitment		X		X			X

FIGURE 1.2

to all of Deming's 14 points. It must be noted that our performance in some of the areas was certainly stronger than others. For example, our Staff Development Center is certainly a strength when it comes to human resource development. On the other hand, we do not have a great deal of latitude in our bidding processes and must go with the low bid unless there is a compelling reason not to do so.

In the end, we won the award because we had developed a value system and culture that was based on quality principles. This was done unknowingly as the total quality movement was not yet part of the developmental efforts in business when we started our school improvement program. It became evident, however, that there were many parallels that only needed to be identified and translated into the language of quality.

And so our voyage in search of the methods and content that will truly make us world class continues. We have been reluctant to call our program anything, as once it is named we face the danger of becoming "it," whatever it is. It is our opinion that we will forever be pursuing the improvement of our schools and that is the way it should be!

SUMMARY

Total Quality Management in education has little meaning without quality results:

Pupil Drop Out rate and Percent of Graduates Continuing their Education show the classroom impact of Total Quality Management. (Figures 1.3 and 1.4.)

Quality outcomes have resulted in Kenmore-Town of Tonawanda Union Free School District serving as a role model for other districts inside and outside New York State. The networking opportunities have benefited everyone.

The following is a partial list of networking districts: Mansfield, Ohio; Washington, Ohio; Plain Loco, Ohio; Bayshore, New York; Hauppauge, New York; Crawford School, Meadville, Pennsylvania; Cranston School, Cranston, Rhode Island.

Total Quality Management means being visionary and setting standards of excellence. Our district is rapidly leading the way toward new assessment in utilizing portfolios' for assessment in both the areas of reading and writing.

Our primary program has discontinued traditional report cards and moved in the direction of outcome-based education where

Ken-Ton Drop-Out Percentage
1984 - 1992

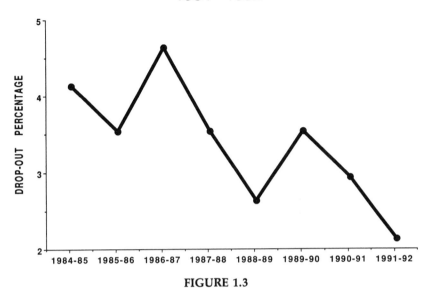

FIGURE 1.3

assessment becomes demonstrated, ideally, along with quantitative assessment.

Our district's success in contract negotiation has demonstrated everyone's commitment to total quality education. Negotiated contract settlements have included:

* An extended elementary day to provide for meeting time
* Peer coaching to satisfy teacher evaluation requirements
* Teachers and administration co-planning for staff development days
* A salary scale stopping at M.S.
* Career Credits ($1,500 yearly for teachers and administrators and $750 for support staff; this is for taking courses provided by the District Staff Development Center)
* Over 92% of staff take 20 or more hours when only paid for up to 15
* Career Credit Option II is available for anyone—teacher/ administrator for writing curriculum or program to benefit the district. Remuneration is the daily rate of pay for up to 5 days

Percent of Ken-Ton Graduates Continuing Their Education

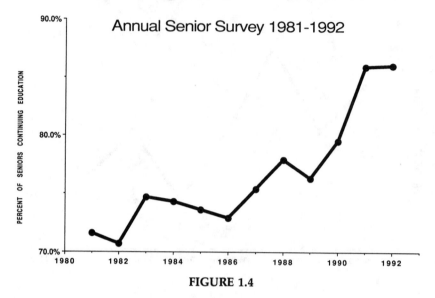

FIGURE 1.4

Approximately 2,000 applications are on file for a small number of possible job openings next year. Low teacher turnover and the district's excellent reputation offer few job openings but make Ken-Ton a very desirable place to work.

Unique to our district is the role that the support staff play:

* Every School Planning Team includes school support staff.
* K-1 Bus Safety Program was organized by the Transportation Department for district students.
* District Employee Handbook was developed by support staff.
* The Staff Development Center Assistant Director is a support staff person.
* Support staff have participated in numerous speaking engagements and presentations statewide and nationally.
* Members of the support staff, who are not school building based, *e.g.*, Food Service, Buildings and Grounds, & Transportation, have their own Planning Teams.
* Facilitator Training for Planning Teams was offered in our district to accommodate the large number of support staff taking the training.

— *2* —

THE TOTAL QUALITY APPROACH IN DICKINSON ISD

Linda Hanson, *Principal, McAdams Junior High School, Dickinson, Texas*

Introduction: *Dickinson is one of the leading school districts in Texas focusing on Total Quality. They co-hosted a highly successful conference in April, 1992, that did much to raise TQ awareness of educators across the State. Bill Borgers, the Superintendent, empowered Linda Hanson to tell the district story for this publication. Linda started her career with IBM before entering teaching and says that is where she learned to put the customer first.*

WHY TOTAL QUALITY?

Interest in the Total Quality Approach in the Dickinson Independent
School District was peaked by several factors:

- A progressive school board that had 4 members involved in
  various stages of the Total Quality Approach in their own
  business careers
- An innovative superintendent always on the cutting edge of
  developments usable to improve the process and product of
  education for the district's most important customers—parents
  and students
- Employees of the district at various levels who were associated with people involved in the quality movement but were
  outside of education
- A supportive and involved bedroom community consisting of
  many workers in various types of businesses and industries
  who were experiencing the thrust of the total quality movement in their own careers
- A new state Commissioner of Education who allowed the idea
  of change to be considered by relaxing the total control and

mandates mindset at the state level to more decentralized control and accountability at the local level.

Once awareness of the Total Quality Approach began to grow both inside and outside the school district, several factors contributed to the approach being looked at more seriously:

* The district, like most districts in the country, continues to see a shrinking of the funds coming from the national level to support education.
* The state continues to be under an unconstitutional funding system for education. The funding at the state level available to support education is continuing to shrink, and the district is faced with an ever increasing proration from the state which must be made up by local tax effort.
* The population of the once predominately white middle class district has changed to one of about 40% lower socio-economic status and about 35% minority population.
* The educational program was not meeting the needs of the bottom 50% of our school district. The dropout rate at both the state and district levels are in the 35-40% range.
* The district competes for employees and students with surrounding districts who can pay more or offer better test scores.

Clearly the system was in need of a fix, and after trying many different "programs" that weren't working, a new way of looking at the system and improvement was needed. Help in a new way of looking at the system and how to improve the system came from some of our business partners—Monsanto Chemical Company, Sterling Chemical Company, Lubrizol, and the Wallace Company, a Malcolm Baldrige Award Winner.

THE FIRST YEAR

Training

We began our first year with one-day-a-month training sessions for the entire administrative staff in the district. This training centered on:

- W. Edwards Deming's 14 Points to total quality
- William Glasser's *The Quality School*
  Lead Management
  Control Theory
  Reality Therapy

- Statistical Process Control (SPC) tools
  Control Charts
  Cause and Effect Diagrams (Fishbone)
  Pareto Charts
  Histograms
  Process Flow Diagrams
  Check Lists
  Performance Indexing

- 7-Step Approach to Problem Solving
  Select a quality opportunity to study
  Analyze the process
  Identify vital causes
  Collect data on vital few cause(s)
  Analyze data and determine improvement strategies
  Monitor and assess
  Decide and act

- Strategic Planning

After having read and discussed William Glasser's book, *The Quality School*, we adopted 4 points for initiating the total quality approach in our district. They are:

(1) Conduct two-way discussions of quality with all administrators, teachers, support staff, students, and parents
(2) Eliminate boss management based on stimulus response theory and use instead lead management based on control theory
(3) Allow workers/students to assess their own work for quality
(4) Develop teams of workers and students to solve problems and continually improve quality

Also, during this first year of training, Glasser came and spent a day in the district discussing total quality.

The Strategic Plan

Much of the training for total quality was provided by, or with the assistance of, the business partners mentioned above. The remainder of the training was conducted by our superintendent who had received training and materials from these same business partners. We ended the year's training by developing a strategic plan for our district with the vision of being a customer driven quality school district by 1996. Components of the strategic plan included:

* Ideal School
* Vision
* Mission Statement
* Beliefs
* Policies to support beliefs
* Opportunities and threats present
* Quality opportunities
* Quality Process Phases
* 1996-97 Outcomes

The Ideal School—The ideal school is defined by brainstorming ideas concerning students, school, organization, people, and facilities/ equipment and placing them in a cause and effect diagram.

Vision—The vision is a statement of where the organization ultimately wants to be or what it wants to accomplish.

Mission Statement—The mission statement is formulated from brainstormed beliefs that have been narrowed down using the Delphi Technique.

Beliefs—Beliefs are things that people in the organization feel strongly about and are not willing to compromise on considering the vision of the organization.

Quality Opportunities—Opportunities are areas to concentrate on regarding student learning and welfare; structure, safety, and policies; facilities; customers/suppliers; people; and quality improvement. The areas are brainstormed and placed in a cause/effect diagram.

Quality Process Phases—Those things that need to be accomplished to achieve total quality are divided into 5 or 6 phases, 1 phase representing 1 year.

Policies—Policies are developed in view of the beliefs and define the things that must be done if the mission is to be achieved.

Opportunities/Threats—Opportunities and threats involve looking at the opportunities already present in the system which would help to achieve the mission and those threats that exist that could deter the accomplishment of the mission.

1996-97 Outcomes—Outcomes expected from implementing the total quality approached are brainstormed and consensus gained.

District-Level Teams

The main outcomes of the plan included the formation of district-level teams, identification of the vital few problems we would solve the next year, and training for all personnel in the district in the Quality School Approach, including the Glasser/Deming philosophy. The district-level teams included:

* The Management Team
* The Curriculum and Instruction Team
* The Quality Improvement Team

Managing the different aspects of the district and chartering teams to solve special problems are the key functions of the Management Team.

The purpose of the Curriculum and Instruction Team is to define exit outcomes, coordinate the curriculum across the district, develop training plans for the different employee classifications, and institute the training required to implement the training plans and quality in our district.

The Quality Improvement Team identifies the few vital problems to be solved in the district and charters teams to solve these problems.

Once the district structure was in place, campuses and support departments began to develop organizational structures to implement the quality process at their respective levels.

Our Goals for the Total Quality Approach

The ultimate goal for implementing the total quality approach is to continuously improve the quality of the district as evidenced by:

* An increase in the quality of student work as shown by grades, achievement test scores, and quality of student port-folios
* An increase in student and personnel attendance

+ An increase in student promotions and graduates
+ An increase in state-mandated test scores
+ An increase in the number of students taking advanced classes
+ External and internal customer satisfaction
+ Schools and departments with a healthy organizational climate
+ A reduction in the number of dropouts and at-risk students
+ A reduction in the number of remedial programs and special at-risk programs
+ A decrease in the number of accidents and injury claims
+ A decrease in disciplinary problems
+ A decrease in the number of students labeled as needing special attention or assistance

THE SECOND YEAR

Training

During the second year of implementation, two major thrusts were initiated. First, all campuses and departments formed a Management Team and, with the help of that team, developed a strategic plan for their respective organizations which correlated with the district strategic plan. Secondly, 30 hours of training were provided to every employee of the district—teachers, clerical and secretarial employees, maintenance workers, transportation and food service employees, and custodial personnel. All of the training was done by the administrators who had been trained the previous year. These 30 hours of training focused on:

+ The Glasser and Deming Philosophy
+ Lead Management and Control Theory
+ Statistical Process Control Tools
+ Team Approach to Problem Solving

Customers and Suppliers

As this training progressed at the campus level, we began to look at who our customers and suppliers were and how we could identify their needs and level of satisfaction with our service. Several strategies were used:

* Meetings between teachers in the 5 academic subject areas at the grade level below us – our suppliers – to coordinate what we wanted and what they could supply us with in the broad area of "need to know" curriculum.
* Meetings between teachers in the 5 academic subject areas at the grade level above us – our customers – to zero in on what they wanted and what we could supply in the "need to know" curriculum.
* Surveys of parents to determine their satisfaction with our school. This survey was passed out to parents at our spring open house so that we could get a large cross section of responses.
* Surveys of students to determine their satisfaction with our school. Every student in the school was surveyed anonymously in May.

Campus-Level Teams

In addition, campuses and support departments began to use teams – a Management Team as already mentioned, an organizational health team, and a performance indexing team.

The Management Team at the campus level consists of curriculum or grade level department chairpersons and other employees elected by the faculty. This team monitors the strategic plan and the implementation of quality at the school level and is the site-based decision committee for the organization.

The Organizational Health Team monitors the organizational health of the campus and develops a plan to improve or maintain the organization's health.

The Performance Indexing Team consists of some members of the management team, parents, community members, and where appropriate students. The team determines areas to be measured to determine continuous improvement (student attendance, test scores, dropouts, etc.). Once the areas, are determined, a weight is assigned to each area (ranging from 0%–100% with the total of all areas being 100%). An index is then formulated for each area (ranging from where the area currently is to the desired goal). A score is determined for each area by multiplying the weight of each area by the current index. The total of all areas can range from 0 to 1000. (The first year's index is usually around 300 since the first year's performances are generally put around 3 on the index scale.) If continuous improvement is being achieved, the score should get larger each year until it approaches 1000. When the score approaches 1000, the goals can be set higher.

Also during the second year of implementation, teams were chartered at the district level by both the Management Team and the Quality Improvement Team to work on quality opportunities. In addition, administrators began to use the statistical process control tools to help in problem solving and to measure student and staff attendance, student discipline, and teacher failures.

THE THIRD YEAR

During the third and current year of implementation two major efforts are being undertaken. First, each campus is spending 1 hour a week with the entire faculty revising and refining the campus strategic plan to implement quality at the classroom level. The original strategic plan was to implement quality at the campus level, and the current emphasis is on bringing quality into the classroom.

To go along with this effort, teachers are beginning to "break out of the box." Students are learning what quality things, quality people, and quality work are. They are learning how to assess quality and are given chances to improve the quality of their work. In addition, they are using some of the statistical process control tools and the 7-step model team approach to problem solving in their own classrooms.

And, finally, the Total Quality Approach is being applied by teachers in their own work situations. In some cases, teams of teachers are using voluntary TAPS circles to work on problems concerning students and learning.

LESSONS TO BE LEARNED

Several things need to be considered before implementing the Total Quality Approach:

+ TQM takes time, and lots of it
+ TQM requires training, and lots of it
+ TQM is difficult for people to accept because it is a new way of thinking and working
+ TQM is a lot of work, but it pays off

About Time

If you are thinking about implementing total quality, don't think it can happen overnight. We are currently in the third year of implementation and are just beginning to see some results of the many long hours worth of work. Our business partners who trained us 3 years ago were in about the third year of their implementation and warned us not to expect results too quickly. Don't expect instant improvement. In fact, don't be surprised if you feel overwhelmed and discouraged instead.

In addition, because total quality requires a tremendous amount of training, planning, and meetings, be prepared to spend a great deal of your working time on total quality. This can sometimes be very frustrating while you are continuing to put out fires from your old way of managing your business. Don't give up!

About Training

The Total Quality Approach can't be learned by going to one workshop or reading a book. It takes training over time, and, as Deming says, "train everyone." Because the concepts are unfamiliar, don't expect to present them once and have everyone understand. Many of the techniques need to be discussed and practiced and presented again so that personnel can actually apply them. In addition, training can be done by your own personnel if you train a core group. You do not have to spend large sums of money hiring someone expensive. Your own personnel will have a better grasp of all the concepts if they can teach them to someone else.

It's a New Way of Thinking and Working

According to William Glasser, the things that really make total quallty work are lead management and control theory. Because total quality and the related concepts are so foreign to traditional American management and our way of doing business, one should expect to get resistance, and lots of it. It requires a new way of thinking and working, and people do not like to change. It's hard work. But more than simple change, total quality requires a new mindset, and most people do not change their minds and beliefs very easily, if at all.

Total Quality Pays Off

As I mentioned previously, we are just beginning to see the results of total quality paying off. Working through a team, our accidents and injuries are down, and our workmen's compensation fund is in good shape. Students are more excited about learning and are discussing what quality work is and trying to achieve it. Staff members have a more positive attitude about work as they experience ownership in trying to "break out of the box." Parents and business partners are more involved and participating in the schools. And finally, in December, our state mandated test scores at one campus went up as shown below:

	Percent Mastering Minimum Expectations 1991–1992	Percent Mastering Minimum Expectations 1992–1993
Writing	52%	69%
Reader	42%	51%
Mathematics	36%	47%

As a result of all of this is, we have had several requests for staff members to speak about total quality. In April, 1992, our district, along with a neighboring district and regional service center, hosted a total quality conference for districts in our surrounding area which featured nationally recognized speakers. More and more schools are becoming involved in the process and are looking for partners to share experiences. The road to total quality has not been an easy road to follow. Many times we became frustrated, but always we persisted. We now believe total quality does pay!

— 3 —

AN APPLICATION CASE STUDY OF THE JOURNEY: TOTAL QUALITY IN THE PARKVIEW SCHOOLS

David Romstad, *Superindendent, Parkview School District, Jamesville, Wisconsin*

Michael Jamison, *Elementary Principal, Director of Special Education*

Introduction: David Romstad cannot begin to respond to all the requests and inquiries about TQM implementation at Parkview. He has become known nationally for his TQM efforts and is in much demand for speaking engagements. We are privileged to bring his story to you in this volume. His district has used the consulting and research organization, GOAL/QPC of Metheun, Massachusetts, in its pursuit of quality. David is a strong believer in GOAL's Seven Management and Planning Tools which are discussed in this chapter.

OPENING

This case study will examine the evolution toward quality systems thinking in Parkview. It is a never ending story. The aim of this chapter is to illustrate how some of our early work on quality indicators has spawned a gradual expansion into other parts of the organization. The underlying challenge for Parkview, as well as for the reader, is to deepen appreciation for, and understanding of, the extraordinarily rich complexity of public schooling systems. The journey has only just begun in Parkview.

THE ORGANIZATION

Parkview is a district in transition. It was created in 1962 by legislation requiring school districts to consolidate. The consolidation was not a good example of a smooth merger. Three distinct communities were not overly pleased with the mandated consolidation mix.

In 1987, the Board of Education searched for a superintendent. The Board's own description of the community was one where people were hardworking, yet with a rather low sense of collective self-esteem. There was certainly a sense of pride internally, but a feeling that the district's reputation wasn't appreciated beyond its boundaries. The Board's direction to its newly hired superintendent involved:

* Improving the quality of education for all kids and
* Enhancing the district's stature beyond its boundaries.

This was partly influenced by a desire to maintain enrollment levels. Student enrollment is the critical determinant of organizational revenue from the State of Wisconsin. Parkview receives approximately 57% of its revenue from State sources.

In 1992, this K-12 district has 1140 students, 89 full-time equivalent professional staff, 7 administrators, 80 support staff, and an operational budget of $7,500,000. The overall state-certified value of taxable district property is $148,000,000. Long-term debt in the district is approximately 2% of its overall value. Facilities are in excellent shape as a result of the prudent, yet assertive, vision of the Board of Education in 1988 and 1989.

THE CHALLENGE: DEVELOPMENT AND IMPLEMENTATION OF QUALITY TEACHING, LEARNING, AND ASSESSMENT SYSTEMS WHICH SATISFY ALL CUSTOMERS (INTERNAL AND EXTERNAL)

In 1987, Parkview Junior/Senior High School staff were frustrated by low test scores, especially 10th grade math. Staff were also concerned with a high academic course failure rate. On average, 29% of all student grades in a given grading period received failing (F) grades. Throughout the 1980's, the school had tried many different interventions. Among these were training for teachers in curriculum writing and mastery teaching. Nothing seemed to work insofar as reducing an alarming failure rate. Therefore, solving the failure rate and low test score problems were the top priorities of the principal.

Don Albright had been the Principal since 1983 and an employee since 1963. He had intense loyalty to the school, the staff, and the community. Successful learning for all students was, and is, his "fire in the belly." He had recruited a talented staff over the previous 4 years which complemented the very able staff already in place. He was also instrumental in the recruitment of the new superintendent in 1987. He viewed this position as critical for supporting the continuation and expansion of an atmosphere of innovation and empowerment. In a way, Albright believed that the strategic decisions about to be made would be the most important in the district's 25 year history.

At about this time, pressure in the state and nation was mounting regarding the quality of performance of public schooling systems. It was becoming increasingly apparent that public concern centered upon the test scores of students and the perceived performance quality of teachers and administrators. Therefore, the district was challenged, by both internal quality concerns and external market and environmental pressure, to decide how to conduct its "business" in a new way.

THE PROBLEM: AN ORGANIZATION LOCKED IN A "STATUS QUO" MODE

During the late 1980's, the leadership team felt the following factors made it difficult for the district to achieve "breakthrough" levels of personal and organizational performance:

♦ Too much emphasis by State regulators on inputs
♦ Disconnections between grade levels and departments
♦ Nonexistent research & development
♦ Cynicism among professional staff that new ideas were only partially developed and then left behind
♦ Organized communications with professional and support staff was intermittent and loose
♦ Too little communication with parents and community regarding their customer voice
♦ Awareness that a "bunker mentality" had set in among teachers and administrators as a result of the previous 15 years of general societal criticism of the "failing schools" problem
♦ The school year afforded little time and the district had little money for staff training and development
♦ Subtle teacher union resistance regarding possible links between student and teacher performance

+ Too much emphasis on standardized tests as "measures" of
  the quality of student learning
+ Staff generally waiting for the "other shoe to drop"

Given these characteristics, Parkview's leadership team sensed
that staff, though intellectually interested in "doing the right thing,"
was culturally prepared to wait out innovation on the premise that
"what goes around comes around." The leadership group, then,
decided to try unfreeze attitudes so that everyone in the system could
begin to look at educational services and processes in a fresh way.

THE EMERGENCE OF SOLUTIONS

Solutions to various process problems began to emerge gradually in
Parkview late in the 1987-88 academic year. This was not due so much
to any particular organizational strategy. Rather, things began to
happen as the leadership group, composed of administrators and
teachers, started jelling as a **team**—with an interest in looking at the
organization as a system composed of many interrelated processes
and groups. The remainder of this chapter will focus upon those
specific things that happened beginning in 1988.

THE QUALITY JOURNEY

Year One (1988-89)

The staff at Parkview Junior/Senior High School identified **homework**
as the root cause of a 29% failure rate each grading period. The
following processes were changed or implemented to address this
root cause:

+ Ninth Period for students with unfinished homework

This period was scheduled for Tuesdays and Thursdays for 30
minutes. The district provided an extra bus for this system requirement. Students not complying with the Ninth Period Rule were
subject to disciplinary process, leading, in some cases, to in-school
suspensions until the parent came to the school for a conference.

+ Peer Tutoring Program (Voluntary)

This program was designed as a For-Credit opportunity for students who functioned as tutors as well as for the tutees. The major thrusts of the program were to provide homework assistance to struggling students and provide opportunities for successful students to expand their skills in working with others. The program has always been voluntary so as to assure that students are committed to self-improvement. This also means that the full-time teacher coordinator is accountable for ensuring that the program meets the needs of the customers.

• Pilot of Remediation Period for Academic teachers

The remediation period was an teacher assignment in their daily schedule just like any other period. This replaced an assignment that was typically for lunchroom or study hall supervision. Its aim was to provide added time and opportunity for an unsuccessful student to consult with the teacher in whose class the student was having difficulty.

• Pilot of an Alternative Education Program (in school)

In 1988, Wisconsin legislation required all students to stay in school until they became 18 years of age (it was formerly 16 years of age). This put added strain on the comprehensive education system which was already being asked to do more for young people with less resources. The alternative education resource teacher dealt only with student clients for whom none of the other in-school assistance options been appropriate. Clients could not participate in any other exceptional education program. Students could participate for one year.

The results of these first efforts at specific process improvements and innovations are as follows:

• **Failure rate** for students (grades 7-12) declined by 50%
• Number of students on Honor Roll increased slightly
• Parents became very supportive of assistance opportunities
• Teachers and administrators felt more empowered

This blend of statistical and anecdotal data marked Parkview's first efforts to match the "voice of its customers" with the "voice of its processes."

Year Two (1989-90)

It became clear to the leadership team that more needed to be done within the infrastructure of the organization as a whole in order to prevent the problems that the high school was having to deal with. While everyone was excited about the significant results for improved student learning behavior, it was also painfully obvious that earlier systematic attention to such things as homework requirements and personal responsibility was going to need to become an organizational imperative. In other words, leadership began to see this as a **system problem**, not a teacher, or student, problem.

Parkview leadership committed to the need to begin the long shift toward a learner outcomes-based education system. This was done for two major reasons. First, a system which focuses upon learner outcomes commits to assuring that the learner outcomes are significant, that appropriate instructional strategies are designed for both the outcome and the student needs, and that assessments are specifically aligned with the learner outcomes of significance. Second, belief statements in a learner-outcomes based system are customer focused. These core beliefs include the following:

+ All students can learn and be successful
+ Success breeds success
+ School can control the conditions of success

The balance of the 1989-90 school year was focused upon district personnel receiving initial training in the concept of a learner-outcomes focus. Additionally, district leadership explored the creation of a strategic alliance with other districts for the purpose of collaborative development of a learner outcomes-based curriculum and assessment system. Lastly, all academic teachers at the high school were given a remediation period assignment in their daily schedule.

Results at the end of 2 years continued to be positive:

+ **Failure rate** in grades 7-12 had declined by 60%
+ Honor Roll (grades 7-12) increased by 50% (28% to 42%)
+ Students planning to continue postsecondary education increased by 40% (from 60% in 1987 to 84% in 1990)

Year Three (1990–91)

The district continued to support and refine the assistance component processes (*e.g.*, 9th Period, Peer Tutoring, Alternative Ed teacher, remediation period) at the Junior/Senior High School. The results continued to improve in terms of student academic performance:

* Failure rate in grades 7-12 declined by 68% (since 1987)
* Honor Roll increased to almost 50% of the student body
* Students continuing postsecondary education increased to 84%
* Student suspensions dropped 40% in just 1 year

The 1990-91 school year was significant for other reasons associated with systems improvement. This was the year that Parkview linked with three other Wisconsin school districts to collaborate around the systematic development of learner outcomes-based curriculum and aligned assessments. They were the Oregon School District (K-12 = 2600), Brodhead School District (K-12 = 1200), and the Beloit Turner School District (K-12 = 1000). This strategic alliance was developed due to several perceived advantages for the districts, the students, and educational reform in general. This was truly undertaken as a systemic transformation effort. The consortium of school districts (now called the Wisconsin Educational Quality Initiative) set out the following elements as the core of a strategic alliance plan:

* Develop high performance learner outcomes and assessments
* Design of training systems needed to sustain the change
* Design management information system for evaluation and research
* Satisfy State input standards with outcomes processes
* Demonstrate alignment with 6 national education goals
* Demonstrate alignment with Business Roundtable goals
* Utilize Malcolm Baldrige criteria as base structure
* Assure successful demonstration of learner mastery for all students (grades 4, 8, and 10) on Gateway Assessments scheduled for Statewide implementation beginning in 1993
* Develop continuous improvement capacity in leadership

A major component of the change process involved the systematic development of a structure for shared governance throughout the district. The entire 1990-91 school year was needed to create the

Curriculum Coordinating Council (CCC). This was necessary to secure deep trust among staff that district administration really did aim to push down decision making and accountability. Once consensus was reached among CCC members, a process was begun to develop a Parkview Mission/Purpose Statement, a Five Year Plan, and a training design. Membership on the CCC was set up to include teachers as the majority. The Parkview Board of Education formally adopted this new, dramatically different governance design in May of 1991.

Results flowing out of the 1990-91 school year related to the transformation process were very encouraging. The membership of the Curriculum Coordinating Council discovered the personal rewards that are associated often with empowerment:

* Improved sense of self-confidence and worth
* Responsibility associated with deployment of resources
* Security of knowing that the future will be planned
* Heightened appreciation for the power of team decisions
* Clear knowledge of just how much there was to do
* Supervising curriculum outcomes/assessment teams

District administrators specifically empowered the CCC by restructuring and combining financial resources available from the state, the federal government, and the General Fund. Enough money was restructured to provide over $60,000 (approximately 1% of the budget for personnel). Subsequent resource deployment decisions were all made with constant attention to the letter and spirit of the Mission Statement (which had been developed by teachers).

The most powerful early CCC strategic decision was to create and plan for 57 hours of training time for each employee. The CCC also monitored and critiqued products and processes associated with the Mathematics Project Team. This was significant because it was teachers supervising teachers as we began the uncertain process of developing the very learner outcomes for which we will hold students accountable—and ultimately for which teachers will hold themselves accountable.

Another story began to emerge during this year that involved our first process-centered project team. What began as a simulation associated with some basic training for administrators in the theory of teams and the use of the Seven Analysis Tools, ended up as a powerful piece of evidence supporting the wisdom of beginning quality teams with real problems to solve. Specifically, this project team, which was headed by the exceptional education director, identified this problem statement:

All kids not demonstrating learning mastery of expected learner outcomes in elementary school are being annually promoted anyway.

The project team employed such tools as flow charting, Ishikawa diagramming, and basic run charts to fully understand the system. The team then recommended a K-6 system for requiring homework and providing client assistance that could comfortably align with the junior/senior high school processes.

Year Four (1991-92)

The transformation process progressed as the following activities continued while other targets of opportunity emerged for attention through project teams:

+ Implementation of 57 hour training plan for all staff
+ Development K-12 science and physical education outcomes
+ Pilot test K-12 mathematics outcomes and assessments
+ Create project team to plan for preschool intervention
+ Create project team to plan district budget reductions
+ Continue assistance components for grades 7-12
+ Create project team for employee-run food service
+ Pilot test assistance components for Grades K-6

The results of this ever-widening, yet natural, process moving to continuous improvement were very encouraging on both the observable and intuitive levels. The following is a list of some resulting improvements/changes:

+ Grade 7-12 failure rate decline reached 73% (from 1987)
+ Grade 7-12 suspension decline reached 60% (from 1990)
+ Changed to full day, everyday kindergarten
+ Strategic alliance with community for quality childcare
+ Strategic alliance with Headstart for in-school program
+ Expanded overall customer focus to ages 0-18
+ Board of Education approved Homework Policy for K-6
+ Food Service Program achieved dramatic financial gains

It is hoped that by this time in the chapter it is a bit clearer how evolutionary this process of continuous improvement has been for Parkview. There has clearly been expanded empowerment of employees at all levels of the organization. Administration learned to let go in appropriate ways but not completely. A new role emerged for leadership. Its new emphasis was to maintain gentle pressure for continuous change and improvement.

An additional component supporting change in two of the project teams was the use, for the first time, of the some of the tools developed by the Japanese in the 1960's and 1970's. These are the so-called "new tools" for management and planning (*i.e.*, the 7 Management & Planning Tools published by GOAL/QPC as the **MEMORY JOGGER PLUS**). Portions of these tools were used by the author in facilitating a project team charged with recommending budget reductions and also used by the Director of Special Education (and co-author of this chapter) in recommending preschool intervention strategies for the district.

The dramatic successes achieved in both the budget reduction process (*e.g.*, no loss of employee or Board of Education morale or trust) and the food service improvement process provided powerful reinforcement for Parkview leadership along the journey.

Year Five (1992–93)

This paper is being written midway through 1992-93. The content, then, is in a "real time" frame for the authors/researchers. We see Year Five of the Journey as a breakthrough opportunity. The many processes and efforts going forward must begin to more fully demonstrate expanded degrees of empowerment. Also, the role of leadership must become more sublime. In effect, the changing face of leadership in Parkview is becoming less visible in the traditional ways—yet more visible within the many fibers woven into the organization.

In the area of changing the design and delivery of curriculum, K-12 accountability-based mathematics is being formally implemented. This is a design product of 2 years of work by vertical teams collaborating with teachers in three other districts. This will be the first opportunity for the Parkview organization to analyze real data regarding student performance to mastery in a curriculum fully designed and developed in the new paradigm. We are eager to begin training teachers, students, and parents in the use of data for continuous improvement purposes, instead of for comparing and ranking purposes. Student learning is our core business. Therefore, it is in this area that we will first begin seriously training teachers in action research skills and procedures.

Additionally, Year Five will involve the systematic introduction of the Seven Management and Planning Tools into both district strategic planning activities and specific process improvement efforts. The Superintendent was the first to be trained in these tools. He is training others in the leadership team. They will train people in their areas of responsibility. Some examples of targets of opportunity for using the tools include:

• District and schoolhouse budget development
• Designing customer satisfaction/need strategies
• Continuing improvement in Food Service operations
• Team-based development of outcomes-based units/lessons

Finally, the breakthrough year will involve intensification of the effort to implement the Management Information System for Effective Schools (MISES) which is being co-developed with the University of Wisconsin–Madison. We see this as the technological environment in which the following can occur in a system-aligned fashion:

• Monitoring of performance-to-mastery data (K-12 math)
• Harmonic coordination and alignment of teacher training with both organization and customer requirements
• Generation of basic correlational statistics comparing student performance with various organizational inputs
• Creation of a macro research plan to benchmark changes

Reflections and Visualizations

It is surely apparent to the reader that the Parkview Journey has not been front-loaded with awareness and training programs designed to skill-load the employees prior to beginning a transformation process. Our effort has been an evolution. Central to the process has been our organizational aim to ensure learning success for all students. Everything is traceable to this centrality.

Throughout the first 5 years, our organizational development has proceeded in the midst of dramatic social, economic, and legislative conflict (external to our organization) concerning the role and aim of public education. This has required that our strategic efforts be continuously aligned and realigned with a dazzling array of players who want "a piece" of the educational pie. These players range from advocates for special education students to state level bureaucrats to national education summits to business and industry interest groups. There is extraordinary confusion attending to what everyone seems to want. We believe that this situation has created the near paralysis which has gripped most school leaders over the past decade.

In Parkview, our strategy has been, and will continue to be, formulated upon our best shot forecasts of likely trends in the often adversarial contexts of social, legislative, and economic interests. In fact, we now believe that whatever success we may enjoy in terms of organizational transformation has been integrally related to our predictions. These predictions have been articulated to the Board of Education when asking for approval of changes in the way we do business such as:

- The structure of school days
- Budget allocations for training and development
- Redeployment of instructional and administrative staff
- Downloading responsibility for decision making to staff
- Changing from curriculum coverage to student learning
- Moving from standardized to criterion referenced tests
- Refocusing attention from input to output quality

Perhaps the most dramatic evidence that the quality journey is for real lies in the broad acceptance among employees that change is the "new constant" in Parkview and in the profession generally. By Year Four, leadership exerted no energy in explanation or defense of why change was needed in our district or in education. There are no metrics for this evidence. We just know.

It seems clear as well that the concept of systems awareness, if not systems thinking, is distributed deeply throughout the Parkview organization and community. Dr. Deming would be proud.

As we visualize the future, we begin to see so many more possibilities emerging as transformation continues. These possibilities are all concepts, practices, and procedures that in the old paradigm would not only have been unimaginable but indeed impracticable. These visualizations, or predictions, of future organizational behavior include the following:

- All students demonstrating mastery at grade level
- All teachers doing research on teaching and learning
- All students doing research on their learning

- All teaching/learning processes successful first time
- All students responsible for their own behavior
- Elimination of punishment as a form of discipline
- Fully operative organizational macro research system
- Our systems and processes seen as "best in class"
- Fluid collaboration with social service agencies
- All staff functioning as entrepreneurs within system
- Customer focus from prenatal to the grave, and,
- Dynamic accountability (horizontally and vertically)

Finally, our quality journey has been much more than an effort to bring statistical and systems thinking into the schoolhouse environment. This has really been a journey deep into our humanity. It is more than an effort to reinvent our quasi-corporate educational organization. It is actually a quest of infinite dimensions to redefine our individual and collective consciences. In truth, the Parkview School District seeks nothing less than to continuously, and forever, **bring quality with a conscience** into all that we do and all that we dream about doing.

— 4 —

USING TOTAL QUALITY MANAGEMENT IN AN INNER CITY SCHOOL

Lewis A. Rappaport, *Principal*

Franklin P. Schargel, *Assistant Principal and Quality Coordinator,*

George Westinghouse Vocational and Technical High School, Brooklyn, New York

Introduction: Lewis Rappaport and Franklin Schargel have become widely known throughout the U.S. because of the transformation they have performed at George Westinghouse. Often, TQM skeptics say it may be fine for affluent suburban schools, but it will never work in inner city urban areas. George Westinghouse proves that not to be the case. The reader is also referred to Chapter 6 which includes some George Westinghouse student perspectives on TQM.

OPENING

George Westinghouse Vocational and Technical High School, located in the heart of downtown Brooklyn, is in many ways a typical urban inner city school. Although the school is open to all city residents, most of our students reside in the inner city neighborhoods of Brooklyn. Of the approximately 1,700 students currently enrolled:

* 75% are Black
* 22% are Hispanic
* 25% are female
* Many come from single-parent low-income families (876 were eligible for the free lunch program)
* Most will be the first high school graduates in their families

Westinghouse has problems typical of many inner city schools:

* A high attrition rate
* An aging faculty
* Students entering with poor reading and math skills
* Students with a lack of motivation

* Low self-esteem, and
* A history of failure

HOW WE BEGAN

Our initial pilot use of Quality began in 1988, after the principal and a volunteer group of teachers took an initial quality training seminar conducted by National Westminster Bank USA. The bank also conducted an all-day workshop for all teachers at the school. The Bank helped us to establish an annual Continuous Improvement Scholarship for one of our most-improved graduates and we began a staff recognition and reward program. A Quality Staff Selection Committee, representing a cross section of the staff, review staff and student nominations and chose a Quality Staff Member of the Month.

Those selected receive:

* A plaque
* A small check
* Their names announced over the public address system, and
* Their names placed on our "Quality Staff" bulletin board for all students, staff, parents, and guests to see

Our involvement with TQM was minimal until our assistant principal attended a GOAL/QPC and National Educational Quality Initiative (NEQI) seminar in the Fall, 1990. He returned to the school convinced that Total Quality Management, used in the instructional process, would make a significant difference in the academic results of the school. The principal agreed and pledged his support. For the next 4 months, we immersed ourselves into reading all we could about quality. Not having many educational models, we decided to benchmark the nation's leading enlightened industrial firms using TQM including:

* Colgate-Palmolive
* Digital Equipment Corporation
* IBM
* Marriott Corporation
* Motorola
* NYNEX, and
* Xerox

They generously shared their expertise by training us in TQM techniques.

In January, 1991, we introduced the concept of Total Quality Management to a skeptical staff, which for years had been told about the latest fads in education which would cure our educational problems. We felt that if we couldn't convince our staff to buy into the process then the process would be doomed to failure.

On January 30, 1991, the principal stood before the faculty and stated: "As long as I am principal, this school will use TQM techniques and tools to address the challenges which we face."

As a result, the staff wrote a mission statement for the school. ("The purpose of George Westinghouse Vocational and Technical High School is to provide quality vocational, technical, and academic educational programs that will maximize each student's full potential in today's changing technological society and prepare students to meet the challenges of our rapidly changing world. In an era of intense international competition, each student will be prepared to meet the demands of the world of work, pursue post-secondary education, and address life's challenges.")

Our first step was the building of a TQM foundation by establishing credibility with the faculty. We developed and delivered several training workshops. With this training, participants became familiar with the Quality philosophy, the actions, tools, and techniques which would help us achieve a better quality product and reduce failure. The faculty pinpointed 23 areas of concern that we should address. They prioritized them, and we agreed to address 1 new obstacle a month while continuing to deal with the previous month's concerns. Since January, 1991, we have directed our energies to removing the root causes of each error factor.

One of the staff's concerns was class cutting. By using TQM techniques and tools we have been able to reduce cutting by 39.9% in a 6-week period. Another major ongoing concern is class failure. On January 30, 1991, we identified 151 students who had failed every class. Again, using the tools and techniques provided by TQM, we were able to reduce the number of students who fail every class from 151 to 11 by June 30, 1991 (an improvement of 92%).

As we progressed, staff members began to see concrete results, i.e., improved school tone, reduced cutting, greater student achievement, etc.

A cross-functional Staff Steering Committee was then formed by volunteers to address, monitor, and institutionalize our quality efforts.

PARENTAL INVOLVEMENT

We felt that without parental support, our process would fail. In the 1991-92 school year, we decided to continue to concentrate on the 23 issues raised by the faculty while giving particular emphasis to parental involvement. Since parents are considered internal customers of our school, we felt we needed to survey them so that we could best meet their needs. A questionnaire was developed and completed by parents at the first Parents-Teachers' Association meeting, an evening orientation for incoming students and their parents. The questionnaire sought to determine the best day and time to conduct P.T.A. meetings and the topics our parents wished discussed at meetings. In addition, a personal profile of our parents' income level, educational achievement, and family composition was developed. The survey results determined that we would continue to conduct P.T.A. Meetings on Wednesdays, but *now* at 6:00 p.m. Our parents wished to select meeting topics and invite guest speakers. When the parents were brought into the decision making process, they found their voice and our P.T.A. was transformed.

In spite of their decision to more than triple P.T.A. dues, membership increased dramatically to over 200 paid members. Monthly attendance at meetings followed suit. For the first time in years, the P.T.A. adopted formal bylaws and leadership positions were contested at the annual election of officers. The parents asked for, and received, training in negotiating with teenagers, conflict resolution, evaluating and selecting colleges, etc. As the school year progressed, parents increasingly internalized the concept of shared responsibility and they became enthusiastic, creative, and pro-active. In response to the social tensions created after the Rodney King verdict, our parents requested and organized a Family Night on June 1, 1992. The event's theme was that we are one family, the Westinghouse High School family, all working to create a caring environment for learning. More than 175 parents, students, and staff shared ethnic food, singing, and dialogue. The overwhelmingly positive response to Family Night convinced us to continue the event as an annual function.

Throughout the school year, the parents received monthly reports on our TQM activities. Since a key TQM component is ongoing training, P.T.A. members were asked to volunteer for a weekend of quality training. Six parent volunteers jointed 25 staff members and 15 students for a weekend at IBM, Palisades, New York. The IBM Corporation generously hosted and conducted quality training geared to our school at this world class facility. These parents now formed the nucleus of the Parent Quality Steering Committee and have subsequently met as a group, facilitated by our quality coordinator. The parents also held a joint meeting with the staff and student steering committees. Thus, the concept of team building, another TQM technique was introduced and nurtured.

CONTINUED STAFF INVOLVEMENT

The continual application of the quality process is best exemplified by the activities and actions of the Quality Staff Steering Committee during the 1991-92 school year. Committee members wanted to improve student achievement by:

* Raising student attendance
* Reducing student lateness and cutting, and
* Developing a consistent schoolwide policy to promote student achievement

As a means of achieving these goals, they drafted a student contract that spelled out requirements to succeed in subject classes. The steering committee began by meeting once a month after school, but soon requested weekly meetings, after their school day had ended, as they worked to hammer out the wording of the proposed student contract. Their only payment was two dozen doughnuts and the opportunity for input into restructuring the school's learning environment. Members of the committee presented the proposed contract at monthly faculty conferences to obtain further input, comments, and suggestions. In June, after months of fine tuning, the student contract was approved by a 75% written vote of the entire faculty. The contract was implemented in September, 1992.

BRINGING TQM TO THE STUDENTS

A key component to changing the instructional process is the bringing of the process to the student level:

* Can we intrinsically motivate our students?
* How can we shift the paradigm from student apathy to student partnership in the learning process?

We established a leadership class for students so that we could begin involving students in the quality process. The class, composed of between 25-30 students, meets 5 days a week and informally serves as the Student Quality Team. The team meets monthly with the principal and tries to locate ways to improve overall student performance at the school. We also developed Quality workshops for students, and some have taken Quality training at National Westminster Bank USA and IBM, Palisades.

In addition to promotion based upon achievement, other total quality principles are being introduced to our student body.

We are driving out fear by eliminating failure:

* Only passing grades will be recorded on student records; no grades will be recorded for failure
* Any student who does not successfully master the material of a course will not receive credit, but will be required to repeat the course
* Promotion will be based on achievement, not time served

Raising student achievement is also one of our goals for the Summer Quality Academy. Two hundred randomly selected incoming ninth-grade students received training in the application of Total Quality processes prior to the start of the 1992-93 school year. The students were taught:

* "How to do it right the first time"
* Critical thinking and decision making
* Listening
* Test taking
* Team building, and
* Time management skills

Facilitators were those staff members and students who had already received Quality training. We are monitoring achievement of this control group during this school year.

Recognition and reward for achievement have been an integral component of our Total Quality efforts:

* During the past school year, each subject area or department has recognized an outstanding departmental achiever as the Quality Student of the Month with his or her name and picture on a bulletin board

* The Quality Students of Westinghouse, those attaining an 85% and above average, are listed on a bulletin board in the hallway outside the Principal's office
* A Quality Student Recognition Ceremony is held each term to honor our high achievers and their parents; parents receive a congratulatory letter from the Principal at the conclusion of each term thanking them for contributing to their youngster's success

SATISFYING OUR EXTERNAL CUSTOMERS

Our external customers in the business community, such as IBM, Colgate-Palmolive, Time-Warner, Xerox, Motorola, the Marriott Corporation, Digital Equipment, and NYNEX have been generous in sharing their TQM expertise. The Ricoh Corporation, a leading Japanese manufacturer of photocopiers and facsimile machines, visited our school and was impressed by our application of the TQM process. Ricoh hosted 60 of our students on a tour of their facilities and followed that up with a partnership offer for our students to repair their products.

The school has raised over $500,000 in new or additional programs and services. The school received several funding grants, including a New York Working Grant, that assured the school of $143,000 a year for 3 years, to establish a year-round on-site employment office, our Career Development and Employment Center. Westinghouse was 1 of only 6 New York City high schools, and the only Vocational and Technical school, to receive this grant. The school recently received 5 IBM computers, donated by the manufacturer, to be used to further the TQM effort. Other important partnerships include:

* National Westminster Bank USA and the Westinghouse Electric Corporation have established multiyear scholarships for the most improved student graduates.
* Polytechnic University and New York City Technical College have agreed to run coordinated programs with Westinghouse High School; Project Care allows our students to take courses at the colleges while they are still attending Westinghouse.
* The 2+2 Tech Prep Program is another college preparatory program that the school has developed with New York City

Technical College; Polytechnic University students now tutor
our students in Scholastic Aptitude Test preparation.
* School-Business Advisory Councils have been established in
the electronics, woodworking, and optical areas; Another is
being developed with the Jewelry industry; Council members—from business, industry, and the faculty—meet regularly with the principal and staff to suggest ways to upgrade
our programs and make our students more employable.
* The school has been visited by numerous business leaders
who have donated equipment and supplies.

ADDITIONAL QUALITY RESULTS

As a result of our efforts in promoting quality concepts during the
past 3 years, we have seen these significant changes:

* Students and teachers have become more involved in the
school; Students provide peer tutoring and assist senior
citizens in shopping.
* School extracurricula activities have grown. We have added
the following clubs: Darts, Chess, Computers, Leadership,
Math, Optical, Asian and African-American Culture, Haitian
Culture, and Hispanic Culture.
* Thirty-five (out of 150) Faculty members—many with 20 or
more years of experience—now participate in unpaid, after
school brainstorming sessions.
* Interdepartmental meetings have been held on a regular basis.
Members of the English and Social Studies department have
held joint meetings to discuss how to coordinate learning
programs and how to implement writing across the curricula.
* The 3 trade departments have held joint meetings to coordinate the ordering of supplies and instructional problems
which they jointly share.
* Teachers in our vocational and technical departments have
redesigned our 9th grade program. Like most high schools,
Westinghouse has more dropouts from its entering class than
any other. Our Apprentice Training Program pairs an entering
freshman with a senior mentor. For 10 weeks freshmen are
assigned to seniors in shop classes. The 9th grader works side
by side with the 12th grader who guides the 9th grader

through class experiments. Freshmen pick up 10th and 11th year skills, and the senior gets leadership responsibilities. Teachers say there is less boredom in classes, thus less disruption and a lot more focus on work. As a result of the pilot year, 28 freshmen in the Apprentice Training program received grades of 85% or better. Of an equal number of those not in the program only 14 received grades of 85% or better. Also, attendance of those freshmen in the Apprentice Training Program was higher. The marked success of the pilot Apprentice Training Program resulted in our expanding it to include all freshmen after the initial experiment.

• Requests for admission to Westinghouse have increased. We currently have more than 10 students applying for every seat.

During the past 3 years we have learned a great deal. We know we are not finished. As a matter of fact, we have just begun. The road ahead is far longer than the road behind. One of the most important things that we have learned is that Quality is not a quick fix but the beginning of a journey with no end.

— Part Two —

PRIMARY LINKS: WORKERS, SUPPLIERS, AND CUSTOMERS

— 5 —

A TEACHER'S PERSPECTIVE ON TQM—HOW TO NURTURE THE SPARK

David P. Langford, *Langford Quality Education, Billings, Montana*

Introduction: *The real test of successful TQM implementation is when it begins to be used at the classroom level. Unless teachers can become excited about the possibilities to enhance learning, the other improvements will not reach full potential. David Langford has been a teacher since 1979. He has taught music, technology, science, and business. In 1985, he joined the staff at Mt. Edgecumbe High School, Sitka, Alaska, as technology teacher/ coordinator. In 1988, he introduced and began implementing TQM, first within his own classes and eventually in all other school functions. David is credited with being one of the first educators to bring quality concepts into school management and the learning process. In 1991, he was featured in the PBS special "Quality . . . or Else." In early 1992, he moved to Billings, Montana, where he is directing Langford Quality Education—sharing his TQM success story and research with hundreds of others, both in the U.S. and abroad.*

BACKGROUND

Before I became involved with Quality methods and philosophies, I strongly felt that as a teacher I was a victim of the education system. I was unable to bring about lasting changes for improvement and felt continually tied to the apron strings of my administrators. It seemed as if every move I made toward improvement required the consent of an administrator or the budget authority of the school board. Over several years, my yearning for taking risks and improving not only my own classrooms, but the entire system, faded. I became less inclined to put effort into new programs aimed at improvement, less inclined to implement new ideas of my own, and less inclined to support the improvement efforts of others. The spark I had for improving education was slowly being replaced by complacency. I began exploring many other interests because the work itself was no longer intrinsically rewarding—only a job. I was learning how to do only what was required to keep my job and as a result my enthusiasm for teaching and the students' enthusiasm for learning suffered.

Several movements for education improvement failed to renew my interest. The school accountability movement, for instance, had worked to place accountability for improvement on the shoulders of both students and teachers in the form of standards and increased pressure for improvement. However, accountability soon became just a fancy word for blame.

The theory went something like this: "We can improve schools if we raise standards, set goals, find out who isn't achieving and replace them." Although this method will usually gain some short term results, fundamental systems study and improvement will be forsaken for the rewards of accountability. Accountability efforts depend largely on inspection processes which are expensive and require increasing levels of inspection to achieve further results. Quality, on the other hand, stems from prevention not inspection.

I was tired and frustrated with the current system of education. I had spent several years as the chief negotiator for the teachers union and was weary of fighting the bureaucracy. I had decided that the only way out of the situation was either to become a superintendent or to get a job in industry. Consequently, during the summer of 1988, I began taking classes at Arizona State University to update my certificate for superintendent. I happened to meet a local high school business teacher, Tricia Euen, who explained that she and Janet Gandy, from the State Department of Education, were beginning to work with McDonnell Douglas Helicopter Corporation on quality improvement applied to education. Tricia invited me to accompany her to McDonnell Douglas to talk with Jim Martin, who at that time was the Continuous Improvement Coordinator. I thought the topic of continuous improvement was intriguing, but I also thought it might be a good chance to get a job in industry and escape the education system shackles.

In about 2 hours, Jim Martin explained the background of quality improvement and its application at McDonnell Douglas. He challenged me to go back and fix the current system with a new philosophy and method of improvement. Jim also gave me a stack of books, articles, and video tapes to start the journey. I studied and learned about the quality movement and became convinced of its potential for education.

THE BEGINNINGS AT MT. EDGECUMBE

When I first introduced Total Quality Management (TQM) to my school administrators, they were interested in the concepts but not in the application to our system. Once again, I felt thwarted and frustrated. I began to hold others accountable for the failure of the system. I blamed administrators for lack of leadership; I blamed colleagues for complacency; and I blamed the students for poor attitudes. I felt justified in my own accountability movement, because it basically let me off the improvement hook. This attitude was compounded by the phrase from Quality leaders that said "Change has to start from the top!" The top in my system was not buying in, therefore I was released from improvement responsibility. Basically, I was to wait for the top to buy in before quality improvement could take place.

I began to reason that I must be the top of something in the organization and perhaps I was the top of the classroom system. If I could not learn to manage my own organization with quality, then how could I expect the administration to suddenly change the operation of the school? Perhaps, by becoming the example, I could be a more effective change agent.

I turned to the students to help me figure out the application of quality in education. These initial students were the catalysts to persuade other teachers and administrators. At first they viewed this as just another assignment, but when this particular assignment never seemed to go away, they began to understand the depth of the process. I enlisted the help of students not only to improve classroom performance, but also to change the entire school and possibly the state and national systems. The students accepted this challenge and we began the study of quality in earnest. The spark had been ignited.

The implementation of Quality methodology promotes, fosters, and facilitates the adoption of responsibility for each individual in the organization. Instead of setting goals, quality methodology studies the system by which results are produced and asks the question: "By what method will new results be achieved?" Accountability is a byproduct. Quality methods allowed me, as a teacher, to take responsibility for my own improvement efforts, monitor and analyze results, and experiment to achieve further improvements. I did not need the permission of anyone in the system to begin this process. I already had the ability and authority to change my own work process. Quality thinking provided new methods for improvement.

It was the students who first began the campaign to improve the school. Once they had grasped the concepts of quality and understood the tools of implementation they put themselves to work as watchdogs of the system. They collected data on the system and analyzed it to form theories for improvement. One example was the project of monitoring systems questions.

A student proposed a way to assess the problems in a system by monitoring the most asked system questions. These recurring questions would point out the problems in the system. We sent out a small army of students into the system to monitor system questions. Each day they would return to class armed with covertly collected data. We would compile this information and draw inferences. The 3 most asked questions were:

What are we going to do today?
Why do we have to do this?
What's my grade?

To us, these questions translated into lack of involvement in the planning process, lack of purpose for the work, and lack of a process to monitor progress. Planning, purpose, and tracking grades were typically all teacher controlled functions. To improve the system, our challenge was to eliminate the need to ask these questions by developing new processes of learning. My role over the years slowly changed from the all-knowing information provider to the system facilitator. I was constantly working on the system of education to give more and more of the responsibility for learning to the students.

(1) Develop an Awareness of the Current Situation.

We began by developing a broad awareness of the need for change in the system. We talked about global economics and the effect on us as individuals. We did product surveys to discover where products in our area were produced. We studied newspapers and magazines to track articles concerning the United States and global economics.

(1) Develop an Awareness of the Current Situation.
(2) Develop a Customer Focus.

Next we began discussing why we existed as classrooms and schools and who were the beneficiaries of our work. We listed internal and external customers of the education system and discussed what it meant to serve a customer such as society and how we would know if we were improving.

(1) Develop an Awareness of the Current Situation.
(2) Develop a Customer Focus.
(3) Develop a Constancy of Purpose.

We then began developing a statement of purpose which would describe why we were all there. This document was not developed overnight, but, instead, was continually discussed and modified to fit our increasing knowledge of the system. Once purpose was established, we worked to create vision statements which would help us all understand where we were headed. Constancy of purpose and vision statements for 3 classes are listed below.

Business Applications

The purpose of Business Applications is to learn the skills and processes necessary to optimize business and personal financial management through constantly improved systems, promoting teamwork, and improving communication.

The vision of Business Applications is to gain as much knowledge as possible in economic management and to provide the optimum amount of satisfaction to our customers and ourselves allowing us to teach businesses and others what we have learned.

Business Management

The purpose of Business Management is to learn and apply the principles, philosophies, and processes of quality management.

The vision of Business Management is to learn to facilitate the continuous improvement of systems in which we work and recreate.

Computer II

The purpose of Computer II is to optimize student use of technology for now and in the future. If the skills are learned, they can be applied throughout life in a constant gain of knowledge and application—where work is quicker, easier, and more enjoyable with the world at our fingertips.

The vision of Computer II students is to demonstrate our commitment to learning on a daily basis. We will become super at spreadsheets, hyper at hypermedia, dynamic at databases, wonderful at word processing, dominant at desktop publishing, and terrific at telecommunications.

These purpose and vision documents helped narrow our focus and defined our reason for existence. It took the students and myself a long time to discover that grades were not the purpose of education. We all had a much higher purpose—learning.

(1) Develop an Awareness of the Current Situation.
(2) Develop a Customer Focus.
(3) Develop a Constancy of Purpose.
(4) Select Quality Measures.

We began to identify the measurements we would use to determine our success based on the needs of both internal and external customers of the system. We determined that a major need for both internal and external customers was on-time performance, both in the sense of being on time for class and in the sense of being able to produce high quality work within a time limit. We determined that grades, as a form of inspection, were a measure of our progress but only if monitored by the students themselves, and not by the teacher. We devised several methods of tracking progress using grades as data points, and after several years came to the conclusion that each of these methods only monitored the grading process, not the learning process. We concluded that a new method for tracking learning was necessary and we found the answer through the study of Quality Function Deployment, whereby a company determines what processes are fundamental to customer satisfaction and then deploys all available resources against these fundamentals. This process was introduced in 1989, and a new method was devised to track progress based on the following statements.

Students and workers can . . .
- Take responsibility for their own learning process;
- Do their own inspection as they work;
- Record discrepancies;
- Keep charts;
- Investigate and analyze causes;
- Correct causes;
- Cooperate freely with other students (workers) and management.

Fortunately, the results from only 1 year of application were impressive enough to school administrators to persuade them to get involved in the application of quality. From 1989 on, they were very supportive of the effort, which support continued to expand throughout the entire system. Some of the most profound improvements such as improved attitudes, joy in learning, and a willingness to scrutinize every aspect of the schoolwork process were not quantifiable. Even though I was de-emphasizing the need for grades, in 1988, I had enough students jump into the "A" or top quality work category to justify to myself and others the potential for continuing to implement quality improvement processes (see Figure 5.1).

As the years progressed, I found new ways to manage the system through quality management philosophies, and eventually moved to a system of either meeting or exceeding quality standards or needing more time to achieve the standard. This resulted in 90%–95% of students achieving what used to be deemed "A" work. Each time we achieved a breakthrough in management, it drove me to search even deeper for the foundations of quality.

I left my teaching position in 1992, to help other individuals and organizations discover the potential of quality improvement. Many of the student leaders have carried the quality torch into other areas of society, including hospitals, the military, businesses, colleges, and universities. A few were so deeply affected by the philosophy of quality that they dedicated their careers to helping others understand the application of quality improvement. I believe that this methodology could be the answer America has been looking for to improve and transform the education system.

It was tough fighting the system, trying to bring about a breakthrough in management technology. In order to foster improvement, supervisors must learn to drop "the prove it to me" syndrome. It may take 6 or more years to prove a new concept in education. That might be a very difficult process if the individual has to continually confront the system of the old management style the entire time. New concepts need to be fostered through supportive leadership within the system.

Improvement is intrinsic to all of us and the spark for quality improvement is lying dormant in each of us. To nurture the spark, supervisors need to assume the role of doctors and nurses leading and helping people to improve instead of forcing people to comply. The next time someone comes to you excited about a new idea, theory or concept, try the following phrase: "That sounds crazy, tell me more." You may be listening to a breakthrough concept which could have tremendous impact on the lives of thousands of students or school employees. If you listen and then follow with the phrase, "How can I help?," you will be nurturing the spark for continuous quality improvement and lifelong learning.

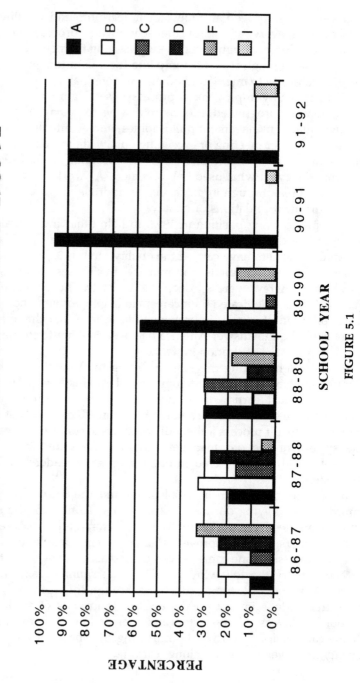

FIGURE 5.1

— 6 —

STUDENTS' THOUGHTS ON TQM—IN THE CLASSROOM AND IN LIFE

Betty L. McCormick, *Austin, Texas*

Introduction: *Both customers and workers, students are a critical link to making any TQM initiative successful. We wanted to find out from students what they thought of their TQM school experience. Several of the schools doing chapters for this book were invited to solicit student comments. Specifically, we wanted to find out what was different about TQM schools, TQM classrooms, the roles of teachers and students, and how the TQM school experience would help them in their future career and life. What advice would they give educators considering TQM implementation? Following are some of the submissions received. In their own words, these students are living testament to the potential for TQM in schools.*

Tina Schaeffer, an 18-Year Old Senior at Mt. Edgecumbe High School, Sitka, Alaska, Writes

TQM in education has given me the opportunity of a lifetime in helping me to improve my daily lifestyle, maximize learning, and carve out the mold for my future goals.

The tools and philosophies of TQM can be applied to enhance any aspect of my daily life. For myself, time management can eliminate a wasted step in a system, thus spare time can be made available. Planning a daily or weekly routine shows me where waste can be avoided, and time used productively. As a result, extra activities or work can fit into my weekly or monthly schedule after planning my activities carefully. TQM focuses on doing things as an individual to working in groups. Group roles modeled and practiced in school are applied to my peer relationships. I have transferred the role of a leader, supporter, and listener when dealing with friends and family from group projects in school. Thus, I am able to see the importance of learning the roles because it's apparent how they apply to other aspects of my life.

Social difficulties or other problems can be solved by using TQM philosophies and tools, such as identifying and analyzing the problem and looking for a root cause. When I encounter a problem with a friend or a problem of my own, I am able to think and look beyond the surface for the root cause to clarify the problem for a solution.

TQM has enabled me to see education as it is and to improve upon it to maximize learning. Project learning, a result of teachers employing TQM to improve education in the classroom, has made education understandable and enjoyable. From biology, using computers to learn human or plant anatomy, to marine science, where students work together to create a small-scale model hatchery, using projects as methods of teaching makes learning fun for students.

We are able to use our creativity and imagination to learn more by using real life applications, such as working in a joint partnership with a company, utilizing computer programs to figure statistical data, or group activities which involve group roles. The competency matrix is a tool used at Mt. Edgecumbe in replacing the existing system of grading. This tool was created using the philosophies of Deming's 14-Points as applicable to education, "work to abolish grading and the harmful effects of rating people." The current system of grading tells nothing about students' knowledge; whereas, the matrix is a spreadsheet used by students and teachers to determine where the students' level of knowledge is at. Implementing the philosophies of TQM are easy and effective methods of improving education for a quality learning experience.

Learning about quality has opened the doors to my future. My involvement with TQM has offered me opportunities for travel and education otherwise impossible. From Boston to Louisiana, other students and myself have been able to give presentations to people throughout the United States. All of which result in great learning experiences. Usually the type of items I've presented are simply scratching the surface of quality in education as I know it, instead of teaching methods of quality management. Giving presentations has shown me the importance and widespread demand of TQM in the business world, and taught me how I would implement TQM in anything that I may do. Presenting has made it possible for me to meet and establish contacts with my audience. Those that I present to offer suggestions such as which college to attend or what field of study would be best to pursue. A few people I've met have offered me jobs or special opportunities for my future. Knowing many different people in various parts of the country exposes me to countless relationships and resources. The philosophies and tools of quality have unlocked a hidden secret leading to a key for the future.

The fortunate young people who learn about TQM before getting into business, experience an irreversible and incomparable advantage to maximize learning and daily living, and hold the key to survival in the ever-existing need of change in traditional education and business management.

I have developed into a strong person by the people that have influenced me, the situations that have shaped me, and by the goals I have planned for my future. My mother and father have influenced me greatly, as has our Native Inupiat Ilitqusiat (Eskimo tribal values). . . . David Langford has taught me the key to survival in the white man's society by introducing me to quality and the widespread importance of its use in business, education, and in my daily life. As an outstanding teacher, he taught me several quality tools of management and opened the door for many others. As a result, my knowledge of quality led to a summer internship in Louisiana with the Neill Corporation. . . .

I have developed into a confident, independent, and supporting person. . . . The presentations I have given developed a stronger confidence in myself. In Boston, a doctor, along with others, spoke to me about how impressed they were after my presentation. Preparing for it was difficult; yet, because my audience expressed wonderful compliments, I felt I would be able to share what I know again. Now, I am totally confident to stand up and give a super presentation. Along with strengthening my confidence, my summer internship taught me to be independent in the work force. This was my first job experience where I was taught and expected to use my mind. I worked on numerous projects which required analysis and thought provoking ideas. In such an atmosphere of work, I was able to find my strength in self-motivation and in analytical thinking. When transferring these skills to the classroom, my involvement in journalism has shown me the power and importance of supporting my fellow workers. I greet my peers as co-workers and my teacher as my employer. Thus, my attitude towards them is that of how I would express it in an actual job. As a result, I am continually supportive of everyone and their work and maintain a positive attitude. The situations that shaped me have me climbing the ladder to success with confidence in myself and with the support of others to have them join me.

My role models and my efforts in achieving my goals lifts me toward a light of opportunities and happiness. With my confidence, open mind, and by supporting others develops me into a leader, contributor, and an encourager for myself and for others to always strive for success.

Terrence T.J. Shanigan, a Student at Mt. Edgecumbe from 1985-89, Comments

As a student at Mt. Edgecumbe, I was given a chance to make decisions for myself. Mr. Langford challenged us to think about why we were going to school and where all of this learning would be relevant in our future. Now students are given the chance to be part of our own curriculum planning process. Students are not as dependent on teachers to tell them what to do. As a student, TQM showed me that the root purpose for a school is to facilitate learning. It's not a place where administrators command and make rules to govern the every movement of its direct customers (students).

The teacher is focused on facilitating not lecturing. He constantly works on finding ways to improve the system even if it seems to be the best. There is no more wasted time inspecting our work, or making us tardy. Instead he keeps track of it and uses this as data which can be turned into ways to make the system better.

I am no longer afraid to go to school. I am no longer criticized for poor work, but rather asked how this could be improved. I feel that there is a purpose for me being there and that learning can be fun when all can be team players.

My mother is extremely envious. She wishes she had the chance to learn in a TQM/TQL atmosphere. She brags to others, knowing that their kids will not be able to compete with me once we leave school. Now my mother is beginning to implement TQM in her daily life at work as well as at home.

In today's' world of business and industry they are not just seeking people with a degree or prior work experience, but people with the knowledge to work on a team, able to understand quality and how important it is to continually improve what may seem to be the best. With a strong background in TQM and a degree, I will be much better suited for a job in any science, math, technological, financial, educational, or industrial field of work.

I have grown in knowledge considerably. I am now better able to assess situations and make faster, more accurate decisions with the data I collect. I will listen to my superiors for guidance, but will not blindly follow them if I am not sure where they are going. I have learned to look outside the American culture for my basic educational foundation.

Many educators are willing to surf, but don't want to ride the wave. TQM/TQL is not an easy thing to start. They must go slow to go fast. When Dr. Deming says "It must start from the top," he means from the top of our classroom. The teacher is at the top. Don't get confused with beginning with the principal or the superintendent, although they are very important players in the implementation of this process. Once the students buy in, it is like an avalanche. All of the teachers will be wanting to find out what is making their students more motivated to learn. Remember that you're not creating a school of TQM/TQL, but creating a school for learning using tools, theory, and TQL philosophy.

Three 9-Year Old Fourth Graders at Edison Elementary School, Kenmore-Town of Tonawanda, New York, Contributed the Following

Richard Ryan

Our school is better than other schools because we have continuous improvement, quality, and everyone takes responsibility.

Andy Vandermeer

I think our school is better because we are improving every day. This will help us in a job. TQM is a great way to get the school together; like parents, students, teachers, and adults. I like what I learn in this school. It will help me in the higher grades.

Jennifer Whelan

I would say to people that it would be a good idea to have TQM in their school because it makes your school a better place.

Jessica Allen, a 15-Year Old Sophomore at Kenmore West High School, writes

With TQM you get more people involved. You're not just a product— you get to see the inside workings of a school, how you come to a decision. It's great being involved. We've made lots of improvements like our Anti-theft Program and Community Club. (Like going to a play and going back stage—it's neat.)

Students here feel that they're getting more attention given to them. They're happier because they're more satisfied and getting results instead of just playing it along like they did before. You see the results, too!

Kevin Mogavero, a 17-Year Old Junior at Kenmore West High School, Added

The outlook here is positive. We received the NY State School of Excellence award by working for continuous improvement. I'd tell other schools to be TQM schools. Try it out—it really does work Our administrators are closer to the teacher-student level and the administration can see our problems at a closer level because we're more closely involved by working together.

Michael Chilungu, a 17-Year Old Junior at Kenmore East High School and Member of School Advisory Team, Writes

It's a comforting feeling to know I have some kind of input in the change process. I know that Kenmore East is very interested in change and suiting the needs of the students. I'm not sure if you'd find that in a school without TQM because there wouldn't be as much interaction between the students and faculty.

Many changes are taking place. We are currently working on de-tracking. I know that students can meet higher standards and most general students can handle Regent's work.

We are also currently recognizing students who exemplify the attitude that Kenmore East wants students to have. Those students who enrich the school and whose efforts improve the school and embody the attitude and spirit to take the school in a positive direction.

Three 16-Year Old Juniors at George Westinghouse Vocational and Technical High School, Brooklyn, New York, Contributed the Following

Rodney Ramlochan

The implementing of TQM to our systematic form of education has basically created a positive reaction in my mind and minds of my fellow colleagues. I see TQM is an excellent strategy plan for pursuing perfection, that can easily be followed by both students in classes and employees in the world of business. TQM is working hard to replace a system in which people are looked upon as numbers, and the normal mentality is one that is satisfied with barely passing. TQM recognizes individual accomplishment with reward and still strives for the strengthening of teamwork.

The introduction of TQM has led to many beneficial programs and changes, but the one that is the most successful in our school is our closely knit steering committee. The George Westinghouse Steering Committee is a combination of concerned staff, students, and parents, all sharing the ideals that lead to becoming the best, and all having the pursuit of perfection branded in their minds. They accomplish these ideals by placing each person in the group in a that is filled with responsibility and at the same moment requires devotion to oneself and team members. Participation is a basic goal to achieve especially when the solving of problems and the creating of ideas are fundamental to the success of our school. The steering committee works hard to solve problems and glitches that arise in the applying of TQM in matters that range from unconcerned students that do not wish to participate to obstacles that block the path of students that wish to be successful. Our TQM steering committee is one of the best in New York and I feel our strong efforts will not only pay off for the people involved presently, but will also pave the road for generations to come.

The role I play as a student has not changed very drastically, since I was always a respectable person and did my share of participating in teamwork. Although, I do see the role of the average student raised under TQM because of the added responsibility of working as a team and looking out for others. The teacher's role assumes its ordinary position as an authority figure and leader of the organization. The only thing that has changed about teachers is their roles have gotten intertwined with those of students on a personal level which may add to the sense of teamwork in class.

One can compare schoolwork as the product of dedication and labor to the quality products manufactured by companies under TQM. My feelings have changed deeply for schoolwork because it is now my understanding that schoolwork not only represents you physically, it literally reflects your inner feelings. TQM has influenced me in making this decision because it has opened my mind to see school not only as a place of learning but as the first place to gain the knowledge and experience that will be necessary in making you the best at what you do in the future years ahead.

My parents are relieved to know that the education I receive goes further than just knowledge, because they understand that intelligence is not the only factor in success. They believe that human relations and cooperation are major points that must be met in a persons life before success can be achieved and here at Westinghouse under the TQM system I am receiving all of the above.

I see my future employment as a direct result of my school experiences. As I mentioned, during these years of high school TQM not only shapes me into a quality student but a quality person. It is the image of a quality person that an employer looks for in choosing their employees.

When asked the question of how TQM has changed me personally, I simply reply, "in every way possible." This may sound funny, but quality is not something a person reminds himself to take to work and then forgets as soon as he's home. No, quality affects the way a person speaks, looks, and works and there is no variation once a person truly undergoes the TQM experience. It is instilled upon a person and will last an eternity.

The only advice that I can give to any educators that are thinking about implementing TQM is that it is the most beneficial program they can ever subject into their school system. TQM is one of the few programs that one can truthfully say that nothing will be lost only gained.

Nicolo G. La Masa

. . . The school seems to have spread the roots of quality into its system and with time and proper care its growth is inevitable. Actions taken by the school staff, teachers, students, and parents clearly demonstrate that the road for a powerful revolutionizing vehicle in education has been paved. One such action is the establishing of a Quality Steering Committee where educators, parents, and students address problems and work for solutions. Questions such as "how do we reduce failure, how do we get more parents involved, how do we use TQM techniques to make Westinghouse more effective?" are answered and then executed.

"Call it a relentless pursuit toward perfectness" were the words I emphasized to fellow students and friends getting ready to speak with groups of incoming freshmen with the sole purpose of welcoming them to our school and introducing them to our programs and quality techniques. This process, which I took part in the beginning of the 1992-1993 scholastic year, was called "Project Welcome." It is a direct product of TQM which I believe is successful in giving teachers the opportunity to communicate with students before regular classes begin. Teachers objectives are simply to answer specific questions about Westinghouse, motivate them, and introduce them to quality in education programs and recognition.

I, as well as my parents, feel confident that this school will prove beneficial for the continuation of my studies in college. This school will also facilitate the ability in succeeding in my career by both providing hands-on experience in the field of interest and a strong academic background, a unique quality that is instilled at Westinghouse. I would define this school as liberal because it allows students to have curricula that best fit their abilities and needs in life while many other schools provide a fixed curriculum where the needs of students in our everyday changing society are not reflected.

Educators thinking of implementing TQM are directed in the right path. Recognizing success and establishing competition between students are incentives that will certainly raise standards internationally and better the never-ending process of education. My advice to them is that is it imperative that they continue their education in order to keep students up-to-date with the rapidly expanding sea of knowledge. This is especially true for educators that teach in subject areas involving technological fields.

Keyur A. Parikh

. . .The teaching methods of many teachers, after the introduction of TQM, has changed at Westinghouse. The change is in how the roles of teachers and students within the classroom are a complete contradiction to regular classes in regular schools.

In regular schools the classrooms consists of a teacher, a blackboard and notes on the board. The notes on the board are expected to be copied by the students for their references for future tests. This method of teaching leaves many students bored. When the students are bored they usually don't pay any attention to what's being taught. The end result of this method of teaching are rooms filled with bored and uneducated students. The basic understanding behind TQM is to work together in solving problems, including the teachers. It seems in methods such as these, the student is the main source of erudition and from this we learn that the teacher must use different methods— methods which allows the student to participate more often, enabling the student to share his or her idea. This method of sharing ideas makes learning fun.

The roles of the teachers in classrooms are very obscure. The teachers are now both the source of information and a student themselves. With this the role of the student has become both a person inclined to learn and a person who hold great source of wisdom. Having the two conjoined we have a school filled with people who share ideas and work concurrently to educate themselves. The key word here is "educate," from the Greek meaning "to learn from within," and I feel with the TQM methods we are.

. . . Having participated in TQM has only enhanced my devotion to my school and school work. I know now that each day spent in school will only intensify my knowledge, for I know that I will learn something new in school and as well teach others from the idea of sharing, networking our ideas.

. . . Experiences such as participating in TQM has trained me for my future occupation, because from this I have learned the basic ideas behind satisfying the consumer. In school the consumers are the students attending the school. The sellers are the teachers within the school. With this idea the seller works together with the consumer to arrive at a final result, a one happy shopper, which is a student learning it and doing it all.

The TQM experience has changed me, for now I am a very sociable person. As my old self, I was very shy and not so sociable with others. After the TQM experience I have learned to be more open with others and learned to show my talents to others. Having changed to a new person I have gained many new friends and among them teachers.

I have learned to share information with my peer groups and teachers. I have seen this newly developed train of mine to be very beneficial. By doing this, both the party that I am speaking with and myself can educate each other. I feel that learning from each other is the key to success in the real world.

After experiencing TQM, I have learned to be more responsible to the needs of others and that of myself. I have began to understand that helping others and not myself only, will in the end prove to be helpful for I know that because when a person is helped the person will never be lost and make a wrong turn or decision in life. By helping students I am assuring myself that the future I will live in will be pleasant, for the students I help today shall be the ones who will run the country tomorrow.

Having mentioned all this, I can truly say that I am a changed man, changed and ready for the real world because I have learned the basic ideas, from participating in TQM to survive in the world today.

The advise I would give to educators thinking about implementing TQM would be do it. . . . The results at Westinghouse are getting better and better. All we have to do now is stick with it. Then and only then shall the 'total' in TQM be achieved.

Following are Several Comments from 6th Grade Students at Dunbar Middle School, Dickinson, Texas, Who did not Identify Themselves

Teachers have told me the quality work I do will be worth extra credit. That really makes me want to work harder.

Last year our teachers did not care if we did not do quality work. This year they take points off if it is not quality.

All the teachers and students are working harder and getting better grades. We try to work more intelligently and so do our teachers.

The teachers talk about putting in quality and working at home on things that we are not succeeding in. Now a lot of the things are done in groups and you are given another chance to do things.

There are mostly good grades for the people that made F's last year. We usually make better grades and the teachers are usually happier. My feelings about school have improved and my school work has definitely changed. My parents feel that I am learning things a lot better. My personality has changed a lot because I believe in myself. TQM can really help all students believe in themselves.

We work more in groups. The students make more decisions and the teachers push us to do quality work. School is more fun when we work in groups.

PARENTS' PERSPECTIVE ON TQM AND KOALATY KID

Betsy Van Dorn, *Editor-in-Chief, Education Today*

Jesseca Timmons, *Editor, Educating Kids, Educational Publishing Group, Inc., Boston, Massachusetts*

Introduction: Parents are both suppliers and customers and without their involvement in the schooling of their children, real substantive educational reform will not be possible. "Education Today" is the nation's largest publication for parents of school age children. Betsy Van Dorn and Jesseca Timmons have contributed a chapter on the exceptional parental involvement found in the Koalaty Kid program. Koalaty Kid was first implemented in Corning, New York, in the early 1970's and has now expanded to over 60 schools across the nation with the support of the American Society for Quality Control. Both Betsy and Jesseca have written extensively on parental involvement and initiatives for school reform. In researching this chapter, they were impressed with the enthusiasm demonstrated by all involved with Koalaty Kid.

Koalaty Kid has gotten the kids excited about reading. It teaches them to do quality work in all their other subjects, too, and teaching quality prepares them for the future. And once kids learn it, it stays with them for life—until they go to work.

—**Carolyn Heitz**, parent and Curriculum Coordinator, Linn-Mar School District, Marion, Iowa

These words summarize the benefits of what may be one of the best TQM programs in the country for elementary schools: The American Society for Quality Control's **Koalaty Kid.**

Koalaty Kid has increased parent involvement, boosted school pride, and sparked enthusiasm at 60 elementary schools around the country. Using volunteers to get kids interested in reading, Koalaty Kid helps students academically while building their sense of community. Koalaty Kid unites parents, teachers, students, and volunteers from business in working toward a single goal: teaching children total quality.

Developed at the Frederick Carder School in Corning, New York, in the 1970's, Koalaty Kid takes its name from the school's koala bear mascot and is overseen by the American Society for Quality Control (ASQC) as a model TQM program for elementary schools. The program has now branched to schools in 17 states, Canada, and Mexico.

PARENT INVOLVEMENT IS KEY TO SUCCESS

Key to success in implementing TQM in schools—particularly elementary schools—is parent involvement. Since up to 91% of children's time is spent outside of school, parents or guardians are the single greatest influence on a child's education. Koalaty Kid recognizes that parents are often the missing link in education, so each Koalaty Kid school concentrates on bringing parents and members of the community into the school to volunteer.

Mary Brockway, a media specialist and parent at the Whitehead Road School, Athens, Georgia, attests to the success of this effort:

> With the business volunteers, the kids have a better sense of community. There is also a lot more parent involvement. The theme in our school is "Every book must be shared." The parents read aloud, share books, and read more themselves. They really listen to the kids. Parents act as role models—this is the best way to teach kids, and it teaches them to do their best forever.
>
> Koalaty Kid really reaches out to parents and the community. It took hours and hours to set up the program and we were able to rely on parents and volunteers.

A TOTAL COMMITMENT

The implementation of Koalaty Kid relies on parent and community volunteers and on the contributions of a school's business partners. Seeking total involvement and commitment from volunteers, the program has been very successful in bringing committed volunteers into schools.

RaeAnn Allen, PTO president and parent at Whitehead Road School, says one of the best things about Koalaty Kid is the role of volunteers:

Parents at our school volunteer as Koalaty Readers in the library and in the classroom. They help figure out the points and the paperwork. Our business partner underwrites the cost of the program and gives teachers mini-grants for special projects, and sends volunteers over to talk to the kids about their careers.

Says **Donna Spengler**, another parent at Whitehead Road School:

I love the fact that we have reading volunteers in the class. My child reads much faster now, which builds her self-esteem. The volunteers help with the weekly awards and with counting the number of books the kids read.

The commitment of Koalaty volunteers is impressive. **Carolyn Heitz** of the Marion, Iowa, Linn-Mar School District reports that:

Community involvement is really the key of Koalaty Kids. We need to reach 1400 students every year, so we need a lot of help. Volunteers have logged over 1,000 hours of volunteer time at our school!

REACHING OUT TO PARENTS AT HOME

What about parents who are unable to volunteer at school during the day? Many Koalaty Kid schools make a special effort to reach parents at home with regular invitations to attend Koalaty Kid Assemblies. The assemblies include awards ceremonies for the Koalaty Kids, and most assemblies are held monthly as yet another way to involve families and community. In addition to helping parents keep track of what's happening, they send a positive message to children: that their education is important—important enough for an auditorium full of adults to come and celebrate their progress.

Marsha Terry, a full-time working mother with children at the Johnson Elementary School, Southlake, Texas, says:

The Koalaty awards ceremony gives school an added dimension. It makes my kids really enthusiastic. . . . I went to the Awards Ceremony and the kids loved it.

The school keeps me in touch with handouts they send home, so I always know what's going on.

Mary Brockway of the Linn-Mar School District points out another benefit of the Koalaty assemblies:

> Another great thing is the assemblies and the pep rallies. The kids have so many assemblies, they're learning good manners for assembly and better listening skills.

Another special event for parents takes place as part of the Koalaty reading program at the Linn-Mar School District. Says **Sally Reck**, a media specialist and parent at Linn-Mar:

> We know that many children in our district are not exposed to reading at home. We want to help these children and their parents. Last year, we had a storyteller come and speak to parents about her stories—and 35 parents showed up.
>
> Another thing we've done is to relax the rules at the school library and the town library, because some homes don't have books. Before, there were limits on how many books a family could take out at one time. Now there are no limits, and circulation is way up. Circulation at the library was up 40% during the Koalaty program last year.

PROGRAM SPURS ENTHUSIASM

According to parents, the greatest result of the Koalaty Kid program is the enthusiasm and love of reading it instills in their children. This enthusiasm in turn inspires parents and volunteers to get involved in Koalaty Kid.

Carla Kerbo, a parent at Jack D. Johnson Elementary School, Southlake, Texas, commends Koalaty Kid for helping her son feel more confident:

> . . . I feel Koalaty Kid has done a lot for my child. He is rewarded for his efforts, instead of just his grades, and the program has boosted his self-esteem. Although he's still not very interested in reading, he feels better about himself and his other school work.
>
> Before Koalaty Kid, the school would publish the honor roll kids in the newspaper. Now, they are moving away from that and toward recognizing all children for their effort, not just kids

who get straight A's. Koalaty Kid focuses on the child's effort instead of just his grade. Now my son is measured on what he can do within his own potential.

I like the fact that they give awards. My child is very happy, so our whole family is happy.

SCHOOLS ACQUIRE FOCUS

Marsha Terry, another Johnson School parent, likes the idea of centrality:

Koalaty Kid has given my child a good attitude and has helped his reading. The program encourages kids to read and it makes them enthusiastic.

I think Koalaty Kid gives kids a theme they can hang on to, and I like the fact that it gives the kids goals they can shoot for.

Vivian Alford, principal of Whitehead Road Elementary, Athens, Georgia, echoes this sense of unity:

Before Koalaty Kid, there was no central program that kids could connect to. There were a few scattered programs here and there, but nothing connected, and nothing that continued.

Now, we even have a Koalaty Kid rap and a song that all the kids sing!

Mary Brockway, a parent at the school, feels the same way:

All the awards and ceremonies are centered around one theme, and all the kids understand it. Before, there were several unconnected programs with no focus. Now there is great school identity with the posters on the walls, awards and pictures of kids, banners—koala bears everywhere!

TOTAL QUALITY READERS

One strong component of Koalaty Kid is the reward system that centers on children's effort, changes in performance, attitude, and achievement in reading. Each child is recognized based on the amount of effort he or she has put into the program, rather than innate academic skills.

Koalaty Kid students are given individual goals in reading and work toward those goals for the entire school year. Parents find that the goals help get children organized and motivated, and that their love of reading soon carries over into the home.

Donna Spengler of Whitehead Road Elementary agrees:

> Parents love Koalaty Kid because it's based on rewards for good behavior. The rewards help kids get through the week, every week. It gives them a goal and something to look forward to.
>
> The reading program has greatly increased the number of books the kids read, with rewards for every 10 books they read. Although my child reads more quickly now, the greatest change I can see has been in her self-esteem.
>
> Our school has even used Koalaty Kid to teach about Australia. The physical education teacher added up the kid's miles in the "Walk for Wellness" program and they used their miles to "walk" all the way to Australia.

RaeAnn Allen, PTO President and parent of a first-grader at Whitehead Road School, has noticed a drastic change in her child's behavior thanks to Koalaty Kid:

> The difference between my child in kindergarten and now is like night and day. In kindergarten she was very quiet and insecure. Now, she is really confident—she goes out of her way to get recognized, to hear her name over the PA system, and to win the awards. She's only in first grade but she's at a third- or fourth-grade reading level. She's not quiet in the classroom anymore.
>
> Koalaty Kid has helped all her other subjects too, because they all stem from reading. The program teaches the kids to read and understand, not just to read fast. They learn reading comprehension.

Nevertheless, **Randy Dillman**, a father at the Arthur Smith School, Grandview, Washington, is amazed at the increase in his daughter's reading speed:

> My daughter is only 8, and she has already read 1,250 books. She loves the awards and certificates they get for reading 10

books or 100 books. They also post pictures of the book club winners in the hallways. . . .

The best part the program is that it gives kids pride in their school. I know not all kids love the program, but you'll never find a program that's perfect for every single kid. But most of the kids love it. It gets them involved and they really care about their school.

ADAPTABILITY

Because every elementary school is slightly different—each with its own unique population, traditions, history, and physical surroundings—ASQC and Koalaty Kid help schools adapt the program to their own needs.

Monte Haag, principal of the Arthur Smith School, Grandview, Washington, attests to the adaptability of Koalaty Kid:

Since we were a pilot school, we were able to modify the program to fit our own needs. It is now pretty much our own program. We offer even more incentives and assemblies, and the kids love it. We were able to combine Koalaty Kid with our own ideas to make a program that is perfect for our school.

TOO MUCH COMPETITION?

At Linn-Mar Schools, some parents and teachers were concerned that students were losing track of the original purpose of the program—teaching quality—and getting too distracted by the material rewards. With the help of the ASQC, teachers adapted the program to their own needs and moved away from competitiveness.

Because constant self-evaluation is a characteristic of TQM programs, changing the program to meet Linn-Mar's needs was not difficult. The Linn-Mar management team analyzed what was happening in the school and designed a new agenda which de-emphasizes material rewards and intense competition among students.

Sally Reck of Linn-Mar Schools describes the evolution of Linn-Mar's Koalaty Kid curriculum:

We were starting to see the kids only think about prizes, instead of reading for the sake of reading. The kids were just getting too competitive. We changed the program so that now we focus on the content of books and stories rather than adding up the numbers of books.

Now kids study books and stories until they know them inside out, and they get really excited about what they're reading. They read aloud with volunteers and parents. For kids who are slower readers, we have mentors. Now the kids think of reading as fun instead of just shooting for awards.

Another problem with all the awards was that they were getting expensive, and the paperwork was taking up a lot of the teachers time.

The kids grumbled at first when we stopped the prizes—so we knew we were doing the right thing! But now they've basically forgotten about it.

Our program has been changing and evolving all along. The ASQC has helped steer us away from competitiveness and helped us design the program that is right for our school.

LEARNING FROM EXPERIENCE

Other parents expressed concern that Koalaty Kid focuses **too** much on measuring change. Some students, such as the children of **Kelly Carissimi** at the Johnson School, Southlake, Texas, do not feel they have benefitted greatly from Koalaty Kid because their performance in school has always been consistently high—thus they don't show any measured results in the Koalaty Kid program. According to Carissimi:

My younger child doesn't like Koalaty Kid, in fact, he has a real problem with it. He never feels he is doing "good enough!" The first few weeks of school this year when they started Koalaty Kid with his class, he was very upset and cried every night.

My fourth grader doesn't seem to care. It hasn't made much difference is his schooling. He is a straight-A student, but he has never won the Koalaty Kid award.

The program seems to be set up so that if you show improvement over a 6-week period, you are rewarded. My kindergartner's performance hasn't changed over the course of

6 weeks, because he was already doing well. He feels that he is the "only one in the class" who hasn't gotten the award. I try to reward him at home instead.

One thing it has affected is his attendance. For example, today he was sick, but he wanted to go to school anyway. He felt he had to in order to win the Koalaty Kid award. So it may improve attendance, but I don't know if that's necessarily a good thing.

Because Koalaty Kid is continually undergoing assessment by the management team and is open to the suggestions of every member of the Koalaty community, problems such the one described by Kelly Carissimi can be addressed. All it takes is a little help from parents, who must make themselves heard. Without the help of parents, Koalaty Kid can't improve.

HOW IT ALL STARTED: THE HISTORY OF KOALATY KID

The Koalaty Kid program came about when a number of teachers at the Frederick Carder School, Corning, New York, decided they needed a competitive initiative to improve morale and achievement. In particular, the teachers felt they needed a program to improve student reading levels. The teachers came up with their own approach to improve reading and motivation at the school and named it after the school's koala bear mascot.

The success of the Carder school was brought to the attention of Corning Incorporated Quality executives by Carder School parents. The executives introduced the program to the ASQC, and urged the ASQC to promote the program nationally. In 1988-89 and 1989-90, the ASQC located 14 pilot schools, and Koalaty Kid began nationally.

Long-Term Success

Since 1988, nearly all the pilot schools are still functioning with successful Koalaty Kid programs. While some schools have ended the program—usually due to changes in personnel—approximately 60 schools are now using it. Long-term success of is evident at the Carder School, where Koalaty Kid has been running with consistently high results for over 15 years.

THE STRUCTURE OF KOALATY KID

Just as Total Quality Management institutes quality at every level in the workplace, Koalaty Kid brings quality to each level of the educational process: Administrative, instructional, and learning. TQM in education, however, offers its own set of challenges. Teachers must find a way to communicate an abstract concept—total quality—in ways children can understand, and then institute quality with specific actions in the classroom.

PROGRAMS ASK FOR A VISION

Koalaty Kid asks the members of a school community: What do we need to do to improve our school, and what do we have to do to achieve the goals we want? While people in business are accustomed to thinking in terms of goals and production, these concepts are harder to implement in education.

For TQM to impact education, teachers must set goals and motivate every child in every classroom to reach them. Koalaty Kid helps teachers in managing a classroom around reaching those objectives, and helps administrators and parents understand the specific needs of an entire school. Once administrators, teachers, students, and parents have a vision of what their school should be, they can set about making it a reality.

THE FIVE CORE PRINCIPLES OF KOALATY KID

1. Student-Centered Objectives

Just as the objectives of total quality management in business focus on optimizing the production of a product or a service, every objective of Koalaty Kid centers on the students. Koalaty Kid's goals for students are:

- ◆ develop healthy self-esteem and a sense of pride.
- ◆ develop a sense of responsibility in every aspect of their lives, at home at school.

- participate as equal members of the Koalaty Kid education team along with teachers, administrators, parents, and adults from the school's business partnership team.
- become self-motivated in reading and to extend that motivation into every other area of learning, both at home and at school.

2. Partnership With Local Business Sponsors

Koalaty Kid schools enter partnerships with local businesses to help finance Koalaty Kid materials, share human resources, and receive guidance from people in business. The school-business partnership is the key to sustaining the **Koalaty Kids** program at minimum cost to schools and at a maximum benefit to business. Setting up a business partnership involves the entire community in the school, which is one of the goals of Koalaty Kid.

Business Partners as Partners in Learning

Koalaty Kid schools benefit from having business partners in a number of ways. Although it is important, the financial assistance schools receive is probably the **least** of the long-term benefits a school gains from a partnership. The greatest advantage of the school-business partnership is that it brings volunteers into the classroom to act as tutors and mentors.

While many volunteers are parents, many are not. The partnerships bring many adults who would not regularly have the opportunity to work with children into the school. Business partner volunteers read stories and books aloud, tutor students one-on-one, and act as mentors for students who may not have strong role models for education at home.

3. Emphasis on Quality Practices

The core of Koalaty Kid is instilling quality in every aspect of a child's education. The elements of implementing quality are:

- emphasizing clear expectations
- establishing standards of excellence
- a process for continuous improvement
- generous use of recognition

The overall goal of implementing each of these practices is to foster **self-esteem**, **motivation**, and **achievement** in elementary-school children.

To implement quality in teaching children to read, teachers develop goals in reading for each child, track the progress of each student, reward children for their achievements and their personal improvement, and welcome the children's input on the progress of Koalaty Kid as a whole.

4. Broad-Based Team Management

Working from the most basic principle of Total Quality Management, Koalaty Kid replaces the traditional school management hierarchy with a team of parents, teachers, administrators, business partners, and students who all have input into the development of the Koalaty Kid curriculum for a school. Teachers in particular are encouraged to voice their opinions in managing the program, since teachers, more than anyone else, understand the learning needs of the students and how to address those needs.

Total Commitment

The success of Koalaty Kid relies on the **total commitment** of the Koalaty Kid team. Each member of the team is valuable for his or her personal insights on what needs need to be met and the effectiveness of the program as it progresses. Koalaty Kid volunteers commit to come into school week after week, month after month for the duration of the school year to **prove** to children that education is a crucial, community-wide concern. It also reinforces the stability of the single theme of Koalaty Kid

It is the input from each of these factions that enables Koalaty Kid to scrutinize every aspect of learning—at home, in school, and in the community, to see which aspects need the most attention.

5. Adaptability

Koalaty Kid and the ASQC recognize that every elementary school and community are distinct. Therefore, the program strives to adapt itself to the needs of every school, large or small. Koalaty Kid schools are free to alter and adapt the Koalaty Kid program to better suit their own purposes.

The Arthur Smith School in Grandview, Washington, and the

Linn-Mar Schools in Marion, Iowa, are just two of many schools that have successfully combined their own ideas with the principles of Koalaty Kid to develop exciting and effective programs.

For more information, contact:

Koalaty Kid
ASQC
611 East Wisconsin Avenue
PO Box 3005
Milwaukee, WI 53201-3005

— 8 —

TQM AND THE ROLE OF THE SCHOOL BOARD

Keith Byrom, *Trustee, Southwest Independent School District, Manager, Quality Process, H.B. Zachry Company, San Antonio, Texas*

Introduction: *An essential ingredient for successful TQM implementation is commitment from the top of the organization. In the case of schools, this means school boards. Some school administrators have indicated that lack of board understanding and support is one of the biggest barriers to TQM implementation. Many such administrators would be eager to have a Keith Byrom on their board. Keith Byrom was first elected to the school board in 1984. As a quality professional, he was eager to share his expertise with both the board and the school district. As you read his chapter, I'm sure you will wonder, as I did, "What if all school boards operated with these concepts in mind?" Keith's relationship with the superintendent is outstanding and they often appear as joint speakers on school improvement at conferences.*

OPENING

It is becoming increasingly clear, that organizations who fail to renew themselves, will probably not survive. The list of those that fail is as impressive as it is long. From auto giants to political parties, those organizations that cannot meet or exceed the expectations of their customers, at a reasonable cost, will be rejected by their customers.

On the other hand, it is equally clear that many organizations actively involved in systematic organizational renewal known by its many names (Total Quality Improvement, Continuous Improvement, Quality Improvement, or Site-Based Management) are having a dramatic renaissance.

But, what applications do the concepts taught by the gurus Deming, Juran, and Crosby have in education? In education, customer expectations are ill-defined and guided by the tri-headed monster of Federal Regulation, State mandated programs, and local political adversarial relationships?

Yet, in spite of ill-defined customer expectations, every school board member of every school district knows that systematic continuous improvement is needed. In fact, we in education must change if our society is going to renew itself.

The question is not whether TQM has application in education.

The question is, how can we implement it and what is the role of the Board of Education in leading TQM?

If renewal in industry requires commitment from its corporate leadership, then renewal in education must begin with the Board.

THE BOARD IS ALSO A TEAM

I first ran for the Board in 1984. In retrospect, I cannot remember exactly why. However, I do remember my platform. I campaigned on the platform that my incumbent opponent had "been there too long, had lost touch with the voters, had failed to produce results, and was only concerned with his own re-election."

Sound familiar? Of course, that is what you say when you run against an incumbent. What are you supposed to say? "My opponent is a Paragon of Virtue and everyone should vote for him."

So, the whole process, win or lose, begins in a confrontational manner, without trust, truth, or vision. Is it any wonder the system is so adversarial?

Most traditional boards are adversarial without an understanding of the importance of consensus. Instead, their objective is, in many cases, to "run" the district. They require final approval of almost everything from when the superintendent leaves his office to what route the buses take.

It is called micromanagement. It often results in low student morale, high teacher turnover, law suits, and administrators and teachers who are afraid to make any decision for fear it will be scrutinized and overturned by the board.

At least, that was our experience. I had won the election. But I joined a board with a long experience of confrontation, finger pointing, fear, and low self-esteem.

Like most adversarial boards, we slipped into stagnation.

COLLABORATIVE DECISION MAKING

But, in response to this stagnation, our Board, in 1985, agreed that we would make all board decisions based on consensus. No more split decisions. We would vote only after consensus was reached.

We defined consensus as:

- Everyone understands the decision.
- Everyone agrees to support the decision.
- Everyone agrees to work for the decision.

In addition:

- The superintendent was to be a part of the team and was also required to support the decision before we voted.
- Consensus was not to be considered achieved simply by a majority vote, a unanimous vote, or when people gave in for the sake of consensus.

The advantages of collaborative decision making versus adversarial decision making are obvious:

- More ideas
- More resources
- More buy-in
- Better chance of successful implementation

If you believe that collaborative decisions are superior to individual decisions (and most people do), then it follows that the single, most effective way to improve decisions is through a collaborative approach.

There are, of course, disadvantages of collaborative decision making:

- Time: The process of working out solutions that can be supported by all members, may, on occasion, take time. However, generally speaking, that time pales in relation to the time required to attempt to implement controversial split decisions on subjects such as budget, tax rates, or bond issues. In fact, split decisions are often impossible to implement (*e.g.*, bond elections).
- Lack of Controversy: Consensus based Board meetings are poorly attended by the media. Once a member of the media commented that "It appears you made the decision before you voted." I said, "Yes, we did." She said, "Isn't that against the law." I said, "Why would it be against the law to reach an

agreement that can be supported by all members before we vote." Our society believes that good decisions are made only in a combative arena. If we are going to improve, we must begin to change that perception. That requires a positive collaborative attitude which must begin with the board.

In 1985, our Board adopted the policy of collaborative decision making. The results since that time have been:

* No split decisions
* No board turnover
* No disrupting community controversy
* Dramatic improvement demonstrated by improved test scores, improved facilities, decrease of teacher turnover, and dramatic increases in student morale and self-esteem

THE MANAGER'S WORSE NIGHTMARE

Most managers are scared to death of consensus. They are mortally afraid that employees will run off and do something that they cannot support. They call it management by committee or management by compromise. True consensus is neither. Remember, in true consensus, everyone, including management, must *understand, support,* and *work* for the decision. Under the guidelines of consensus, the group cannot "run off."

On the other hand, employees are always afraid that managers will dominate and make a decision they cannot support. With true consensus, that is not possible either. The key to true consensus is that everyone must be encouraged and allowed to participate. Participants must express their disagreements. Consensus (Collaborative Decision Making) fails when a person "gives up" for the sake of consensus.

PUSHING DECISION MAKING TO THE PEOPLE DOING THE WORK

My first year on the Board was one of confrontation and an adversarial relationship with the superintendent. In 1985, after a year of confrontation, our superintendent resigned. In response, we adopted *consensus* as our decision making option and agreed that if we ever found a superintendent that would work for us, we *would let him run the schools.* Some call that pushing the decision making process to the people who do the work. Some call it decentralizing. We called it desperation. Talk about decentralization, today we only make two important *content* decisions:

• To elect the superintendent (a very important responsibility)
• To decide if the band uniform should be light green or dark green

When I tell this to board members from other school districts, they get angry. "You must not make any important decisions, like the budget, building programs, or bond elections," they say.

Is approving a budget, building program, or bond issue a content decision or is it approving a process based on content decisions made by people who are actually doing the work? As a Board, we approve many processes, but we can make very few *content* decisions. How can we? We are not doing the work. The people who know the most about the content are the people who do the work. How can board members know how many text books are needed for the new library, how many students are projected for next year, how many pounds of hamburger meat are needed next month, or how many new classrooms need to be built. Board members rely on the people doing the work to decide content.

This principle should govern the relationship between board and superintendent, superintendent and principal, principal and teacher, teacher and student.

The Board has to take the lead in defining vision and insisting that the people who do the work make decisions about content and are accountable for that decision. At the same time, the Board must ensure processes and systems are producing desired results.

If collaborative decision making is superior to individual decision making and content decisions are best made by the people doing the work, the next logical progression is cross-functional teams utilizing consensus to make *content* decisions to improve work processes approved by their leaders.

As a result of this principle, employees in our district have created cross-functional teams utilizing collaborative decision making. They have been authorized to make decisions with regard to the content of their work, provided:

• They reach their decisions through consensus
• Their supervisor is part of that consensus
• They develop performance measures before any change is instituted
• They are within the constraints of the process approved by the Board

CREATING THE ENVIRONMENT FOR IMPROVEMENT

When I first ran for the Board, I had a standard speech. Everyone has one. I would begin by saying "Our educational system had failed and we needed:

• To improve our facilities;
• To improve the quality of our teachers;
• To improve the educational process, so that when kids graduate, they can step immediately into a productive role in society."

Once, when I had finished my speech, the guy that spoke after me began by saying: "He couldn't have said it any better. But, what we really need is a football team that has pride. If the team will have pride in themselves, the kids will have pride in themselves and quit writing on the walls. The parents will start coming to the school and the teachers will stop quitting. Then, and only then, will the community let you make the improvements you think are so important."

How outdated, I thought. How does the football team relate to improving the facilities in our schools?

I have since concluded, that I was missing the point. Until we can reinstitute pride, improve self-esteem, and drive fear out of education, we will never be able to renew or improve.

Lack of pride is a function of 3 factors:

• Pervasive fear in the organization
• Low self-esteem
• Negativism and finger pointing

These characteristics describe the environment in many of our schools. Unfortunately, most school boards, through adversarial approaches, only foster this kind of environment.

Education is criticized constantly by politicians, the media, and the community. Teachers are described as lazy and incompetent. If education is going to renew itself, then it must begin by changing the environment from one of confrontation, finger pointing, and adversarial relationships to one of collaboration and *recognition* of success.

Typical school board meetings consist of 2 hours of debate and discussions and 2 hours of confrontation and criticism.

Our school board meetings consist of 1-hour approving and disapproving processes and 1-hour recognizing achievement in the District.

Recognizing achievement in education is not that hard to do. In spite of constant criticism by everyone, our schools continue to produce an exceptional product. Look at all of the successful people in this county: Doctors, lawyers, housewives, plumbers. Where did they come from? They came from our educational system.

Look at the majority of students today: Aggressive, well-mannered, achievers. Not all students. Some are just "average;" they go to school, make "C's" and go on to be good citizens. So what is wrong with that? Who said all kids should make an "A." If a "C" means average and average means half are above and half are below, what is wrong with an average kid. We have built the strongest country in the world with everyday, average people. Only half of all board members are above average. There will always be average kids. *So how can we criticize education because only half of all of our kids are above average kids.* To do so, would defy the law of mathematics.

If a "C" does not mean average, then what does it mean? If we do not know, then why do we have it?

I play golf, but not very well. In fact, I am about average and will probably never be much above average. However, I continue to play and do my best. But if I were criticized every time I played for being "only average," it would not be long before I gave up. That is what many of our kids are doing. Test scores are part of our system and that will probably never change. However, no matter what the test score is, our approach should be to help the student improve. To criticize the kid or the teacher only perpetuates a fearful environment.

But what about the "Bad Kids." What about the gang members and drug runners and other failures. Should we condemn all teachers for these failures?

First, whose failures are these anyway? Perhaps society or family. But, clearly not the educational system.

Second, what percentage of the kids are we talking about? 5%? 10%? 15%? 25%? 50%? It does not matter. The point is, we should not be emphasizing society's failures, but instead its successes, because our successes are spectacular. We should examine the reasons for our failures, develop plans for improvement, measure our improvements, and revise our plans. However, to dwell on failure instead of success is counter productive.

THAT VISION THING AGAIN

The Board's responsibility in TQM is to create a positive environment, a positive collaborative attitude, push content decisions to the people doing the work and create a vision of what we want our schools to look like in the future. Although vision begins with the Board, it must be shared with administrators, teachers, staff, students, and community leaders. The vision must be comprehensive and include input from all of these groups.

The vision must then be translated into goals and teams created to develop comprehensive strategies to achieve these goals. These teams must be cross-functional and include representatives of stakeholders from each affected group.

Based on the district vision, campuses must create an even more specific vision. Campus vision is then translated into action plans and teams created to develop solutions utilizing collaborative decision making. All employees of every campus should be expected to serve on some type of improvement team.

These campus teams develop solutions to new ideas. They should include teachers, students and parents.

They require special skills, including:

- Effective meeting techniques
- Scientific problem solving
- Collaborative decision making
- Trust

It should be clear that training is needed. In fact, training probably never ends. But then again, this is education.

TRAINING, TRAINING, TRAINING

By June, 1992, our district had completed its vision for systematic improvement, completed 1 year with a pilot school, and implemented and adjusted its districtwide improvement plan based on the experience of the pilot school. We were now ready to implement the process district wide.

Our goal was to train 660 teachers and administrators, involve all employees in employee improvement teams, and develop performance measures.

The only practical approach was to teach teachers to teach the concepts of continuous improvement and collaborative decision making. Figure 8.1 displays the actual agenda for the training in the district.

MEASUREMENT: HOW DO WE KNOW IF WE IMPROVED?

Most TQM gurus emphasize the necessity of utilizing scientific Statistical Process Control in order to identify processes for scientific problem solving and improvement, discover core reasons for problems, and to baseline and measure results of process improvements.

Once we had developed a vision, instituted collaborative decision making, and decentralized content decisions, it was time to introduce the concept of performance measures. But when we asked people to measure improvement or to use measurement to identify opportunities for improvement, they resisted.

The introduction of measurement in and of itself created fear. Measurement has been used for years to club students and teachers over the head. All of the gains in improving the environment can be lost if measurement is not introduced properly. Every school kid and teacher knows what it means to fail a test. So when we fail, we learn to hide it or blame others. How can we ever improve if we are not allowed to fail and to learn from that failure? Unless we show people that it is ok to learn from our mistakes, we are doomed to mediocrity.

Subsequently, as our first campus teams began to recommend process changes, we began to require the identification of *predetermined performance measures* in order to determine the results of process changes. Measurements must be established prior to the

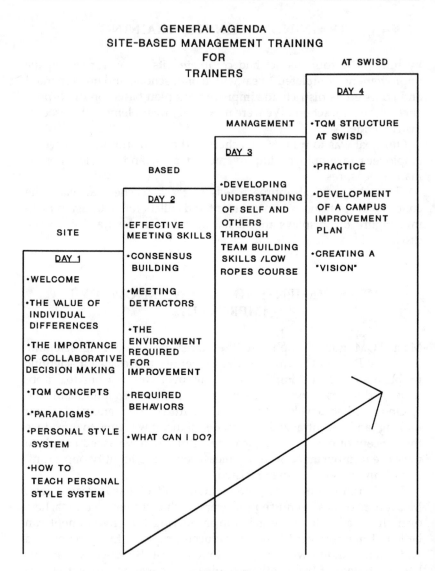

GENERAL AGENDA
SITE-BASED MANAGEMENT TRAINING
FOR
TRAINERS
AT SWISD

FIGURE 8.1

initiation of change in order to baseline the process. Figure 8.2 is a
control chart of the first process improvement in our district.

In this example, the team has used brainstorming to identify ideas
for improvement. Not surprisingly, they chose discipline. Through
use of the problem solving tools, they developed and implemented a

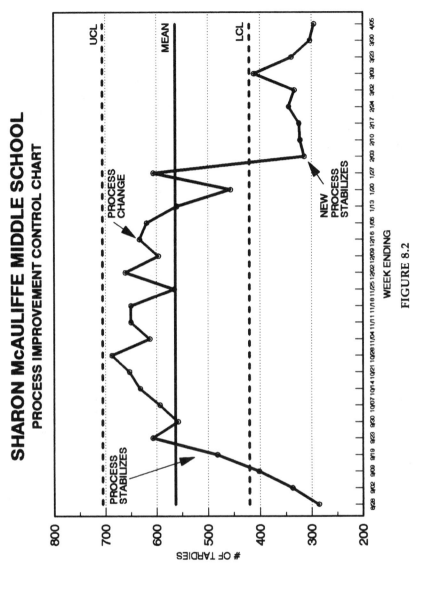

FIGURE 8.2

plan with full buy-in of the teachers. (Note: The process change required more work for teachers and buy-in would have been hard to accomplish had the decision been made in the traditional *manager decide and announce* fashion.)

With the requirement of predetermined performance measures, the team chose to chart the *total* number of tardies (not tardies by teacher). The plan was implemented on January 6, 1992, and resulted in obvious improvement. In fact, the number of tardies was reduced over time and, in effect, process control limits were established. The control chart provided the team and teachers with a scoreboard.

In addition, the teachers took ownership and responsibility for discipline at the school. They can no longer blame the problem on the kids or the principal.

The effect of the chart was dramatic:

- It demonstrated how a process can be baselined
- How a control chart can measure a trend
- How predetermined performance measures can be used without creating fear
- It became a standard for measurement in the District

THE ROLE OF THE LEADER

In implementing TQM, managers are tempted to push concepts, control behaviors and inspect compliance with the TQM structure. However, to do so is contrary to the concepts of an improvement process. Individuality and creativity must be encouraged.

In addition, teachers tend to be skeptical. They have seen a lot of new programs before. Decades of fear and mistrust cannot be erased overnight or even over years. Teams are suspicious of the principal and the principal is often suspicious of the teams. The culture that we grew up with says that managers tell workers what to do. That's their job, that's what they were hired to do.

Our culture teaches that managers are supposed to:

- Know everything
- Control everything
- Direct everything

There is only one problem. It is impossible. Nobody can know everything, control everything, or direct everything. So, we have set our leaders up for failure. It is no wonder managers are so frustrated and stressed-out.

Unfortunately, we require the same of our teachers. They, too, must know, control, and direct everything. It is little wonder that education is such a hostile environment.

If an improvement process is going to succeed, the principal and administration must change from managers to leaders.

♦ Leaders lead improvement by:
  • Teaching improvement concepts
  • Identifying opportunities for improvement
  • Pushing content decisions to the people doing the work

♦ Leaders teach people how to improve processes through:
  • Collaborative decision making
  • Predetermined performance measures
  • Scientific problem solving

♦ Leaders provide support by:
  • Helping people get what they need in order to improve their jobs
  • Providing encouragement

♦ Leaders define the expectations of their customers by:
  • Developing processes to identify those expectations
  • Developing strategies to meet or exceed these expectations

♦ Leaders create a safe environment by:
  • Modeling required behaviors
  • Recognizing successes
  • Providing consequences and accountability for behavior

CONTINUOUS IMPROVEMENT – THE ULTIMATE GOAL

When things are going well, it is easy to get caught up in the excitement of teams and the euphoria of empowerment.

But, the ultimate goal of improvement is improvement. Improvement must manifest itself in measurable results. Measurement of the processes tells you what to improve or how a specific process is acting. If you improve the process, test scores will improve in a corresponding fashion. Results must focus on both processes and test scores. Test scores are only one measure of improvement.

The Board must lead this aspect of the process. They must insist on measurement and baseline the major processes which require improvement. In addition, board members must participate on improvement teams. Consensus requires their input and buy-in.

It is a difficult compilation of complicated concepts that require time, commitment, and common sense. It also requires an understanding that life is not a series of unrelated events. There is order to the universe. It is the Board's role through collaboration with those that do the work to discover that order and to continuously improve our responses to it. It is difficult and requires real change. But it is achievable.

The option of doing nothing is unacceptable. The customers of education like the customers of any other process will ultimately make the final decision as to which suppliers will survive and which will not.

Part Three

SECONDARY LINKS: CUSTOMERS AND SUPPLIERS

— 9 —

BUSINESS PARTNERSHIPS IN TOTAL QUALITY SCHOOLS

Paul Bailey, *Quality Assurance and Distribution Superintendent, Sterling Chemical Company, Texas City, Texas*

Introduction: Businesses and other employers represent one of education's biggest customers. A close customer/supplier relationship can be one of the keys to successful school restructuring. Paul Bailey was suggested for this chapter by one of the superintendents who has been a partner with Sterling Chemical. Very often business/education partnerships are the domain of corporate human resources, public/community affairs or communications staffs. The move toward total quality management demands the involvement of corporate quality staffs. As you will see from this chapter, the impetus for this partnership started with Sterling Chemical's quality staff. They knew they had a responsibility to work with all their suppliers and schools were their biggest supplier of human resources. Through the involvement of Paul and others, a Houston area Quality Council has been formed to help all public sector organizations begin the quality pursuit. Paul's chapter follows the model of the Baldrige's National Quality Award Criteria—pointing out how businesses can help schools in each area.

OPENING

Imagine former students returning to a school where they had ignored teacher guidance a generation earlier. They now desperately need the same teacher's help to survive. Such was the case when W. Edwards Deming, the quality guru, returned to his native America in the early 1980s to help major auto manufactures survive against the Japanese competition. Deming helped Japan when no one in America would listen.

HOW STERLING CHEMICALS STARTED QUALITY

Deming's return to America brought him in contact with major auto manufacturers such as Ford. Ford began to require that its suppliers follow their lead toward total quality. Failure to do so meant decertification as a supplier. One Ford supplier, Sterling Chemicals, Texas City, Texas, listened to Ford's mandate and started implementing a total quality system in the mid-1980s. After receiving advice from a quality consultant, Qual Pro, Sterling developed a total quality plan.

STERLING'S INVOLVEMENT WITH LOCAL SCHOOLS

In keeping with the Deming philosophy, it was necessary that Sterling make sure that its suppliers were committed to total quality. Some of its key suppliers were the area school systems that provide Sterling with its most important resource, its people. At Sterling, 3 full-time Quality Facilitators support the 950 person workforce in the quality effort. Since 1988, 5 employees have rotated through the Quality Facilitator job (Rob Fransham, Harry Conrad, Brian Kam, Paula Clemens, and Paul Bailey). Each of the 5 has played an important role in helping schools understand the quality principles.

Similar help has come from businesses across the nation that understand how important it is to develop a partnership with educational institutions in the areas where they reside. Quality has become a common language between business and education. Employers become motivated when they see local job applicants not having the skills needed to work in their plants or offices. Supporting the school systems and becoming involved is helping the schools.

A MODEL FOR IMPROVEMENT

Business can provide a good role model for improving the quality of education. Some valuable lessons can be shared with education on what to do and what not to do when implementing quality in education. A management guide for improvement in business that will work well in education is the Malcolm Baldrige National Quality Award criteria. Several educational systems have already discovered how the award criteria can apply to education. With slight modifications it can be easily adapted to Total Quality in education. There are 7 key areas addressed in the Baldrige criteria. They are:

Leadership
Information & Analysis
Strategic Quality Planning
Human Resource Utilization
Quality Assurance
Quality Results
Customer Satisfaction

All elements are necessary to achieve total quality and continuous improvement. This is not another program, it is a better way of doing business.

A guide or road map for total quality leadership is shown in Figure 9.1. This flow chart will be used to explain how each Baldrige key area can be applied to education and how business partnerships can help this process. Each of the blocks in the flow chart represents a numbered step. Numbered steps followed by letters indicate items that may be implemented at the same time. The diamond shapes represent decision points with yes or no decisions. When answering the question in the diamond, be sure to consider supporting information. Getting through this road map may take years.

Step 1—Quality Philosophy

In Sterling's initial contact with a school district, the district was exposed to Sterling's quality philosophy, that of W. Edwards Deming. In teaching this philosophy, Sterling used a set of Dr. Deming's 14-Points customized for education.[1] This modification of the 14-Points was developed for educators to help them see how the philosophy applies to education. The 14-Points for education are as follows:

1. CREATE CONSTANCY OF PURPOSE TOWARD IMPROVEMENT OF THE ENTIRE SCHOOL SYSTEM AND ITS SERVICES.
2. ADOPT THE NEW PHILOSOPHY. WE ARE IN A NEW ECONOMIC AGE.
3. CEASE DEPENDENCE ON TESTS AND GRADES TO MEASURE QUALITY.
4. CEASE DEPENDENCE ON PRICE WHEN SELECTING THE CURRICULUM, TEXT, EQUIPMENT, AND SUPPLIES FOR THE SYSTEM.
5. IMPROVE CONSTANTLY AND FOREVER EVERY PROCESS FOR PLANNING, TEACHING, LEARNING, AND SERVICE.
6. INSTITUTE MORE THOROUGH, BETTER JOB-RELATED TRAINING.
7. INSTITUTE LEADERSHIP.

---

[1] James F. Leonard, "Transformation 101: Introduction to a Deming Roadmap for Improving Our Schools," presented as a paper on applying quality in education, 1990.

TOTAL QUALITY LEADERSHIP

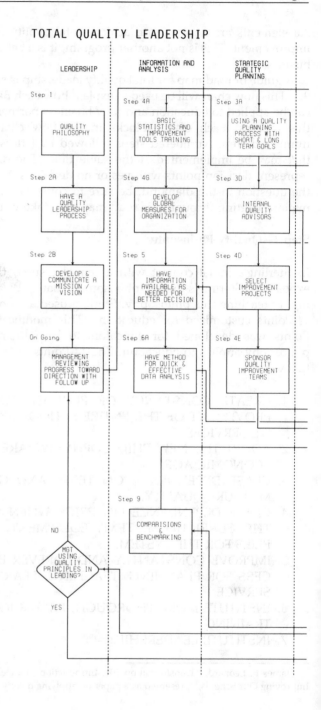

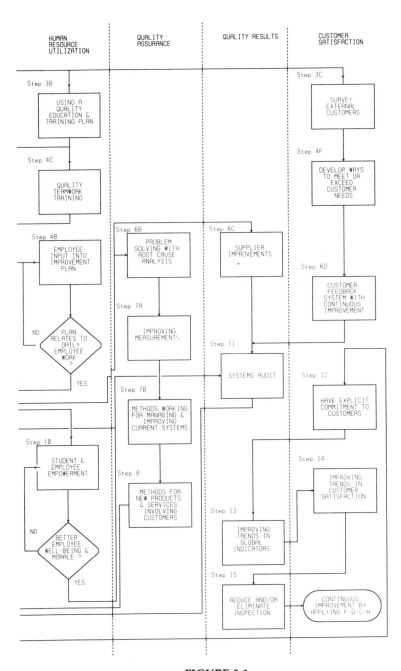

FIGURE 9.1

8. DRIVE OUT FEAR.
9. BREAK DOWN BARRIERS BETWEEN GROUPS IN THE SCHOOL SYSTEM.
10. ELIMINATE THE USE OF GOALS, TARGETS, AND SLO-GANS TO ENCOURAGE PERFORMANCE.
11. CLOSELY EXAMINE THE IMPACT OF TEACHING STAN-DARDS AND THE SYSTEM OF GRADING STUDENT PERFORMANCE.
12. REMOVE BARRIERS THAT ROB STAFF AND ADMINIS-TRATORS OF PRIDE OF WORKMANSHIP AND ROB STUDENTS OF THE JOY OF LEARNING.
13. INSTITUTE A VIGOROUS PROGRAM OF EDUCATION AND SELF-IMPROVEMENT FOR EVERYONE IN THE SYSTEM.
14. PLAN AND TAKE ACTION TO ACCOMPLISH THE TRANSFORMATION.

Step 2A—Have a Quality Leadership Process

It is important to have a process for integrating quality values into day-to-day operations. One of the first things done in implementing Total Quality Leadership in the school system is to develop a method for making quality happen. This can only occur by training top leadership in a school district in quality leadership and then demon-strating understanding by providing guidance and direction. This is normally done through a quality committee or committees. The committee may be called a quality council, steering committee, executive committee, etc., but its purpose is the same: To get a quality leadership process started. The purpose of this committee is to establish a leadership system and an organizational culture to assure customer satisfaction. Top management MUST lead this effort; there-fore, Sterling insisted upon working with leaders.

This initial approach will grow into a leadership model applicable at every level in the school district. Quality leadership involves top leaders focusing on mid- and long-term planning and removing obstacles to success. This group must verify that plans are carried out and that continuous improvement becomes standard practice.

Schools getting started in quality improvement often have prob-lems defining the quality process they need or selecting objectives. This is where a business partnership can be helpful. Frequently, businesses within the school district have developed quality systems that can be shared with the school district. Several school districts have used Sterling Chemical's quality structure as a guide in developing their system.

Step 2B—Develop and Communicate a Mission and Vision

Everyone in the school district must understand the direction of the quality effort. For that reason, a clear mission and vision is imperative. It is important that the mission be well thought out and be committed to by the entire school district. This takes time, but is well worth the effort. Confusion can result later during the implementation of a quality system when this step has not been done well. The mission is the school district's purpose for existing. The vision is where the organization wants to be in the future.

This mission and vision must be deployed throughout the school district. They must be in writing and clearly understood by everyone. Some organizations check for understanding and acceptance by surveying the employees. However, the real test of these statements is whether they are helpful in providing direction.

Sterling developed a model that was shared with the school districts (Figure 9.2). The mission is developed first and is followed by the vision. Based on the vision, plans that involve short-term action are developed. The organization implements the plan, checks the results, and takes follow up action. The Plan-Do-Check-Act cycle is repeated as often as necessary, always referring back to the vision for guidance.

Step 3A—Using a Quality Planning Process with Short and Long-Term Goals

It is necessary to develop a strategic plan that addresses the priorities of the school district. This is nothing more than a business plan that is quality driven. The quality process will, therefore, be integrated with the strategic plan. The plan must be in place to achieve the vision. It must list goals that are planned steps for directing the district toward that vision. Caution should be exercised when developing goals because arbitrary goals are difficult to understand and resources required to reach the goal may not be fully realized. If a plan exists to improve something, there must be a method to determine that it has improved.

Balance must exist so the school district looks at the short-term as well as where it wants to be in the future. This balance can be achieved by using the Plan-Do-Check-Act cycle, shown in Figure 9.2,

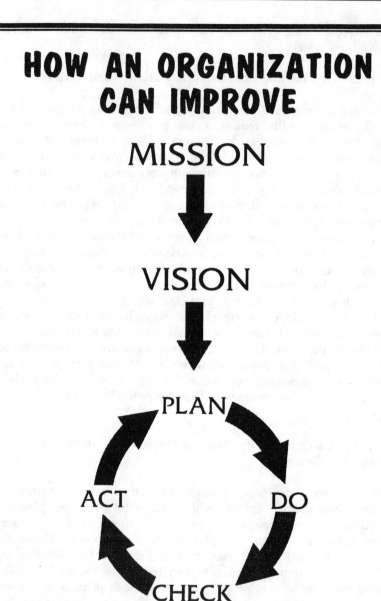

FIGURE 9.2

on at least an annual basis, while using the vision to guide the school on a longer-term basis.

The organization's direction is set by the top leaders with input from employees and customers. Departments within the organization translate those directions (plans) into specific departmental targets and define the means to reach them. As with setting direction, employees and customers should be involved.

Industry has developed business strategies and plans for years. However, integration of quality into the strategy and plan is new. School districts can learn from these businesses by following their examples.

Step 3B—Using a Quality Education and Training Plan

Quality education and training is the first step to change the culture of the school district toward total quality. Training must relate to the organization's long term vision in order to be effective. Training curriculum should include the quality philosophy, statistical methods, problem solving, team building, and leadership.

Training, like other processes, should be constantly improved. Business partners can be helpful in providing quality training. Much of the training used by businesses can be easily adapted for use by schools. Sometimes it may be possible to include school personnel in internal corporate training courses. Also, school systems may reciprocate by including business personnel in training opportunities within the school. Finding time for training in schools requires some innovative thinking. Most of the schools Sterling has assisted started with teacher in-service training time. As quality becomes part of the curriculum, regular classroom time can be used for training.

Step 3C—Survey External Customers

Educators often have a problem using the word "customer." There are many "customers" in the education system, including students, parents, business employers, government, and others. This requires asking the right questions to find out what is important to each of the customers. The school may use surveys, focus groups, interviews, and other methods to determine what the customer expects. Successful organizations have been able to anticipate customer needs and provide improvement even before the customer recognizes the need.

The school can benefit from surveying techniques used by industry, but must customize surveys to fit their situation. They first must identify their customers. The survey will reveal how well they are meeting their needs. This becomes vital input to an improvement plan. Some schools have invited their customers to spend time with them so administrators and teachers can find out how satisfied their customers are and what their expectations are for the future.

Sterling Chemicals has participated with an industry group which invites school counselors, administrators, and teachers to spend a day in the plant. Employees in entry level jobs talk with the school representatives about their jobs. Sterling management talks about current and future expectations of potential employees. This has been very helpful to the school in adjusting their curriculum and providing guidance to students on industry needs.

Step 3D—Internal Quality Advisors

To become self-sufficient in the quality effort, it is necessary to develop internal support to help in adopting the new quality philosophy. A quality advisor, sometimes called a facilitator, has responsibility for helping explain the new philosophy, helping others apply quality tools, working with teams to apply the team process, and supporting continuous improvement efforts.

The quality advisor should have strong people skills, teaching skills, and technical skills. Schools are generally full of good candidates for this position. Caring teachers that relate well with students are ideal candidates to consider.

Step 4A—Basic Statistics and Improvement Tool Training

The statistical techniques used in quality systems are practical and require little effort to apply. School personnel must have an understanding of the statistical methods used to achieve and maintain improvements. EVERYONE, including top leadership, must understand these simple statistical methods and be proficient in using them.

To change the existing culture, understanding and use of the quality tools are essential. The school can get excellent help from its business partner. Good business partners have developed training packages on quality tools for their employees. Sterling Chemicals has included school personnel in its 2-day employee training session on quality tools.

Step 4B—Employee Input into Improvement Plan

Getting commitment to any plan is directly related to involvement. What are the opportunities for employees to get involved in quality improvement? Involvement can start on day one. Successful design of the quality system should include a cross section of employees from the schools. Organizations that have done this step effectively have had cross functional reviews and critiques of the plan before finalizing.

Businesses are learning to get more up-front input in planning by including a cross section of employees on all permanent quality committees. Employee involvement on quality committees is an excellent way to gain commitment to quality improvement.

Step 4C—Quality Teamwork Training

Major gains in improvement often result from teams of people who are an active part of a system. The quality team is usually a temporary decision making group existing to improve a process, to solve a specific problem, or to make a specific decision. A process exists for having a successful team. Well trained, chartered, and focused teams are ingredients for success. Teams are a very important part of the culture change that must occur for improvement. Having a process for management of quality teams will ensure the school district gets desired results from teams.

Again, business partners may have a successful approach for providing team training to the school districts. In addition to training, school districts can profit by lessons learned in business. This can save countless hours of time and resources.

Making the transformation toward total quality will require a solid teamwork process that is clearly understood and supported by school management.

Step 4D—Select Improvement Projects

Proper selection of improvement projects requires a clear view of organizational direction and the plan that was developed in STEP 3. This, along with the team process, will get desired results.

Effective project selection requires definition of a system that has clear boundaries. Early in the quality process, however, it is recommended that leaders select relatively easy projects for teams so that the quality effort will achieve early successes. Hopefully, the early project will fit into the organizational plan.

Sterling selects improvement projects utilizing a matrix system to categorize possible improvement items called "The Most Pressing Needs." As projects are completed they are removed and new ones added. The matrix is reprioritized each year and new projects are added to it: Projects that support the organizational direction. This ensures that resources are applied to projects of highest priority.

Step 4E— Sponsor Quality Improvement Teams

The leadership of the school district must clearly communicate the team assignments. They must assist and nurture the teams if the teams are to succeed.

The team process requires that leaders make certain the team is progressing as expected. This is normally accomplished by having the project team report to a guidance group such as a quality steering committee. This guidance group charters the team, checks on progress, makes sure recommendations are accomplished and the intended results are achieved. Schools can learn much from business partners about successful team management.

Step 4F—Develop Ways to Meet or Exceed Customer Needs

What do you do to satisfy your customers? The answer to this question may come from results of customer surveys. There are other ways, however, to learn your customer's needs. Knowledge of customer requirements and expectations extend beyond the routine survey. Data from various sources, such as customer complaints, have value. Face-to-face discussions with your customers is another way to obtain feedback. Data received from the customer must be accepted at face value because it is either fact or represents the customers' perception.

The most effective business techniques have involved getting closer to the customer. Forming business partnerships is a way of accomplishing this. The purpose of the partnership is to develop a complete understanding of each other's needs, strengths, and weaknesses, leading to a cooperative working arrangement. In selecting business partners the school may discover some companies who decline the schools request for help. The company probably doesn't have a good quality program yet. Most companies will gladly help schools if they have something to offer.

Step 4G—Develop Global Measures for the School District

Key organizational indicators are important for determining the effectiveness of improvements. These indicators or global measures include those items the school district said were important in their direction setting and planning. This information can be useful in focusing improvement efforts on systems that are not performing at the expected level.

The following criteria may be applied when selecting global measures:

(1) It must be of major importance to organizational long-term success.
(2) The school district leadership has agreed that the key measure is important to the customers.
(3) The item is measurable. If you can measure it, you can manage it.
(4) The measurement must be reliable. Bad data may be worse than no data.

It is advisable to keep the list of global measures short. Schools that do a good job of developing and improving a few key measures are better off than those having many measures that are not consistently tracked.

Step 5—Have Information Available as Needed for Better Decision Making

Obtaining and maintaining reliable data requires a good method for consistently providing and recording the data. Effectively using the data to prevent problems before they occur is far better than using the data to detect problems after they occur. This enables an organization to manage systems rather than just reacting to them.

What are the key types of data needed for quality improvement in the school district? How does this data relate back to the direction and plans discussed in STEP 3A? Connection back to the leadership model discussed in STEP 2 is essential. The routine review of key data in making decisions helps make "management by fact" a reality. Having reliable information is key for getting quality teams started with facts rather than opinions.

Step 6A—Have Method for Quick and Effective Data Analysis

When working with schools, it is often found that they have plenty of data but that it is not organized well for use in continuous improvement.

Having a good system for providing data is useless if nothing is done with the data. Business is learning that methods must be developed for ensuring that data is routinely tracked and analyzed. The methods are used to measure current levels of quality, to identify areas for immediate corrective action, and to provide input for taking preventive measures to avoid recurrence of problems.

Step 6B—Problem Solving with Root Cause Analysis

Effort is wasted by jumping to conclusions without understanding the root causes of problems. Problem solving techniques are available to make sure that this does not occur. Many approaches to problem solving exist. One of the school districts Sterling worked with, Dickinson Independent School District, developed a Team Approach to Problem Solving (TAPS). This process involved a 7-step cycle for problem solving:

(1) Identify the problem
(2) Analyze the process
(3) Identify the vital few causes
(4) Collect data on vital few causes
(5) Analyze data and determine improvement strategies
(6) Monitor and assess
(7) Decide and act

Step 6C—Supplier Improvements

When considering total quality in the school district, the most important resource supplied is the student. Schools should be responsible for trying to improve the students coming into its system. This is much like industry, continuously working with their suppliers to improve incoming resources. Industry has been surprised by the successes in improving the performance of their suppliers. As stated earlier, it was the Ford Motor Company that provided the motivation for Sterling (a supplier to Ford) to implement a quality system. It is important for the school to recognize this early and develop plans. Some schools that Sterling has worked with have tried to improve students in the first few years of elementary school by providing one-on-one reading help. Sterling volunteers and others give 1 hour per week helping students who are behind in reading skills. This is just one example of how schools can improve incoming students if emphasis is placed on doing this.

The school district has many other traditional suppliers with whom a long-term relationship of loyalty and trust must be developed. Fewer suppliers will be used when:

* Schools insist on evidence of quality
* Schools reward those who do the job right with increased business and discontinue doing business with those who are not willing to change

Step 6D—Customer Feedback System with Continuous Improvement

How does the school know if its customers are satisfied? Certainly long standing business partnerships are good indicators. Customers are telling schools daily if they are satisfied. For example, why do some students leave and go to other schools? Lost customers reveal important information.

Other indications may come from the results of actions taken to meet or exceed customer needs (STEP 4F). After analysis of customer satisfaction/dissatisfaction feedback, the information must be translated into quality improvement activities. Students, parents, employers, and other customers will become nonsupportive if they feel nothing happens with their feedback. Total quality should result in schools trying to please the customer not the administrator, superintendent, or school board.

Step 7A—Improving Measurements

Once key measures are developed, attention should be given to make sure they are accurate and precise. If the drop out rate for schools is being measured, would 2 people measuring the drop out rate get the same answer? A critical item is sometimes repeatedly measured in industry to ensure the reliability of the measurement. Plots of data may show strange patterns that must be investigated. A faulty measurement system may be giving incorrect results that could lead to incorrect conclusions.

Industry has adopted techniques for identifying faulty measurement systems. Also, methods are available and used in industry that allow measurements to be made for systems where data is not apparent.

Step 7B—Methods Working for Managing and Improving Current Systems

Many processes in need of improvement are not well defined. The product of the learning process is knowledge conveyed to students. Industry frequently refers to this as "value added." There are techniques available to analyze the learning process, simplify it, and reduce waste. One tool that can be used is to flow chart the learning process. It becomes clear, for example, that the 3rd grade teachers are internal suppliers to 4th grade teachers, the 4th to the 5th, and so on.

Successful quality organizations have developed methods for controlling and improving their key processes. Sharing these techniques with schools can be a valuable part of partnerships, between businesses and schools.

Step 8—Methods for New Products and Services Involving Customers

The school should have a method for designing courses and new services that considers customer requirements. For example, if lack of homework assistance was reported to be a problem based on student and parent feedback, then a method must be found for addressing this concern. Perhaps time before or after school can be made available with tutors. When a change is made, measurements to determine if the effort was successful are needed. For the homework example, the school may want to measure improvements in homework or changes in failure rates.

Business partners are using various techniques to provide superior new products and services. One such process, called Quality Function Deployment, may have some application in schools.

Step 9—Comparisons and Benchmarking

Another tool that is becoming increasingly popular in business is benchmarking. Benchmarking involves identification of the world's best performers for the global measures the organization has chosen to measure. Information is acquired from these world class organizations about the processes they use to achieve that level of performance.

Benchmarking requires having systems in place and working before looking at others. Schools need to know and understand their own systems before benchmarking. One such technique already mentioned is flow charting. Once systems are understood, it is easier to adopt new systems through benchmarking. Benchmarking, when done correctly, can result in step-change improvements. Benchmarking, however, is an unfamiliar concept for most schools and data is difficult to obtain.

Business has a resource for benchmarking, the International Benchmarking Clearinghouse, which is a service of the American Productivity & Quality Center in Houston. This Clearinghouse is a leader in promoting, facilitating, and improving benchmarking. Perhaps a similar approach in education could provide some useful help for educational benchmarking in areas not covered through established benchmarking channels. For example, if school districts kept data on the percentage of their graduates employed, information would be available to benchmark against for those who consider graduate employment a key measure.

Step 10—Student and Employee Empowerment

One quality area in which schools have shown impressive knowledge from which business can learn is empowerment.

Some of the better resources for empowerment are from education. William Glasser, author of *The Quality School*, provides guidance in empowerment in schools. David Langford, a former classroom teacher at Mt. Edgecumbe High School in Sitka, Alaska, and now director of Langford Quality Education, Billings, Montana (see Chapter 5), provides real evidence that empowerment works in his examples of class room involvement of students.[2] William C. Byham has written a book, *Zapp! The Lightning of Empowerment*, that explains empowerment well.

Both business and education must move from a highly autocratic environment to one of local autonomy. For schools this will bring local school management into a working reality with its employees and customers.

---

[2]David P. Langford, "The Deming of Education," presented as a paper on how to use the Deming philosophy in the classroom.

Step 11—Systems Audit

Audits have become a way of life in industry. Customer audits occur almost weekly. Business can be helpful in developing and helping conduct school system audits. Studies have been conducted that conclude that the Malcolm Baldrige National Quality Award criteria applies to education. The Baldrige Award criteria can provide a common way for auditing school progress.

Several states are developing state quality awards around the Baldrige criteria for education. A great deal of expertise exists in industry for helping schools understand Baldrige criteria, developing assessments, and helping conduct audits.

Step 12—Have Explicit Commitment to Customers

The school district should have explicit educational commitments to students, parents, employers, taxpayers, and other customers. Some schools back up these commitments by offering Student-Back guarantees. Educational warranties work much like those for products. If an employer finds that a recent graduate is unable to read, write, or calculate proficiently, the school district will offer free remedial instruction.

In business, companies improve their product or service, then improve their warranties. A business that provides a better warranty without improving systems for providing the product or service will soon go out of business. Schools should understand that real system improvement must occur before warranty improvement.

Local business partners can help in determining the school system's commitment. However, schools must become innovative in other ways to provide commitment to customers other than the traditional warranty.

Step 13—Improving Trends in Global Measures

Properly selected global measures are the key to long-term improvement. Those school districts who accomplish dramatic improvement know how to improve their systems. School districts who continuously improve will properly manage both the improvement of existing systems and the design and development of new systems.

Industry has discovered some interesting facts when performing long-term improvement correctly. Quality, productivity, and competitive position start improving from the time the quality improvement effort begins. To the surprise of many, costs go down because waste is reduced. Industry has discovered that many things they thought were critical add little, if any, value. The elimination of this waste ends up reducing cost. Quality experts agree that a great amount of waste exists in every organization.

Step 14—Improving Trends in Customer Satisfaction

Global measures that are focused on pleasing the customer have proven to be invaluable. As quality improves and cost goes down, industry has found that the results delight the customer. Improving trends in concerns voiced by the customer through the feedback system in STEP 6D is a way of finding out if things are getting better. Customer satisfaction trends indicate whether or not the quality effort is working. Customer satisfaction trends should be monitored. Graphical representation is an excellent way to portray these trends.

With help from their business partners, schools can develop ways of determining trends in satisfaction. One technique used in industry is to have outside consultants compare them with the customer's other suppliers. Malcolm Baldrige Award examiners have criticized companies for not surveying noncustomers or lost customers. Similarly, schools should know if they are losing students to other schools, whether they are public or private, and why.

Top performing Baldrige Award applicants have productive means of measuring customer satisfaction beyond measurement of complaints, returns, and warranty rate. Use of measurement tools such as third party market surveys are common.

Step 15—Reduce and/or Eliminate Inspection

When suppliers are able to demonstrate that they are committed to quality and have in place a system of prevention and continuous improvement, they are normally rewarded with increased business. With demonstrated performance, it then becomes unnecessary for the customer to inspect. This relationship might work well for school districts with textbook, equipment, and training suppliers.

One measure for key suppliers might be the skill and ability of incoming students. With demonstrated performance from students, reduced testing of students is appropriate. Some progressive schools are starting to experiment with reduced testing.

Final Step—Continuous Improvement by Applying P-D-C-A

The Total Quality Leadership steps listed above are guidelines for implementing a quality system. The criteria in the Baldrige award also provides excellent guidelines for a Total Quality Leadership system. The basis for any quality effort is continuous improvement and that call for using the Plan-Do-Check-Act cycle. The cycle involves the following steps:

PLAN a change aimed at improvement
Carry it out, perhaps on a small scale (DO)
CHECK the results for what was learned
ACT by adopting the change, abandoning it, or. . . .

The cycle is repeated again and again until other systems require more attention.

The Baldrige criteria is more like a road map that measures where schools are in their quest for total quality. It will help schools to see where their deficiencies exist. This model should be coupled with the Deming philosophy, a philosophy that will provide principles to guide school action toward improvement. The Total Quality Leadership model is a suggested approach only. Dr. Deming frequently says "An example studied without theory teaches nothing." However, seeing a model of how Total Quality Leadership can occur might encourage others to start a quality effort. It should not be thought of as the only path to Total Quality. Many paths can lead to the same destination. It is necessary for each school to select its path and move forward toward continuous, never ending improvement.

The school systems that Sterling has helped have all been very excited about quality. So far results and implementation of concepts taught have been mixed. Some school districts have accomplished much while others are still having problems getting started. Size does play a part in the speed at which quality occurs. The larger the school district, the more difficult quality is to implement. The quality culture change takes much longer to achieve in larger organizations. The same thing happens in businesses. Quality is hard work! There are no short cuts.

As Lloyd Dobyns said, in the PBS series "Quality . . . Or Else," "Change is difficult; not changing is worse!" Business and schools owe it to America to improve the educational system. It is our hope for the future of this great nation.

— 10 —

THE ROLE OF COLLEGES OF EDUCATION IN THE QUALITY TRANSFORMATION OF EDUCATION

Bryan R. Cole, *Associate Professor, Education Administration, Texas A&M University, College Station, Texas*

Jane A. Stallings, *Dean, College of Education, Texas A&M University, College Station, Texas*

Introduction: *Colleges of education are both suppliers to and customers of schools. For systemic initiatives such as TQM to make an impact, their concepts must be part of teacher and administrator training. Bryan Cole and Jane Stallings have been leaders in Texas in rethinking the role of colleges of education in light of the quality interest in schools. Jane Stallings was also a member of the Texas Quality Education Award Task Force in 1991. Texas A&M is working with 13 other colleges of education in restructuring teacher and administrator programs. Their chapter lays out a new role for the college which provides a model for others.*

OPENING

Everything we do, save for a few involuntary muscle responses, is based on a decision. Decisions are based on values. Source values provide the ethical, professional and personal parameters that give direction to thought and deed. The quality movement causes one to question and evaluate the fundamental values (and assumptions) upon which decisions are made and actions are taken. Education is a value based enterprise. Educators, daily, make hundreds of value laden decisions that directly impact the lives of others. Therefore, it is imperative that educators clearly understand the educational values and underlying assumptions upon which their professional decisions are made and with what results. Furthermore, educators must understand the interrelationship between these value decisions and the entire educational system.

When something comes along that suggests that the educational values that we have been taught and practiced for years may be based on faulty assumptions, there is naturally cause for concern and uncertainty. Such is the case with the introduction of Total Quality Management (TQM) principles and tenets into education. Colleges of education are reluctant to embrace "efficiency principles of business" into the more "humane" enterprise of education. However, Total

Quality Management offers much more to the educational scene than simply efficiency measures—indeed it offers a whole new way of thinking about education, about management styles and about other people including students. Chaffee and Sherr point out why TQM can work in higher education:

(1) TQM is a comprehensive philosophy, with principles and tools. Unlike many administrative innovations, TQM is not a recipe of ingredients and steps that must be followed slavishly to produce the intended result. Rather, TQM is more like a well-equipped, well-stocked kitchen. TQM has the ingredients and the mechanisms of good management, from which organizations select those that suit their needs and purposes.
(2) TQM has face validity. TQM uses many known principles and tools of good management. Perhaps its major contribution to practice is that it makes good management clear and understandable. It contains all the essential elements in one consistent package. It rejects some ingredients that have proven ineffective but remain common in practice, and it adds some ingredients that organizations have typically overlooked.
(3) TQM is already working in a number of similar enterprises and a few colleges and universities. (pp. 7–9)

Accordingly, colleges of education must take a proactive role in the examination of the rich opportunities for improvement that Total Quality Management affords, not only for their own management, but for the significant potential improvement of education in general. Indeed, colleges of education must provide the leadership in the transformation of education (some refer to it as restructuring) and in the preparation of teachers and administrators to be educational leaders of quality schools. This transformation/restructuring will not be effectively addressed through such movements as the extended school day, year-round education, and other similar methods designed primarily on "more is better." Rather, a transformation/ restructuring resulting in significant improvement in student achievement and development can only occur through fundamental changes in the way we design and manage educational systems. And a dedicated commitment to the principles and full implementation of Total Quality Management provides the opportunity for that transformation.

To effect this transformation, colleges of education must reassess their mission, their constituents, their programs, indeed, every aspect of the way they currently conduct business. It is with this realization that the Texas A&M University College of Education has begun the process of understanding and applying Total Quality Management in fulfilling its responsibilities.

First, it is recognized that making the fundamental changes that Total Quality Management would suggest is a long term commitment and requires comprehensive planning and close articulation with the other components of the various systems with which the College interacts—schools, agencies, the university, the profession, business, and industry.

Secondly, it is recognized that the very mission of the College, as well as the methodologies by which that mission is carried out, may fundamentally change.

With these two points in mind, this writing will share some of the experiences of the College to date in "beginning the journey" of implementing Total Quality Management and outline some of the thinking and issues that have emerged and that are anticipated to emerge "down the path."

BEGINNING THE JOURNEY

A Five-Year Strategic Total Quality Management Plan was drafted to begin understanding the role and scope of implementing TQM in the College. The Plan was divided into 4 major areas—managing the college, curriculum, research, and propagation. Significant activities and timelines were developed for each of these areas. As a result of this strategic plan, a preliminary Total Quality Management Action Plan was developed. The plan called for multiple phases that included:

- Reviewing vision and mission statements;
- Faculty and staff training;
- Identification of pilot processes to be studied;
- Team formation;
- Conduct of pilot process studies; and
- Rebuilding of the College strategic plan based on critical processes.

At best, the plan was naive and incomplete. However, it did serve as an effective point of departure for discussion, for initiating training, and for stimulating thinking throughout the College. As a result of this initial planning, a Total Quality Management Leadership Steering Committee was established consisting of the following members:

Dean of the College
Associate Deans (4)
Department Heads (5)
Chair of the College Faculty Advisory Committee
Chair of the College International Program Committee
College Business Officer

A 1-day TQM awareness training workshop was conducted with this group to provide an orientation to TQM and to discuss and assess the receptivity and advisability of implementing TQM in the college on a broad scale. As a result of this session, the Steering Committee enthusiastically endorsed the wisdom and potential of TQM for college operations. This session also served as the impetus for a 1 1/2 day, collegewide retreat that was designed to accomplish several purposes:

- Create an environment so that everyone feels valued and a part of the College vision and mission;
- Foster communication, trust, and empowerment among the faculty;
- Enable faculty to share their individual goals, professional values, and individual visions for the College;
- Familiarize faculty with the concepts of Total Quality Management as a process framework for attaining individual and College goals;
- Begin building a College vision of inclusivity.

The retreat provided significant input to the Dean to begin building a College vision of inclusivity. Additionally, 7 critical issues were preliminarily identified as process improvement candidates. These issues included:

- Improvement of communication within the College
- Balancing multiple roles and expectations (*e.g.*, research and teaching)

- Faculty/staff involvement in decision making
- Maintaining one's autonomy while contributing to program, departmental and college missions
- Faculty recognition
- Budget
- Restructuring the College

The involvement of everyone in the College in this process was critical due to the diverse and comprehensive nature of the College. Over 100 faculty and staff subsequently offered to serve as a member on the Process Improvement Teams to address these 7 areas. One senior faculty member in the College, Professor Robert Shutes, reflected on the College retreat—

As I sat down to capture my reflections on the fall retreat, I thought I would be polite to those faculty members who didn't know me yet and state my departmental affiliation. Once I centered and spelled out my department's name, however, I realized that it made my department appear more important to me than the college, whereas the retreat had just the opposite effect. By forming each working group with representatives from every department, the planners decreased our sense of departmental identification and emphasized collective involvement in a common enterprise. That is the dominant impression I carried away from the retreat, and that is why I replaced my department affiliation with my sense of relationship to you (the faculty and staff of the College).

As our separate departments have grown in numbers of students, faculty, and staff, and responded to demands and requirements of the Texas Higher Education Coordinating Board, accrediting agencies, legislators, the Texas Education Agency, the State Board of Education, and various university pressures, we have been steadily driven into almost paranoid preoccupation with our separate responses to the interlocking bureaucracies and have increasingly lost the sense of family we once enjoyed when the college and the university were smaller and the pace of our lives seemed more manageable. In my view, this retreat took a big step toward reestablishing our sense of oneness and marshalling our collective abilities again to support some common goals.

The retreat also served to remind everyone of how much talent and brain power our college contains, of what interesting and attractive personalities populate every department, and of how exciting it is to interact with diverse colleagues in solving problems. That is especially so when the problems involve redefining who we are as a college and formulating a new vision for our future contributions to our university and our society. Those problems were, in fact, the focus of our challenge at the retreat, and everyone attending, including a number of talented lecturers and graduate students, worked together to pool their ideas, their insights, and their abilities to capture them in ringing phrases.

The retreat began the process but did not finish it. Several poster pads worth of distilled ideas, many three by five cards crammed with proposals, and many facilitators' summaries of consensus came back to campus to be analyzed and synthesized, debated and refined. Anyone who was unable to attend can still participate in the derivation of our new vision for ourselves, our new goals for the 21st century, and the new means we must develop to attain them. There is also plenty of room for everyone who attended the retreat to stay involved and monitor the results. I hope you will because not only will your contribution improve the quality of the product, we haven't all met yet!

From this, it is clear that something very important within the College has begun.

We are defining the College vision as a statement to our internal customers of what we wish to create and what we want to become. The mission statement, on the other hand, is a statement to our external customers of what we do and how we go about accomplishing it. The vision is providing a shared framework and sense of commonality with which each individual in the College can feel a sense of belonging and professional investment in the direction of the College and relate how his or her personal vision is supported and nurtured by the College vision. The College vision is also giving direction to the review of the College mission as well as the departments' vision and mission statements. In this regard, the College is attempting to take heed from Senge's guidance:

That personal vision, by itself, is not the key to more effective creativity. The key is "creative tension," the tension between vision and reality. The most effective people are those who can "hold" their vision while remaining committed to seeing current reality clearly. This principle is no less true for organization. The hallmark of a learning organization is not lovely visions floating in space, but a relentless willingness to examine "what is" in light of our vision. (p. 226)

Sensitivity to this tension is critical among all faculty and staff in light of resource limitations, increased and multiple expectations, and the reality of the broader educational system in which we strive to have our work make a difference.

THE CHALLENGE OF A SHIFT IN MISSION

The current mission of the College of Education, which has not been changed since the decision to begin implementation of TQM was made, is as follows:

The mission of the College of Education is to develop a citizenry that can participate, thrive, and contribute to a free and democratic society. To this end, the College of Education will develop professionals who can contribute to shaping the structures which determine the quality of the process and content of education within the public and private schooling systems and the workplace. These professionals will contribute significantly to the dialogues of society. Within the broad purpose and mission of Texas A&M University, the College of Education has three primary functions: Research, Teaching, and Service.

In reviewing the mission statement in light of TQM principles and tenets, there are multiple directions upon which the statement can focus, and thereby establish direction and priorities for the College, as well as communicate to our external customers what they can expect as clients (students) and customers (school districts and other employers, and graduate and professional schools). While we are examining and studying these multiple directions and the implications thereof, 3 tenets and their interrelated dynamics pose quite interesting challenges and questions for a college of education.

1. Organizational Design

The first tenet relates to organizational design. In *Designing Organizations for High Performance*, David P. Hanna states:

All organizations are perfectly designed to get the results they get; if you don't like the results you are getting, look at the organizational design. (p. 38)

Couple this with the point that TQM is about improving the total behavior of an organization—it's enabling an organization to actually do through cultural change and continuous process improvement what it wants to do and should be doing. These thoughts would suggest that colleges of education ought to be about preparing educators that can design and manage effective educational organizations (at the appropriate level consistent with their training and experience). Whereas the emphasis now is on recognizing and attending to individual learning styles, this shift would suggest an emphasis on educational process design. This shift would be consistent with other TQM tenets that purport that when problems arise or you are not getting the results expected or desired, you should focus on the process as the source of deficiency rather that the ability or motivation of the individual. If the process is the "right" process, then the student can achieve the desired level of progress. But, of course, TQM tenets also purport that the process, to be the correct process, has to give high priority to the client/customer—in this case, the student. So it becomes a matter of perspective and balance. Nonetheless, focusing on the process design versus the individual is an important issue when dealing with a limited number of professional education courses in a curriculum.

2. Profound Knowledge

The second tenet is that of Deming's profound knowledge. Profound knowledge consists of 4 parts:

- Understanding of a system and systems theory;
- An appreciation of variance (knowledge of statistics);
- A knowledge of psychology;
- A theory of knowledge.

In transforming education, be it colleges of education, or education in general, educational leaders must have a thorough understanding of these elements, their interdependence, and the implications for education of managing the transformation through the application of profound knowledge. While only a few key points relating to profound knowledge will be related here, the reader is referred to W. Edwards Deming's *Out of Crisis* and *Quality, Productivity and Competitive Position* for a complete treatment of these concepts.

Colleges of education must foster an understanding by their students of systems and systems theory. In applying this concept, we must change our own, as well as our students'. thinking away from a concept of organizations as machines made up of separate replaceable parts and come to view them as dynamic, living systems. We must see each system, be it a child, a school district, or a college of education, in relation to other systems and in relation to what makes up each of those other systems. In order to effectively educate the child or manage the educational system, we must understand the systemic dynamics that are functioning within and across that system.

In developing an appreciation for variance, we must acknowledge that systems and systems' components differ. The implications of this acknowledgement is that we accept everyone where they are and begin their improvement from that point. We move away from standardized testing that is norm-based and that creates the conditions for failure because no matter what, 50% of those being tested will be "below average" and will be viewed as nonsuccessful. We do the same thing in the evaluation of teachers, faculty, staff, etc. We create win-lose situations. Colleges of education must be the leader in teaching people how to create educational and managerial situations in which all people win. Variances dealing with affective dimensions cannot be quantified, so we should not expend energy and resources trying to measure what is unmeasurable. Rather, we should nurture and support people where they are and collaboratively work with them toward improvement. Some variance can be quantified, and we should do so in order to study the variance, to determine the source of that variance, and to implement continuous improvement methodologies to correct the source of variance. Educational managers at all levels must fully understand the implications of variance and how to interpret variance.

Included within the profound knowledge dimension of psychology is the understanding of how people are motivated, how people interact with each other, and again the recognition that people are different. Educators must be aware of these differences and develop these differences to the optimization of the individual and the system. We must move from encouraging competitive learning and working environments to creating cooperative and collaborative learning and working environments where each individual feels valued and supported. Grading must be restructured to acknowledge individuals and their worth and not used to compare and demean.

Understanding the theory of knowledge and its application provides educators with the ability to predict, based on sound educational theory, and then to modify that prediction based on observed, and where appropriate, measurable outcomes. Educators must be taught how to use theory in conjunction with the other dimensions of profound knowledge as a means of managing continuous improvement for individuals and organizations.

The above comments on the application of profound knowledge to the improvement of education and educational management only begin to scratch the surface. Colleges of education in conjunction with the schools must conduct the needed research to realize the significant potential for education that lies within a full understanding and application of profound knowledge.

3. Environmental Sanctioning

The third tenet is an appreciation that all organizations are sanctioned by the environment in which they are located. If they do not meet the expectations of that environment, they will not survive. Colleges of education must become much more in tune with their environment and the environments in which schools operate. Similarly, preparation programs must reflect these environmental concerns and provide students with the knowledge and skills to educate and manage effectively in these environments. On one level, this tenet is addressing the TQM principle of achieving customer satisfaction. However, on a higher level, this tenet recognizes the dramatic changes that are occurring in our society and begs colleges of education to build a sensitivity and knowledge of these changes into preparation programs.

IMPLICATIONS OF TQM TENETS FOR COLLEGES OF EDUCATION

Integrating these 3 tenets—organizational design, profound knowledge, and environmental sanctioning— indeed presents major challenges for education in general and colleges of education in particular. Recognizing that work redesign is a major component of TQM, these tenets suggest not just "renovation," but full redesign is needed that includes changes in the very foundations upon which our theory and practice of education and educational management are now based. This redesign will challenge the vested interest and bias of every individual involved and will cause colleges of education to dramatically change the way they do business. This transformation, however, will enable educational leaders at all levels to be prepared to manage the high quality educational systems of the future rather than simply to continue to manage existing failing structures.

Accordingly, colleges of education must consider, as we are, a mission statement that addresses these 3 tenets and that might be worded as follows:

The mission of the College of Education is to develop professionals who are ethical, moral, and environmentally sensitive, and who can design and manage effective educational systems by using profound knowledge and continuous improvement methodologies.

The transformation to this mission from a more traditional mission offers exciting opportunities for individual renewal, breakthrough thinking, and significant improvement at all levels of education, and presents a challenge of the highest order to colleges of education.

CHANGING RELATIONSHIPS WITH SCHOOLS

Even during the short time that the College of Education has been involved in Total Quality Management, school districts are seeing a difference in the way we approach school restructuring efforts. With changed assumptions come changed relationships. Over the next 5 years in working with schools, the Texas A&M University College of Education will focus on the following critical areas:

* Creation of partnerships with school districts with an emphasis on using exemplary schools for teacher education;
* Rewarding faculty involvement in local schools through changes in the tenure and promotion criteria;
* Recruitment and preparation of minority teachers;
* Development of a "pre-ed" curriculum similar to that of the "pre-med" curriculum of physicians.

Integrating the Accelerated Schools Model into the Total Quality Management framework will provide a powerfully synergistic restructuring effort of untold potential. The commonality of purpose between these two paradigms offers unique opportunities for improvement of educational systems through a sound educational theoretical and management approach. As one superintendent stated, "For the first time in years, I am excited about the potential for significant positive change in education." Two brief examples of the changing relationships that are taking place will be cited.

The collaborative efforts at Jane Long Middle School, Bryan, Texas, reflect school university partnerships and middle school education. A school-university team representing Texas A&M University College of Education and Jane Long Middle School faculty completed accelerated schools training in the summer of 1991. The team's goal is to integrate science, math, language arts, and social studies throughout the middle school curriculum. During the Fall, 1991, semester, the university faculty and middle school faculty designed methods courses that are presently being taught to the first cohort of future teachers. At the same time, our student teachers presented an interdisciplinary thematic unit based on the outcomes of this collaborative planning. The school-university faculties provided each other with information and input to help them establish their goals. A series of regular meetings, discussions, and shared inservices provided both groups with the information that supported their instructional planning. Additionally, another university and middle school faculty collaboratively planned thematic unit on the Mayan culture has been developed and taught by our student teachers. This instructional unit was particularly relevant because of the large number of Hispanic students in the Jane Long Middle School. The school-university partnership resulted in university courses and middle school integrated instructional units developed and taught in a cooperative manner. All teachers involved served as a mentor to 1 or 2 of the 24 university students who completed the block. The next phase of the project is to integrate Total Quality Management components into the management and continuous improvement aspects of the project.

A second initiative is in conjunction with the Goose Creek CISD, Baytown, Texas. The goal of PROJECT 2000—Performance STANDARDS Based Curriculum—is to develop a pilot Performance STANDARDS Based Curriculum and Assessment model in which students in the high school graduating Class of 2000 can demonstrate competency in the outcomes collaboratively identified by Texas A&M University professors, Lee College (a community college serving the Baytown area) professors, and Goose Creek CISD educators. The project's strategic plan will be developed collaboratively by representatives of Texas A&M University, Goose Creek CISD, Texas Education Agency, Texas Higher Education Coordinating Board, Lee College, and Exxon Corporation (a major industry in the Baytown community) during 1993. This pilot project is designed to demonstrate that students who participate in a collaboratively developed, clearly focused Performance STANDARDS Based educational experience, based upon principles of Performance Based Curriculum, systematic change, and total quality management, perform better than students subjected to traditional time-based, course driven, SAT, and class rank assessment procedures.

CONTINUING THE JOURNEY

The transformation to date has been exciting. The excitement is greatly enhanced by knowing that other major components of the "total educational system," including government and business and industry, are beginning to see the value of adopting and applying TQM in education. For once, we may all have a common framework whereupon we agree upon missions, methodologies, and outcomes. Such a common framework can nurture an educational system of cooperation, enhanced student achievement and development, and more effective use of limited resources.

The Texas A&M University College of Education, as a "learning organization," is like many others feeling its way through the transformation. At this point and for the foreseeable future, there are more questions than answers. But working together to answer these questions will make the transformation to quality education a reality. While our plans provide us with a "theory of knowledge" for implementing TQM in educational systems, we recognize that they too are dynamic and will be modified as we learn. The challenges of collaboratively identifying and addressing critical processes in managing the college, in curriculum, in research, and in propagation offer this and other colleges of education the signal opportunity to develop preparation programs that can indeed result in an educational system that meets and exceeds the needs of all students and creates and nurtures a truly democratic and economically viable society.

REFERENCES

Chaffee, Ellen Earle, and Sherr, Lawrence A., *Quality: Transforming Postsecondary Education*. ASHE-ERIC Higher Education Report No. 3. Washington, D.C.: The George Washington University School of Education and Human Development (1992).

Deming, W. Edwards, *Quality, Productivity and Competitive Position*. Cambridge MA: Massachusetts Institute of Technology Center for Advanced Engineering (1982).

Deming, W. Edwards, *Out of Crisis*. Cambridge, MA: Massachusetts Institute of Technology Center for Advanced Engineering (1986).

Hanna, David P., *Designing Organizations for High Performance*. Reading, MA: Addison-Wesley Publishers (1988).

Senge, Peter M., *The Fifth Discipline: The Art & Practice of The Learning Organization*. New York: Doubleday Currency (1990).

— 11 —

CHOOSING AND WORKING WITH A CONSULTANT

Susan Leddick, *Profound Knowledge Resources, Inc., Dallas, TX*

Introduction: *Consultants can be a key supplier in initiating TQM in schools and there are many to choose from. Susan Leddick is one of the nationally known quality consultants who have worked many years in the private sector. She has recently been drawn back into the school environment where she started her career as a high school teacher. The demand for skilled quality consultants in education is growing and it is rare to find one who also has experience as an educator. Susan is also assisting the American Association of School Administrators in developing a quality curriculum for schools. Her chapter here provides valuable tips to educators as they begin to consider procuring consultant assistance.*

WHY A CONSULTANT? CAN'T WE DO THIS OURSELVES?

So much about the transformation to a new way of managing school districts, local schools, the classroom, and support services seems to make so much sense that some people think that they should just be able to figure it out on their own. That's misleading. Dr. Deming often reminds his audiences that profound knowledge—the stuff of transformation—"must come from the outside, and by invitation." From systems theory we know "that each organization evolved in relation to a larger whole, that closed systems cannot change or grow. Management "teams" who talk only among themselves often develop personal insights and warm relationships. They cannot transform their [organizations]."[1]

When I think about consultants, I always remember the same incident. One afternoon years ago, when the kids were little and I was an at-home mom, the electric range in the kitchen ceased to function. Undaunted, I hauled the *Reader's Digest Home Repair Book* and *You Can Fix Almost Anything* off the shelf. While the kids napped,

---

[1] Weisbord, Marvin R., *Discovering Common Ground*. San Francisco: Berrett-Koehler Publishers, Inc., p. 50 (1992).

161

I played appliance repair Sherlock Holmes. "It's the thermostat, for sure," I announced to my husband at dinner that night. "They have new ones at Central Hardware and it shows here how to replace it."

He did his best. The control panel was trickier than it looked, and there was a maze of wires, to boot. But finally he triumphed—the old thermostat lay in the cardboard box and the shiny new one was ready to rouse the electric range to life.

It was not to be. We finally called the repairman, who commented on the nice new thermostat. He found the real trouble in the wiring and fixed it in a matter of minutes. It took some special tools and know-how. We had managed to spend twice what it would have cost to have called him in the first place. I learned a valuable lesson about consultants.

Consultants Can See What We Can't See, and They Can See It Fast

A set of objective eyes and practice based on theory are the real value of your consultant. Deming goes to great length to demonstrate that the system cannot transform itself. For most of us, it is sufficient to think of times we have called in a professional to help change a car part, write a will, or conduct a surgery. Given enough time and money, we might be able to do what those professionals do, but we haven't that luxury at the start. It's the same with the transformation—busy school practitioners need help from the outside to begin their learning.

There's More to the Transformation Than Meets the Eye

There is a substantial body of knowledge. This is not a body of knowledge handily codified in a set of how-to books. It is, instead, a deep understanding of customers, systems, variation, knowledge, planned change, and people. It is the mastery of this body of theory that separates the best consultants from those who can add less value.

There's Only One First Time Try

I've seen too often how hard it is to build up momentum and excitement for the transformation *the second time*. It's better to optimize your chances. Get help from the beginning. Don't wait until everybody can see that the thermostat was the wrong call. Of course, no consultant worth his or her salt would tell you that there's only one right way to transform your school or classroom or district or department, but every one of them can give some good avoidance tactics and good strategies based on theory.

CHOOSING THE CONSULTANT

When Will You Need the Consultant?

Fullan's change model[2] contains 3 phases: Initiation, implementation, continuation. *Initiation* is the start-up and awareness phase. In initiation people become intrigued about a new way of doing things. *Implementation* is the tryout phase where they test whether the new way can work "around here." *Continuation* is the institutionalization or integration phase where the new way has become the routine way. All 3 phases of change can be eased with good consultation. Regardless of stage, a strategy is required. By "strategy" I mean a decision where there may be a time lag of a year or more between the decision and an organizational response.[3] The consultant can be helpful in reviewing strategies, and in helping to decide when short-term action is needed. The simple diagram in Figure 11.1 explains the general role of the consultant at each of these phases. We will return to the 3 phases as we discuss working with the consultant.

What Should You Look For?

Someone Who Can Stay the Course – Not a One-Shot Deal

Because of the complexity and depth of change that is afoot, you want someone who can be your colleague and guide over the long haul – as much as 3-5 years or more, in some cases. You will have minimal impact from 1-day presentations to large groups (even though the cost per head declines dramatically that way!). Think, instead, of a close and lasting working relationship.

---

[2]Fullan, Michael G. and Stiegelbauer, Suzanne, *The New Meaning of Educational Change*. Columbia University: Teachers College Press (1992).
[3]Tribus, Myron. Personal communication, November, 1992.

PHASES OF CHANGE	ROLE OF THE CONSULTANT
	Your consultant offers seminars, workshops, and start-up planning.
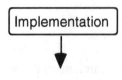	Your consultant provides technical assistance to implementers and helps solve real problems.
Continuation	Your consultant's role changes as people master the new way of doing things and make it the way everyone works all the time. The relationship may end or evolve.

FIGURE 11.1

Someone with Personal Experience and Credentials in the Quality Field

It may sound callous, but there are a number of people today who have read a few books, attended a couple of workshops, and declared themselves to be quality consultants. Be careful. Ask questions like these and listen hard for the answers:

♦ With which of the quality leaders and theorists have you studied directly?
♦ For how long?
♦ What prepares you to consult with our system?
♦ What are the theoretical principles from which you guide your work?
♦ How will you help us with planning, with measurement, with allocating resources to improvement priorities?
♦ By what method should we make improvements, design new systems, or standardize existing systems?
♦ What tools shall we use?
♦ How will you prepare us to stand on our own?
♦ What training materials do you use?

• If you can't help us on something, can you refer us to other people who can?

Listen for answers that indicate that your prospective consultant has had substantial and legitimate preparation. (The American Association of School Administrators (AASA) is preparing a certification process that will soon be of some help to you, but it is just beginning in early 1993.) Listen for answers that indicate the use of an integrated system of theory, process (or method), and tools. These should be reflected in the materials used for training and during consultation. Note that training and consultation are not the same thing. Listen for answers that indicate that you are not being led into what I call "learned dependency." You have every right to learn to stand on your own feet and become self-sufficient.

In addition to the credentials, your prospective consultant should be able to relate to people at all levels of the organization—community, board, faculty, administrators, support staff, and students.

Expect that a prospect will ask you a number of questions, too. Be wary of anyone who does not inquire of your unique situations, your progress, your challenges, your history.

Call all references. People will tell you things over the phone that they will not write on paper.

Many people prefer that their consultant be a former teacher or administrator. I have not found this to be a significant issue (even though I have been both in my own career). Let me explain. Good quality consultants work from a universal set of theoretical principles that guide them in manufacturing plants, retail stores, government offices, or public schools. Certainly every organization is unique, and every organization proclaims to outsiders "Yes, but we're *different!*" That's the world of the consultant. Every day is spent going from setting to setting, assessing the uniqueness, and rediscovering the universals. The consultant learns to listen for key points, and people often comment "How could he know so much about our business so fast?" This goes for schools, too. My advice: Don't turn down someone who has the other credentials and personal traits you want on the basis of her not having been a schoolteacher at some point in her life.

Just one final note on what to look for: Sometimes you may face the decision of working with several consultants from a single firm vs. working with multiple consultants vs. working with a single consultant. Look for consistency in any case. Several consultants from a single firm can be effective if they work from the same theory, processes, and tools (they most likely will), and if they communicate about your organization among themselves. Expect to invest some time, energy, and money in coordinating their work—meeting with them as a group and doing joint planning.

Working with multiple consultants can be a bit more difficult since they are not formally part of the same organization, but it can be done. Sometimes, for instance, you find someone who relates really well to your teachers but not so well to your administrators. Someone else may be just the opposite. By coordinating their work and being sure that they are heading in the same direction (and, of course, working from the same theoretical concepts) you can have the best of both. Please do not assume that they will do this coordination without your prompting it; you must manage the interactions so you all stay focused on purpose.

Working with a single consultant is probably the simplest of the 3 options, but sometimes it is hard to find one person who has both the credentials and the time to dedicate. As always, good people are in high demand. Expect to schedule a year's work at a time if you are looking to establish a working relationship with people with national or international practices.

Where Should You Look?

Word-of-mouth

Word-of-mouth is a reliable source. Find people who have been working with consultants and ask whom they recommend. Be sure to ask why.

Professional Organizations

AASA and other professional organizations such as the American Society for Quality Control (ASQC.) Expect that AASA will be able to give you names of consultants who have already begun to work with schools. ASQC, which has local chapters in most cities, can refer you to working consultants in your area. These people may not have done any prior work with schools, but may be happy to help you and are quite skilled in quality principles.

Community Colleges

Community colleges are sources of good trainers and consultants. Since 1984, the Transformation of American Industry National Community Colleges Training Project, headquartered at Jackson Community College, Jackson, Michigan, has been training trainers in community colleges around the country. Most of these trainers have worked primarily with local businesses and industrial firms, but several are beginning to respond to inquiries for help from schools. A special version of training materials for schools has been developed through the Transformation project.[4]

In the state of Iowa a statewide voluntary initiative began in January, 1993, to prepare an existing group of community college trainers to work with public schools. They partnered with local Area Education Agencies to develop trainers within the AEA's during joint consultation with schools.

Several other states are considering doing the same thing as Iowa. In the meantime, individual community college trainers in Minnesota, South Carolina, Michigan, and other states are beginning to serve schools.

Do You Have to Like the Consultant?

It helps. Dr. Myron Tribus comments on this point: "Liking comes from success together. Respect is the place to start."

What Should You Expect in a Proposal?

A proposal should be developed jointly between you and the consultant. It may require a couple of reviews and revisions before you are both happy with it and it adequately describes your work together. Agree on the method of payment, the schedule, and other logistics. The completed proposal should include at least the following things.

Activities for All Levels of the Organization

Look for breadth and depth. There should be a clear purpose for all activities—activity and progress are different, so be sure the proposed activities are likely to move your organization forward, not just keep it busy.

---

[4]For information contact Carole Schwinn, Project Director, Jackson Community College, Jackson, MI, (517) 787-0080.

A Plan for Making You Self-Sufficient

Training of internal trainers and facilitators is absolutely essential. Look for a plan that allows your internal trainers to work side-by-side with the consultant to get coaching as they begin to practice.

And . . .

Itemized costs for consultation, travel, training, development, and materials.

Time allotments on a monthly basis. Expect that the consultant will be with you every month to keep the momentum going.

A year-long commitment, minimum, with renewal options.

What Will It Cost?

$1500 and up per day for well-qualified professionals. This price is probably already discounted for work with not-for-profit organizations.

Daily fee plus travel plus materials. Some charge for travel time; some charge for preparation or development. (On development: If you're asking for a customized session, expect to pay extra. Some consultants charge equal numbers of days for consultation and preparation.)

You will probably pay less for people associated with a community college. In no way is the lower price reflective of lower quality. You may pay nothing for the help of a local business partner.

How Will You Pay for It?

Grant Money

Research shows that it's much more difficult to get to the continuation phase in grant-funded projects. It's not hard to tell why. Don't you spend your birthday money differently from the way you spend your paycheck? If you take this route, be even more sure to write in a training of trainers option. Having your own trainers will help assure that you can carry on after the money has dried up.

Hard Money

Most people take it from staff development. Or sometimes from special discretionary funds.

Sponsors

Primarily these are business partners in the community. This form of support usually comes as service, but it may also come as grants to support events like conferences or training projects. Servicemaster, for example, supported the Pasadena, Texas, conference on quality in education in the spring of 1992. The conference drew almost 700 attendees.

Combined Hard and Soft Money

Probably the best combination because it may have a better chance to lead to permanent change.

Collaboration with Other Districts

Most consultants are happy to work with more than 1 district at a time, allowing them to share costs. Several districts in a region can form a strong network, reducing costs and creating support for follow-up during implementation.

WORKING WITH THE CONSULTANT

What are the Keys to a Good Working Relationship?

Establishing a Contact Person

The higher in the management hierarchy the liaison for the consultant can be, the better. Some consultants require that the superintendent or an assistant superintendent be this contact. Whoever it is should have intimate knowledge of how the organization works, should be influential and respected in the organization, and should be committed to the transformation. This is the person who will schedule the consultant's time, announce and organize meetings, strategize during planning, and be the front line for assessing progress with the consultant.

Understanding Whose Job is What

You hire consultants to help you, not to do your job for you. Expect your consultant to guide, to test practices against theory, and to help you see what you cannot see about your organization. The job of implementation or application is still yours. The job of creating a shared vision is still yours. The day-to-day operations of the organization are still yours. Refer again to the 3 phases of change to remind yourself of the special consulting needs of each phase. The clearer the responsibilities are, the less likely you will run into trouble and accusations that someone isn't holding up his end of the bargain.

Close Communication

Expect to talk with your consultant weekly, and maybe more often at the beginning. (By the way, these calls should not be "billable" for the consultant. The proposal or contract should explicitly allow such communication to be part of the deal between you.) The consultant will be relying on you to keep her up to date with the current events in the organization. It does neither of you any good if the consultant seems "out of it" when she talks to people about what's going on and planned. The opportunity to learn by joint planning before a visit and debriefing after should not be discounted, and time should always be allocated to encourage these discussions. Send your consultant copies of important documents or news clippings. Expect that your consultant will do the same for you—sharing new work, new materials, and new learning.

Frequent Face-to-Face Encounters

Monthly visits are a good place to start. Depending on the phase, shorter or longer spacing may be appropriate. Certainly one of the advantages to having a local consultant is that it is easier to meet face-to-face more frequently. You can call on short notice and ask that the consultant attend a meeting. (A bonus is associated with local providers: Less money spent on travel, leaving more for direct service delivery.)

What's Off Limits?

Personnel Judgments

Inevitably, it happens. A client asks "What do you think of so-and-so? I'm thinking of moving him to a position of whatever." Please do not ask your consultant to make such off-the-cuff judgments of your staff. Now, if you want the consultant to interview the person, to help review qualifications for a new position, or make a formal assessment, that's different. What's off limits is casual judgments that may be ill-founded. Gossip rarely serves any good purpose.

Anything Unethical or Illegal

"Well, that's obvious!" you say. Is it? I know of consultants who have been asked to dummy their expense reports, to pad or scrape their billings . . . and so on. Expect that your consultant will have the highest integrity, and respect that position.

How Should the Time be Budgeted?

Split the time between the staff and the schools. Without visiting the schools and interacting with the building staff, teachers, and students, the consultant can become too removed from the real work of the district. On the other hand, without regularly consulting with the district management and school board, it will be impossible for the consultant to contribute much to systemwide transformation. It is, in fact, the leaders of the organization who will make the transformation possible and who must be dedicated to its success.

Recognize that there is a difference between training and consultation. Sometimes there will be a need to train—conduct internal seminars. Often, however, the consultant will consult with small groups in planning or in reviewing progress and giving feedback. Dedicate time for the consultant to help with systemwide planning, improvement of the measurement system, and coaching on the new demands on leaders as their roles change.

It's important for people throughout the organization to be able to interact with the consultant, requesting time on the schedule as they need it, but maintaining the overall time allocation agreed on during the proposal writing.

What is a Typical Routine Cycle of Consultation Like?

The activities of consultation change over time and depend on where the organization is in the change process. At the beginning, the focus is on creating awareness and helping to identify "early implementers" who are eager to try out their new learning. Many training sessions are held at this stage. Later, the focus is on giving technical assistance to those early implementers, helping to reinforce their new work, and helping leaders understand and model leadership for the transformation. There will be time spent with internal trainers and facilitators, coaching them through rough spots, encouraging their efforts, and applauding their successes. Eventually the consultant is needed less and less as the organization becomes more self-sufficient. Sometimes special projects evolve at this stage. The consultant continues to share new advances in the field and learns with the organization through their own experience.

Is There a Fatal Error to Make?

Yes. Failing to integrate your quality process immediately with the "real work" of the school system is a sure road to ultimate failure. Be sure that your consultant does not encourage a separate organization for quality. Work through what already exists. You already do staff meetings, for example, where improvement opportunities can be identified and resources allocated. You do staff development where the theory, process, and tools can be integrated into the courses you provide. You may have site-based decision making bodies who are in need of a method and tools for their work. Teachers and students work together every day to improve the teaching/learning system. They should be using the theory, process, and tools of quality along the way. Treating your work for quality as a separate "program" to be integrated somewhere down the road will only make it more vulnerable to attack and more likely to be considered temporary or faddish.

SUMMARY

Consultants can help during all 3 phases of change: Initiation, implementation, and continuation. A list of questions can help to identify those consultants whose experience and credentials are sound. Begin to work with your consultant during the proposal writing stage and continue frequent contact throughout the term of the engagement. Maintain close contact through a well placed individual who will be the liaison throughout. Schedule the consultant's time between central office and the buildings or classroom to assure that the quality process is impacting the real work of the school system. And, above all, integrate the quality process with your everyday work.

Following the guidelines and considering the issues offered here can help you to enjoy a productive and valuable working relationship with your quality consultant – and help you both make a contribution to the transformation of your school system.

— 12 —

RETHINKING THE CONNECTIONS BETWEEN SECONDARY AND HIGHER EDUCATION

Richard D. DeCosmo, *President*
Jerome Parker, *Executive Assistant to the President*
Louis Scott, *Special Assistant to the President*
Susanna Staas, *Quality Coordinator*

Delaware County Community College, Media, Pennsylvania

Introduction: *Another potential critical link for schools are community colleges. They are obviously customers for school graduates, but, as this chapter shows, they can also be suppliers of TQM training and support. Delaware County Community College enrolls 25,000 students each year in its credit and community service programs. It is located in suburban Philadelphia. The staff of DCCC has totally rethought the concept of supplier/customer relationships in the educational system. As such, they can be a model for other community colleges across the country. They have accomplished this without creating fear or competition among their supplier schools. Figure 12.1 represents their concept of education as a "seamless garment," which should be a common vision for everyone involved in education.*

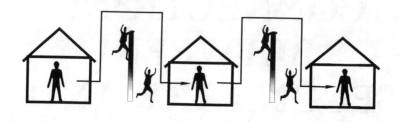

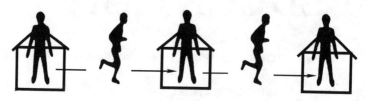

FIGURE 12.1
Removing the barriers between levels of education.

OPENING

Two of the most serious challenges for educational institutions in the 1990s are:

* Achieving and maintaining quality
* Acquiring and maximizing the essential resources to fulfill their respective missions.

Delaware County Community College chose to embrace the principles of Total Quality Management as a way of dealing with both of these issues. Since its inception in 1986, the College's transformation to Total Quality Management has progressed through a number of steps including:

* Implementing a small number of project improvement teams as a mechanism for introducing TQM and solving some long-standing administrative problems.
* Integrating strategic planning with daily process management by identifying, measuring, and selectively improving fundamental processes of the college and each of its departments.

* Developing educational training programs and a certificate program in TQM, which the college offers to the community and internally.
* Involving faculty in adapting TQ techniques to improve the teaching/learning process.

While preparing to create the strategic plan for the '90s, DCCC's staff studied the future and the College's place in it. It soon became clear that the College, like its corporate brethren, must develop closer relationships—even partnerships—with its suppliers. It was evident that the most important partnerships to develop first were with the most important "suppliers," the area school districts. The synergy resulting from these partnerships could help all to be better educators than we could be individually.

Although these relationships with student "suppliers" are analogous to supplier/customer relationships between companies in the private sector, the differences are still substantial. For example, the College does not and should not select only a small set of "quality" suppliers and establish a long-term partnership with them, as some TQ leaders recommend. A community college must work with all of its "suppliers," and they with the college. We all serve the same set of stakeholders. The challenge is to create partnerships that work to the benefit of students.

Delaware County Community College takes the challenge of developing partnerships with area school districts seriously as part of its Total Quality Management philosophy. The College staff believes that these partnerships will improve learning at all levels of the educational system. We believe strongly that we are all part of one system and that we owe a debt to our stakeholders to make that system work better. We are committed to making that system produce better faculty and better students, in short, a quality educational process while making the most effective use of often limited resources.

The College has developed a number of strategies in the last 2 years to create these partnerships. The most promising ones are described in the following material.

TRADITIONAL VS. SYSTEMS VIEW OF EDUCATION

DCCC has maintained a traditional relationship with the 20 high schools—15 public and 5 parochial—within its primary service area.

Delaware County is highly diverse; these schools range from Radnor High School at the affluent, "everybody-goes-to-college" end to Chester High School at the poor, "hardly any-one-goes-to college" end. Typically, as a community college, DCCC has enjoyed its closest connections with the high schools in the middle of these extremes, that is, in high schools where most seniors go on to college; but cost is a major factor in choosing where. The College's relationship with these "middle-range" schools seldom goes beyond regular contacts with high school guidance counselors and good turnouts at college nights.

The College's relationship with the local high schools has been a function of the traditional view of education as a set of discrete sectors or units working in isolation, with little understanding of how their work impacts each other's efforts or the ultimate outcome. Even though it is recognized that this kind of educational isolationism is often dysfunctional, historically there has been formidable resistance to breaking down the barriers. The inviolate view until now has been that of schools, defined in age ranges, as the educational unit, rather than students.

Traditional Relationships in Education

From working with TQM in education at DCCC, we have become convinced that just as TQM has brought about fundamental recon-ceptualizing and restructuring in the business world by putting the customer first, it can do the same for education by putting the student first. This requires that we see education as a system "from the perspective of the people who move through it." (Hodgkinson, p.1.) From this perspective the interrelatedness of the now separate units becomes self-evident.

By adopting this new systems perspective DCCC has taken signif-icant first steps in redefining its own internal relationships with the College's students and staff, as well as steps in redefining relation-ships with its feeder schools.

Systems View of Education

Embedded in the idea of education as a system is the concept that the system consists of numerous interlinking processes, whose common purpose is to "add value" (knowledge, skills, etc.) to students as their common purpose. Between and among these processes are the supplier-customer relationships which are vital to achieving this common purpose. For DCCC, redefining its school-college relationships in this way has centered around 3 activities:

* Sharing student follow-up information
* Implementing 2 Tech Prep initiatives
* Introducing local school districts to Total Quality Management

In 1990, President Richard DeCosmo hired a special assistant responsible for forming partnerships with the local school districts. This position has been instrumental in focusing the college's efforts on implementing these three efforts.

SHARING STUDENT FOLLOW-UP INFORMATION

New students at DCCC are required to take a series of placement tests in English, math, and reading to gauge their readiness to proceed with college-level work. Because DCCC is an "open door" institution, placement testing is necessary to place students in classes at levels appropriate to their abilities. Semester after semester, nearly 2/3 of entering students require some degree of remediation in at least one of these basic skill areas. The College has always accepted this reality as a part of its mission. "Open door" colleges take students from wherever they are and move them closer to their educational goals, even if it requires reteaching subject matter that students should have learned in high school. Such passive acceptance of this reality is clearly a symptom of the traditional "isolationist" paradigm.

In contrast, the "education as a system" view regards this ongoing need for remediation as a breakdown in the system. According to the systems view, the College is the "customer" and the high schools are "suppliers." The matriculating students are the "outputs" of the educational process in the high schools and in turn become "inputs" of the College's educational process.

In this context the College's placement test data is important feedback which tells the schools how well their process is working in relation to the needs of the students and the requirements of the next process. Such process performance data can be invaluable in showing where process improvements can and should be made in the high school.

Utility of Presenting Three Years of Data per Graduating Class

In order to fulfill its obligation as a responsible "customer," the College initiated a program, in 1991, to provide each high school with the placement test profiles of DCCC students who graduated from that high school in the past 3 years. By providing this information on students from the previous *three* graduating classes, the College is able to give each high school a much more reliable record of how many of their graduates actually attend DCCC and how well they do at entry.

Because many students enroll at DCCC after enrolling at another college or working a year or two, it is not uncommon for the number of DCCC students from a given senior class to double in the course of 3 years.

A student profile covering 3 years, therefore, presents a representative picture of the postgraduate educational experience of each school's seniors. Many students that the high schools considered "noncollege material," as well as many expected to attend a selective 4-year college, find their way to DCCC. This 3-year enrollment information is altering the high schools' assumptions about both their students and their educational process.

Utility of Placement Test Information

From placement test information high schools can learn which of their former students require remediation in the different skill areas. At each school, staff can compare each graduate's placement test results with his or her academic histories. For most schools with whom DCCC shares this data, the number of students involved is a sufficient control for individual differences.

Procedures for Sharing Data

Because of the sensitivity of the data, appointments are made with high school principals and, in most instances, their curriculum assistant and their director of guidance. Great care is taken to communicate the constructive purpose of the data sharing. No comparisons are made with other schools. The information is solely intended for each school's internal use. DCCC emphasizes that the College's faculty and staff stand ready to team up with each high school's staff for cooperative curriculum planning or design activities that might arise from the analysis of the data.

Without exception the information has been welcomed and appreciated. We know from follow-up inquiries about the structure and contents of our placement tests that the schools are making use of the data. The data for 1992 has already been prepared and is being shared on a scheduled basis.

We hope that by regularly sharing this data, the high schools and DCCC will begin to work collaboratively to integrate our teaching/ learning processes for the greater good of our collective student bodies.

TECH PREP: A MODEL OF SYSTEMS THINKING

The nationwide Tech Prep initiative predates the College's adoption of TQM. However, DCCC has recently begun to develop 2 such programs: One in conjunction with a consortium of the Delaware County Intermediate Unit and 11 Delaware County high schools, and a second directly with Upper Darby High School. Although the exact form that Tech Prep takes can vary considerably, the basic intent and design is to provide a 2+2 curriculum track for students interested in advanced technical fields that require skill development beyond high school.

At DCCC, Tech Prep is becoming a model of system thinking that cuts across traditional educational boundaries. The Upper Darby initiative has relied on a joint planning team of administrators and teachers from the College and Upper Darby high school to develop the scope and structure of their Tech Prep program, including:

- Areas of study to be pursued by the high school students
- An articulated curriculum
- Shared materials
- Outcomes
- Business contacts

We expect the consortium's program to follow suit with joint planning and curriculum development.

INTRODUCING LOCAL SCHOOL DISTRICTS TO TQM

Early in 1990, the Suburban Schools Study Council, a professional organization of local school superintendents (of which Richard De-Cosmo is a member) invited the College to present an overview of DCCC's experience with implementing Total Quality Management. As a result of this initial presentation, considerable interest in TQM was expressed by the members of the Study Council, in particular by Roger Place, Superintendent of the Springfield school district.

The Council's president seized upon this interest as a way to involve members of the Study Council and organized a conference to enable local school personnel to explore TQ. Income from very modest fees ($50 per person) for the conference, support from the Study Council, and sponsorship by DCCC brought outstanding speakers from school districts that were experimenting with TQM. Members of the School Study Council spent a full day with the keynote speaker, Larrae Rocheleau, Superintendent of Mt. Edge-cumbe School District, Sitka, Alaska.

From this beginning, representatives from 9 school districts whose students enroll at DCCC have attended further introductory training in TQ. This training has been provided by the College at no cost to the school districts. Two local school districts, Springfield and Wallingford-Swarthmore, have pursued active involvement with TQM. DCCC has provided training and consultation to both school districts as their implementation has progressed.

The Springfield School District: A Case Study

The superintendent of the Springfield school district, and several staff members initially attended courses at DCCC in Total Quality. Over the last 2 1/2 years, more than 20 faculty and administrators from Springfield have attended these courses. They, in turn, have returned to the district and taught others on their staff.

The superintendent has formed an administrative team of staff interested in TQ to oversee the effort and to provide a forum for their own study and development. Six administrators and 4 faculty members presently serve on this team. Early in the district's implementation initiative, Dr. Place charged each major administrative organization in the district to identify, chart, measure, and improve 3 processes or problems that are critical to the success of their organizations.

Many TQ projects have been initiated; the following are representative:

Reducing Disciplinary Referrals for Student Lateness

Statement of the problem: During 1990-91, Springfield High School handled 373 disciplinary referrals for student lateness. The Principal, Joseph O'Brien, worked with the school's disciplinarian first to analyze the problem, and then to attempt to reduce the number of referrals. A simple chart (Figure 12.2) showed that eleventh grade students were most often late; and that the principal transgressions by all students involved the sign-in procedure and truancy.

Mr. O'Brien and his staff attempted 2 simple intervention strategies to address the sign-in procedure:

- They made it simpler and encouraged the secretaries who monitored the process not to scold the students who signed in late.
- They increased the penalties for failure to sign in.

To address the problem of truancy, they enlisted the help of the local magistrate and began vigorously to follow up each truancy incident. The results in 1991-92 are shown in Figure 12.2 after the slash (/). Statistics for 1992-93 are not yet compiled.

Another project pursued by Springfield High School is a good example of the importance of monitoring an improvement to prevent regression.

Reduce Percentage of Failing Grades Earned by Ninth Grade Students

Statement of the Problem: In Fall 1991, 62 ninth graders in Springfield High School failed one or more courses. From 210 ninth graders, this represented 29.5% of the class. The ninth graders failed 173 separate courses, a failure rate of approximately 13.7%.

Intervention: Mr. O'Brien and the guidance staff met separately with students and faculty to gather opinions on the reasons for the failure rate. The teachers tended to blame the students; the students

		1990.91/1991.92			
Grade	Late to class	no sign-in	late to lunch	truant	total
9	19/17	24/11	2/4	10/4	55/36
10	4/4	24/8	5/2	26/12	59/26
11	2/3	66/22	4/6	84/21	156/52
12	0/1	40/14	1/3	62/11	103/29

FIGURE 12.2

and parents tended to blame the difficulty of the transition from middle school to high school.

The guidance staff developed an orientation program for ninth graders. The guidance staff, the reading specialist, and the principal developed an early-intervention process: Students whose early progress reports warned of impending failure met with a member of the staff and were advised of available services such as tutoring, special reading assistance, etc.

Results—Fall, 1991: Of 249 ninth graders, 43 students failed 85 courses. These numbers translated to 17.2% of the class members who failed (compared to 29.5% in 1990), and 6.7% of courses that were failed (compared to 13.7% in 1990).

Follow-up 1992: This Fall, although the orientation program was offered again, the early intervention process did not take place. Data shows that 62 students, from 250 ninth graders, have failed at least one course. In Mr. O'Brien's words:

> "What an example of the importance of monitoring improvement efforts; and what proof that this improvement effort is an effective one!"

The school reinstated the intervention effort in January, 1993, and will make it a permanent program in the fall.

At Delaware County Community College, we hope that between these 3 efforts—*sharing information about graduates' placement test results, Tech Prep,* and *introducing local school districts to TQM*—more and more staff and faculty of both the school districts and the College will come to understand that they function as educational colleagues within a larger interdependent educational system. As a result of such knowledge, we hope that it will become indisputable that improved performance by all sectors or levels improves the performance and success of all parts of the educational system.

The beneficiaries, of these efforts, of course, are not only the successful students themselves, but the public which benefits from better qualified and more highly skilled people in the workforce, and the taxpayers who benefit from an effective and efficient educational system that uses resources wisely.

REFERENCES

Hodgkinson, Harold L. *All One System: Demographics of Education, Kindergarten through Graduate School* (1985). Washington D.C.: Institute for Educational Leadership, Inc.

— 13 —

CENTER FOR TOTAL QUALITY SCHOOLS

William T. Hartman, *Professor-in-Charge, Education Administration, Pennsylvania State University, University Park, Pennsylvania*

Seldon V. Whitaker, Jr., *Superintendent of Schools, State College School District, University Park, Pennsylvania*

Introduction: *Penn State provides another example of how a College of Education can facilitate school TQM implementation. Bill Hartman is Director, Center for Total Quality Schools, in the Department of Education Administration, College of Education, Penn State University. He and Seldon Whitaker have formed a unique bond to work together to bring quality principles to school districts in the State.*

OPENING

The Center for Total Quality Schools (CTQS) at Penn State University is the first university-based project devoted exclusively to providing K-12 teachers and administrators with the training, support, and research base necessary to implement total quality management in education. Located within the College of Education, the Center maintains close ties with the Educational Administration Program and the Department of Curriculum and Instruction in the College and with other University units involved in total quality.

The CTQS has developed from an initial concept to an active functioning unit in less than 1 year. In reviewing the creation of the Center, several key factors are identifiable as crucial to its success:

- A FIRM BELIEF IN TOTAL QUALITY MANAGEMENT
- STRONG ENCOURAGEMENT FROM BUSINESS
- PARTNERSHIP WITH SCHOOL DISTRICT
- LOCATED IN EDUCATIONAL ADMINISTRATION PRO-GRAM AT UNIVERSITY
- SUPPORT FROM UNIVERSITY ADMINISTRATION

BELIEF IN TQM

Initiating a new unit devoted to introducing total quality management
into educational organizations is not an effort to be undertaken
lightly. Education is notorious for resisting efforts for change, particularly those coming from the business community. Numerous road-
blocks can be thrown up by those skeptical of "just another fad which
will soon fade away." A variety of obstacles must be overcome,
including the short-term focus of most school personnel, concern
over loss of authority by administrators, satisfaction with the known
current situation, fear of the unknown caused by change, and
resistance to the work involved in making changes of the magnitude
implied by total quality management.

All of these objections, and more, were encountered during the
early development of the Center. Without a strong and frequently
voiced belief in the importance of total quality management as the
most feasible approach to improving education, it would have been
impossible to maintain the extra effort needed to start the Center and
to convince others of the unique opportunity provided by total quality
management for education.

ENCOURAGEMENT FROM BUSINESS

Total quality management envisions systemic change in organizations. School districts are arguably among the purest practitioners of
the Taylorist management style. School administrators who aspire to
fostering systemic change can expect resistance and should have
allies in the community. Therefore, linkages with progressive business leaders can provide the necessary community support for
successfully implementing total quality management in the public
schools.

Many members of the business community have aided the initiation of the Center and continue to support its activities. The idea for
the Center was broached by the authors at a meeting with representatives from Hershey Foods Corporation, IBM Corporation, and the
Philadelphia Area Council for Excellence who were seeking ways to
encourage school districts to implement total quality management
practices. As a part of Penn State, the Center offered the capability to
provide training in total quality management with an educational

orientation to schools. The status of Penn State legitimated the program and provided businesses a means of assisting their local school districts to initiate total quality management in their operations without the taint of business control.

One of the early supporters of the Center was the total Quality Council of Central Pennsylvania (TQCCP), the local community quality council. Both Penn State and the State College Area School District were founding members of the council, along with many of the local businesses. Through these interactions it became clear that the business community viewed both K-12 and higher education as prime "suppliers" of human resources and that they recognized the importance of ensuring that graduates became aware of the importance of quality issues throughout their educational experiences. Consequently, a proposal for the council to provide a grant to the CTQS to "jump-start" initial activities in the development phases was readily approved.

The first public program of the CTQS was a seminar, in the Spring of 1992, on total quality management in education. The purpose of the seminar was to provide an orientation to total quality management for 20 selected school districts and to ascertain their interest in participating in a more extensive training program. Each district sent a 4-person team consisting of the district superintendent, the school board president, the local association or union president, and an executive of a local business. The enthusiasm of the business participants for their districts' interest in total quality management was very clear and created a highly supportive environment for districts. The seminar was fully funded by businesses and educational interest groups so that there was no cost to the districts. The principal supporters included the Total Quality Council of Central Pennsylvania, Rohm and Haas, Hershey Foods, IBM, Pennsylvania League of Urban Schools (an organization of the largest districts in the Commonwealth which sponsored their attending members), Council for Public Education (the education/business partnership in the Harrisburg area), Philadelphia Area Council for Excellence, and Penn State Continuing Education.

Throughout the Center's existence it has been an ongoing recipient of direct and indirect support from the business community. Examples include:

• Provision of nationally recognized speakers at Center training programs;

- Use of consultants;
- Advice on development and offers to serve as internal "champions" for funding within corporations;
- Use of high technology facilities;
- Loans of equipment;
- Extending opportunities for exposure of the Center and its mission; and
- Financial support for districts attending Center training programs.

PARTNERSHIP WITH SCHOOL DISTRICT

For any university-based training program for school personnel a key issue is credibility; the training must be perceived as valuable and helping schools to improve or it will be viewed as an academic, ivory tower exercise. One of the primary reasons for achieving credibility is the strong partnership between top administrators of the local school district and the university faculty in the Center. In fact, the Center is a joint project involving commitment from both sides. This builds on a history of close working relationships between the Educational Administration Program at Penn State and the State College Area School District.

The district is a leader in embracing and implementing total quality management within its operation. Through early involvement in the TQCCP, the superintendent, along with several other district administrators, was part of the initial school district team to be trained in total quality management. As a result, he has taken an active leadership role in bringing the principles and practices of total quality management into the school district through direct training of employees. The district developed and carried out innovative in-house training programs for district staff beginning in 1991-92 school year. The initial project was a monthly training series for 85 first-line supervisors; the training group included:

- All members of the administrative team;
- Subject area coordinators, most of whom are also part-time classroom teachers;
- Physical plant supervisors;
- Cafeteria managers.

In addition, the 9 members of the school board were invited to attend and did so as their schedules permitted. The training series was co-led by the superintendent and the president of the teachers association.

This training program became the prototype for the Center's Leadership Training Program. Many of the approaches, activities, and materials piloted in the district program were employed in the Center's program. In addition, the district serves as a beta test site for new materials located by the Center and considered for use. In this way both partners benefit; the district has the opportunity to remain in the forefront with its training and implementation activities, while the Center receives the experience of pilot testing in an educational setting.

LOCATED IN EDUCATIONAL ADMINISTRATION PROGRAM AT UNIVERSITY

For total quality management to be successful in transforming any organization, top management must be visibly committed and not only accept, but encourage, the necessary changes. The top management positions in school districts are the superintendents, assistant superintendents, central office administrators, and principals. People enrolled in the administrative certification programs within the Educational Administration Program at Penn State are training for these positions. Consequently, the Educational Administration Program is a logical place for the Center to be housed. The connection is a close one since the Director of the Center is also the professor-in-charge of the Educational Administration Program. Additionally, the State College district superintendent is an adjunct associate professor in the Educational Administration Program and is teaching a graduate course on total quality management in education.

The acceptance of the Center is furthered by the positive reputation of the Educational Administration Program, which is one of the leading programs of its kind in the country. It serves as an excellent platform for assessing the implications of total quality management for the effective administration of public schools.

SUPPORT FROM UNIVERSITY ADMINISTRATION

The establishment of the Center for Total Quality Schools was strongly supported and encouraged by the university administration as a tangible product of the university's commitment to total quality management. At Penn State, the University Provost has taken leadership of the universitywide effort for continuous quality improvement. He has attended both the initial Spring introductory seminar and the opening session of the Center's Leadership Training Program. In both instances, his presence and supportive remarks to the assembled participants provided a visible signal of the importance that the university attaches to the Center.

Within the College of Education, the Dean has offered encouragement and assistance with funding to the Center. Broadening the base beyond educational administration, the Center planning staff was expanded to include the department head of Curriculum and Instruction; similar to the administrator strategy, orienting prospective teachers to total quality management in education is a task that can be effectively accomplished through the teacher training program at Penn State.

Additional alliances have been and are being made in other areas of the University where there is an active interest in total quality management, including the Department of Vocational and Industrial Education, College of Business, College of Engineering, and the Office of Continuous Quality Improvement.

THE CENTER

Mission

The mission of the Center is twofold. First, it has assumed a leadership role in introducing the concepts of total quality to elementary and secondary education. This involves being a visible force for promoting the importance and acceptance of total quality in schools. The second component of the mission is practical and action-oriented; it is to assist schools in implementing the principles and practices of total quality in their operations.

> PROMOTE TOTAL QUALITY IN SCHOOLS
> ASSIST SCHOOLS TO IMPLEMENT TOTAL QUALITY
> LEADERSHIP IN THEIR OPERATIONS

Vision

The vision for the Center is that it will become a focal point for training and research on total quality in schools. Already, it is a place for school personnel to come for a structured training program in total quality in education. In this role it links in a positive way the interests of businesses and communities in improving their local schools with schools' efforts at reform. The research being conducted by the Center is incorporated into future training programs to ensure that they are both current and appropriate for schools.

FOCAL POINT FOR TRAINING AND RESEARCH
CONNECTION BETWEEN SCHOOLS AND THEIR COMMU-
NITIES AND LOCAL BUSINESSES

Purpose

To carry out its mission and to achieve its vision, the specific purpose of Center activities can be grouped into 3 major areas: **Training, research**, and **support**. The reason for providing training and support and conducting research is to enable practitioners to implement total quality leadership practices in elementary and secondary schools.

PROVIDE TRAINING, RESEARCH, AND SUPPORT TO
SCHOOLS
ENABLE SCHOOL PERSONNEL TO IMPLEMENT TOTAL
QUALITY LEADERSHIP PRACTICES

Goal

The ultimate goal of the Center is to have schools practice total quality in their operations and to teach the principles to their students. It is not a goal that the Center can impose on schools nor do for schools. Rather, it is a goal to be achieved through inspiring school personnel to adopt total quality as their own way of operation and by assisting them in understanding and implementing total quality within their organization.

Three Major Tasks of the Center

Out of the purpose established for the Center come the 3 principal tasks or areas of activities in which the Center is engaged:

TRAINING
RESEARCH
SUPPORT

Training

Providing training in total quality leadership is a principal activity of the Center. A full range of training programs has been developed by Center personnel to meet a variety of district needs, ranging from first introduction to advanced instruction. The programs include:

ORIENTATION TO TOTAL QUALITY PRESENTATIONS
INTRODUCTORY WORKSHOPS
COMPLETE LEADERSHIP TRAINING PROGRAM FOR SCHOOL LEADERS
ADVANCED SEMINARS FOR TRAINERS
GRADUATE AND UNDERGRADUATE COURSES

The orientation sessions and introductory workshops are designed to provide an overview of the concepts and practices of total quality to school district personnel. Typically, these have been requested by superintendents who are interested in exploring total quality leadership for their district. They have also been provided for districts in which the superintendent wished to introduce school board members, administrators, teachers, and other personnel to total quality leadership in anticipation of beginning their own implementation program.

The major training effort of the Center is the **LEADERSHIP TRAINING PROGRAM** (LTP), an intensive year-long program for districts beginning their involvement with total quality. The program consists of 10 monthly training sessions, 1 day per month. Sessions begin at noon on day one and end at noon on day two and include evening activities, so participants have a full schedule. School districts send a team of 4 members:

+ Superintendent;
+ Association president;
+ Building principal;
+ Classroom teacher.

This provides a cross section of leaders in the school district. A "train the trainers" strategy is employed in the program. The members of each district team form the core group to lead the district's own training and implementation efforts. In addition to school districts, the LTP includes intermediate unit (IU) teams consisting of the executive director and 3 specialists chosen for their skills and interest. Since the IUs are regional educational units, they can serve as an excellent vehicle for leveraging their own training by assisting their associated school districts.

The districts and intermediate units which are enrolled in the initial LTP for the 1992-93 school year are:

School Districts

> Butler Area School District
> Central Dauphin School District (Harrisburg)
> Central York School District
> Derry Township School District (Hershey)
> Harrisburg City School District
> Lebanon School District
> Unionville-Chadds Ford School District
> Williamsport Area School District
> York City School District
> York County Area Vocational Technical School

Intermediate Units

> BLaST Intermediate Unit #17 (Williamsport)
> Bucks County Intermediate Unit #22 (Doylestown)
> Central Intermediate Unit #10 (West Decatur)
> Lincoln Intermediate Unit #12 (New Oxford)

Many of the district teams are sponsored by 1 or more local businesses interested in promoting total quality in their schools. In one instance, the local teachers' association is also a sponsor, demonstrating their commitment to school improvement in a concrete way. Business sponsorship benefits districts in 2 ways:

* The obvious financial assistance in a time of tight budgets;
* The accountability created by the sponsorship.

District teams frequently meet with business sponsors following the LTP sessions to review with them the session content and how the district is planning to utilize their training within the district. This communication fosters greater cooperation and leads to direct business assistance in district training and improvement activities by providing speakers on specific aspects of total quality and technical assistance from qualified practitioners.

The monthly topics for the 1992-93 LTP are shown in Figure 13.1. They begin with an overview of the importance of quality to schools and continue with the basic concepts and principles of total quality. Great care is taken to translate the material into educational terms and applications. A simplistic overlay of business and industry approaches onto education would be a sure-fire method of squelching any enthusiasm from educators, particularly at this early stage in training. In these sessions emphasis is continually placed on the need to transform the entire organization to the new philosophy of quality. The concept of customers has proven to be a very powerful one in helping school personnel understand the fundamental concepts of total quality and what changes are necessary.

LEADERSHIP TRAINING PROGRAM

MONTHLY SESSION TOPICS

SEPTEMBER	QUALITY: THE CHALLENGE OF THE 1990s
OCTOBER	TRANSFORMATIONAL LEADERSHIP
NOVEMBER	CUSTOMER-DRIVEN ORGANIZATION
DECEMBER	SYSTEMS AND VARIATIONS
JANUARY	CONTINUOUS QUALITY IMPROVEMENT
FEBRUARY	TEAMS AND TEAMWORK
MARCH	QUALITY SCHOOLS AND CLASSROOMS
APRIL	QUALITY MEASUREMENT AND ASSESSMENT
MAY	PLANNING FOR QUALITY
JUNE	PARTNERSHIP FOR QUALITY IMPROVEMENT

FIGURE 13.1

The next group of sessions move into the tools for implementing quality within an educational organization. These provide the participants with exposure to and practice in using scientific and organizational tools to institute continuous quality improvement. The tools include techniques such as flow charts, control charts, Pareto diagrams, scatter diagrams, cause and effect diagrams, force field analysis, nominal group technique, team building, and problem solving. With these tools in place, the focus of the sessions shifts to specific educational applications; sessions concentrate on achieving quality at the building and classroom levels. The final session involves not only the district teams, but their business partners in planning how to work together to continue the effort beyond the initial LTP training year. In between each of the sessions, teams have assignments to explore, develop, practice, and implement the concepts and activities which are presented. The assignments range from simple (Do something to delight a customer) to more complex and time consuming (Develop a deployment flow chart of a process in your district). In addition to having team members stay involved with total quality leadership activities between sessions, the assignments also are used by the teams to have others in their organizations begin participation in total quality.

The extended training period of the LTP over ten months is important. Instituting total quality leadership involves a radical change in the culture of an educational organization; this does not happen overnight. Time is required to absorb the new philosophy and to adopt the new behaviors needed to implement it. The ten months of active involvement with the LTP provide the knowledge of total quality leadership and a regular monthly reinforcement of that learning. Participation in the LTP represents a substantial commitment of district financial and personnel resources. This translates into a commitment to utilize the training from the program to improve district operations. Additionally, monthly association with other districts who have made a commitment to total quality leadership creates an automatic network and support group for the participants.

One of the most encouraging features of the monthly sessions are the Quality Stories. Each month several districts share with the entire group one (or more) success stories with total quality leadership in their district. Examples include: A streamlined kindergarten enrollment process based on accommodating parents' schedules; involving high school students in designing changes to improve completion of homework assignments; a third grade teacher obtaining suggestions from her students for a more efficient way to distribute and collect books; and use of LTP training activities for intermediate unit staff. These serve to illustrate the applicability of total quality leadership and to encourage other districts to try new improvement projects.

Another aspect of the LTP is the development of appropriate materials to utilize in training programs. This involves both looking outside for possible materials, as well as development of materials by Center personnel. Benchmarking is a helpful concept in this area as the Center first looks for existing materials to shorten the development time. For example, the Center utilized a series of descriptions and examples of total quality leadership tools developed specifically for education by PQ Systems, Inc. In return for their use, the LTP served as a beta test site for the materials to the benefit of both parties. When not found from other sources, the Center develops the needed training materials either by adapting business examples for use in educational settings or creating presentations and activities itself.

Research

Research is an integral part of the Center in both concept and practice. Total quality leadership in education is a new field and relatively little is known about it. Consequently, an important function of the Center is to examine how total quality leadership applies to education and to develop a research base which can be used by those in education studying and practicing total quality leadership. Additionally, the research activities keep the Center on the cutting edge of the best practices in the field. The results and findings from research are incorporated into the training programs to keep them up to date. The research initiatives take a variety of forms:

- Grants from corporate sponsors;
- Federal and state grants;
- Dissertation studies; and
- Individual and joint faculty projects.

The research projects are focused on the application of total quality leadership in education. They range from conceptual or theoretical examinations of total quality leadership, to development of field tests for new practices, and evaluation of applications. Examples of existing and planned research areas are:

Competencies needed by high school graduates to be successful in Colleges of Business and Engineering

To develop its proposal in response to the IBM grant initiative for total quality management in higher education, Penn State created a cross-functional team that included members for the Colleges of Business, Education, and Engineering. A unique feature of the successful Penn State proposal was the development of special working relationships with its suppliers, K-12 school systems, to review and improve preparation of incoming students.

Customer analysis and feedback

Development of a system for identifying the specific customers of high schools (businesses and higher education institutions), determining the customer-desired competencies for the incoming high school graduates, measuring the level of competency attainment by high school graduates and integrating that information into the school's curriculum.

Continuous measurement of educational progress

Development of a system for ongoing monitoring of student progress and linking results with instructional programs.

Development and field testing of total quality leadership instructional programs and materials

Design, preparation, and evaluation of effective approaches for providing training in total quality leadership. Included are inservice programs for current educational personnel, preservice programs for administrators and teachers, and classroom instruction for schools.

Linkage of total quality leadership with outcome-based education

Use of total quality leadership practices as the approach to achieve the desired results in education.

Management practices and implementation strategies

Effective and ineffective methods and practices for instituting total quality leadership in schools. Focusing on individual positions—superintendent, principal, teacher—and on organizational culture.

Support

One of the critical tasks of the Center is to provide support for successful implementation of total quality in schools. Support takes a variety of forms:

ASSISTANCE TO DISTRICT TRAINERS
SOURCE OF QUALIFIED EXPERTS
DEVELOPMENT AND TESTING OF TRAINING MATE-
RIALS
NETWORK OF TOTAL QUALITY PRACTITIONERS

Supporting school trainers is crucial to the effective transfer of training from the Center to school district programs. For districts in the LTP, this task is begun in their second year. The first major activity is a workshop for district trainers to prepare them for their own training initiative. The focus of the workshop is planning an ongoing district program with a schedule, topics, people involved, and required resources.

Other Center services for these and other districts wishing assistance include:

* Direct training from Center staff;
* Locating qualified experts to assist local training;
* Locating or developing, validating, and maintaining a library of instructional materials for district trainers and classroom teachers; and
* Creating and maintaining an active network of total quality practitioners.

Support is an ongoing activity for the Center and districts avail themselves of the services which they need and cannot provide for themselves.

CTQS ORGANIZATION

The organization of the Center is structured around the major activities to be performed. These responsibilities include:

MANAGEMENT
LEADERSHIP/DEVELOPMENT
TRAINING
RESEARCH
INSTRUCTIONAL SYSTEMS
LIAISON WITH EDUCATIONAL GROUPS

As a way of modeling an organization operating according to the principles of total quality, the actual functioning of the Center utilizes a team approach with individuals assigned primary responsibility for each function, but with issues discussed among all team members and decisions reached by consensus. The Center planning team consists of:

* University faculty (Educational Administration and Curriculum and Instruction);
* School district personnel (superintendent, curriculum development and research, association president, and teacher);

* Intermediate unit staff (staff development); and
* An educational assessment consultant.

Advisory Board

An Advisory Board will be created to assist the Center in setting priorities, establishing policies, and implementing programs. The board will include representatives of:

SPONSORING CORPORATIONS
PENNSYLVANIA DEPARTMENT OF EDUCATION
PROFESSIONAL EDUCATIONAL ASSOCIATIONS
ALUMNI OF CENTER FOR TOTAL QUALITY IN SCHOOLS
   PROGRAMS
PENN STATE COLLEGE OF EDUCATION

CONCLUSION

The Center for Total Quality Schools provides a new and innovative approach for improving schools. Focusing on the principles and practices of total quality management, the Center serves school districts through a variety of training programs, support activities, and research projects. It is the catalyst for districts to become involved with total quality management and a partner in assisting them with implementation. With the focus on education and the selection of superior management practices, it represents the very best in university-school district-business collaboration.

— Part Four —

STATE LEVEL
LINKS

— 14 —

STATE AGENCY AS A CATALYST FOR CHANGE

Joseph A. Spagnolo, Jr., *Superintendent of Public Instruction, Commonwealth of Virginia, Richmond, Virginia*

James C. Chancey, Jr., *Grant Director, Quality Project*

Introduction: *Virginia is one of the first states to explore TQM from a state agency perspective. Having this kind of support from the state can be a real catalyst for change within the schools. The Virginia school districts involved have substantially changed their culture—effective changes have occurred from the classroom to the central office. Virginia also is a model for business partnerships at the state level. Xerox, with it's management training facility headquartered there, has provided significant assistance in raising TQM awareness throughout the state.*

OPENING

"The real voyage of discovery consists not in seeking new lands,
but in seeing with new eyes."

Marcel Proust

Quality in education. What does it mean? Where does it fit? How
do we get there? How can we measure it? These and other questions
are common when the discussion centers on the concept of quality
and education.

In Virginia we have debated, struggled, and experimented with
implementing quality processes into the Department of Education,
the local school districts, and the classrooms. We would like to share
our perspective concerning the role of a state agency in the process of
quality deployment in an educational system.

The COMMITMENT TO QUALITY project is a business partner-
ship between the Virginia Department of Education (VDOE) and
Xerox Corporation. It is the product of 2 years of negotiation.
Approached by letter (November, 1988), David Kearns, then Xerox
CEO, responded favorably to VDOE's request for help in restruc-
turing schools.

Looking at site-based management as one way schools were
restructuring, Xerox internally conducted a study of 7 school districts

in the U.S. and Canada which were extensively involved in site-based management. The purpose of their study was to answer one question:

> Could the "Leadership Through Quality" training assist schools
> in implementing site-based management?

In each school included in the study, a common finding was consistently observed. School personnel that were in the process of restructuring for site-based management lacked the skills and tools necessary to function effectively as a team and make decisions. Xerox concluded that their "Leadership Through Quality" training would be very helpful in this effort.

Figure 14.1 displays the relationship between teamwork requirements and the skill and tools utilized in the "Leadership Through Quality" training.

All partners agreed that while site-based management is one way schools could use Quality, there are many other avenues for infusing Quality. It is the prerogative of school districts to find the best way to use Quality. The Quality strategies represent a process to implement and enhance current restructuring movements such as:

- The effective schools research;
- The school renewal program;
- Site-based management;

RELATIONSHIP BETWEEN TEAMWORK REQUIREMENTS AND QUALITY TRAINING

Teamwork Requirements	Quality Strategy
• Effective communication	• Interaction skills
• Effective team leadership	• Facilitation skills
• Equitable participation	• Team meeting techniques
• Ability to implement decisions/take action	• Role assignments
• Efficient consensus building	• Quality improvement process
• Problem-solving/decision-making models	• Quality tools
• Group process training	• Quality improvement process, Interaction skills
• Technical assistance	• Follow-up technical assistance and inspection

FIGURE 14.1

- Curriculum design;
- Teacher Expectations Student Achievement (TESA)
- School business partnerships; and
- Team-based teaching.

Continued funding for the COMMITMENT TO QUALITY project was secured when the partnership was awarded a 4-year grant (1990-1994) from the United States Department of Education, Educational Partnerships Program.

POLICY DEPLOYMENT

Functional Policy Deployment, the process by which policy is translated into action throughout the system begins with a clear vision statement.

"All children will learn and will learn sufficiently well to possess the knowledge, skills and abilities to lead happy, productive lives in an increasingly technological world."

Virginia Board of Education

The Department's mission then becomes one of:

- Increasing student learning and achievement by improving the teaching and learning process, and
- Providing essential services to schools in order to accomplish the goal.

The Virginia Board of Education has embarked on a bold initiative to provide ALL children with the education they need through the development of a world class education system.

The Board's 10-year program—called World Class Education Initiative—is a long range program of research, experimentation, and evaluation of results. The World Class Education (WEC) Initiative includes 3 components:

(1) Common Core of Learning (CCL);
(2) Outcome based assessment (Outcome Accountability Project [OAP] for schools and Virginia Assessment System [VAS] for students; and
(3) Transformation school sites.

As the administrative agent of the Board of Education, the Virginia Department of Education is charged with creating change in the structure of the education system. Meaningful educational change must occur at all levels, the Department of Education, the local level, school level, and classroom level in order to successfully implement Virginia's WCE Initiative. It is the role of the Department of Education to implement this change.

In implementing this change, the Department has had to change its basic work processes. The Department itself has undergone a transformation. It reorganized, downsized, and is changing its culture to become more customer and service orientated. This transformation has led us to quality management processes. The general elements of quality processes now embodied within the Department include:

+ A customer orientation;
+ Leadership and strategic management;
+ Total organizational involvement;
+ Continuous improvement;
+ Organizational/cultural change; and
+ World class products, processes, and services.

The COMMITMENT TO QUALITY training provides the VDOE with the technical skills to function in teams and processes for consensus decision making. Continued study of W. Edwards Deming's 14-Points and Profound Knowledge concepts provides the new leadership philosophy needed for the transformation. And the inclusion of Peter Senge's Learning Organization theory provides an organizational development process to improve the transformation.

A new and better appreciation of a system has developed. Policy deployment and change are now viewed within the context of a system (see Figure 14.2). The WCE is viewed as interconnected foci and initiatives rather than add-on events or special occurrences in educational reform (see Figure 14.3).

The continuing transformation process is no easy task but cultural change at the Department has resulted in:

+ The establishment of long-term goals with successive short-term objectives;
+ A participative and open style;
+ Greater cooperation and common missions;
+ Disciplined; participative group problem solving;

POLICY DEPLOYMENT SYSTEM

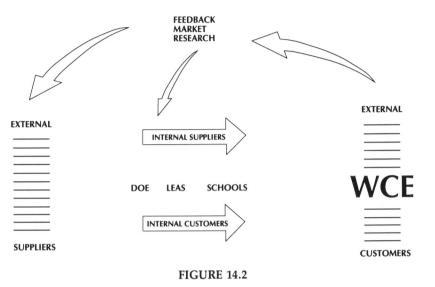

FIGURE 14.2

* Striving to do things right the first time;
* Systematic approach to customer requirements;
* Commitment to continuous improvement by everybody;
* Power shared with everybody;
* Analytical/fact based decision making; and
* Employees working in teams.

CHANGE PROCESS

"It is not necessary to change; survival is not mandatory."

W. Edwards Deming

Quality management is a different way to organize the efforts of people. It introduces a significant change in the relationship between those who manage and those who actually do the work (Tribus, M., *Quality Management in Education*). The *School Administrator* (December

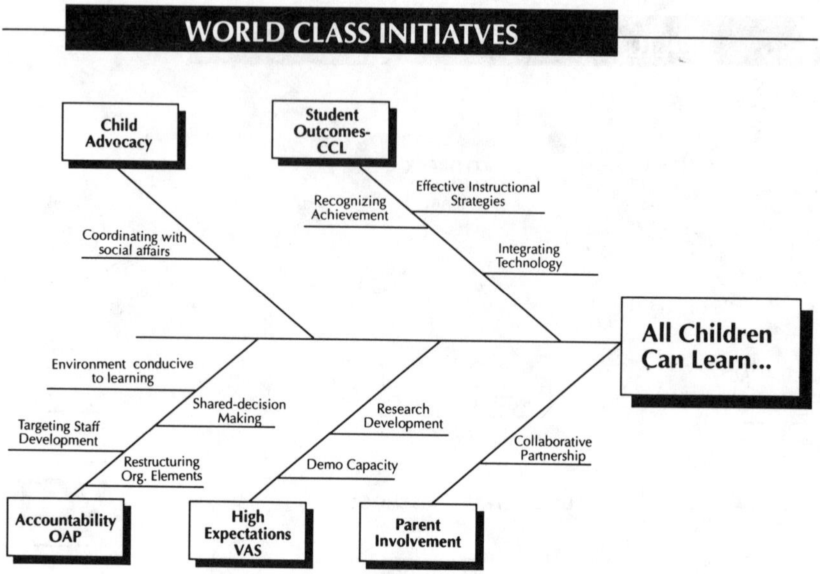

WORLD CLASS INITIATVES

Child
Advocacy

Student
Outcomes-
CCL

Effective Instructional
Strategies

Recognizing
Achievement

Coordinating with
social affairs

Integrating
Technology

Environment conducive
to learning

**All Children
Can Learn...**

Shared-decision
Making

Research
Development

Targeting Staff
Development

Restructuring
Org. Elements

Demo Capacity

Collaborative
Partnership

Accountability
OAP

High
Expectations
VAS

Parent
Involvement

FIGURE 14.3

1990), lists the following perceptual barriers to accepting a business approach to quality:

+ A fear [distrust] of industrial models;
+ Poor knowledge of the work, workers, and work processes in schools; and
+ Unquestioned beliefs.

In transferring the quality processes from business to education, the basic principles are unchanged. It is the application of the quality principles to the differing components of education that must be determined by the educators. One such component and difference that must be established is that students are not the product but it is their education that is the product of the system.

One good answer to facing the dynamics of change is the adoption of a process to deal with change. When implementing quality processes, certain procedures should be followed. They are:

+ Plan timing to avoid conflicts
+ Start small to avoid surprises

- Involve all those affected by the change
- Provide time to acclimatize
- Use role playing to sensitize those affected
- Deal directly with resistance—don't avoid it
- Treat all involved with respect and dignity

Quality implementation requires attention to a model of Behavior Change Steps to help leaders understand how organizational change occurs (see Figure 14.4).

In implementing a Quality process within an organization it is necessary to recognize that one role of the leadership is to facilitate the change process. *Taking Charge of Change* (Hord, Shirley, *et al.*, 1987) provides leaders involved in institutional change a valuable resource when adopting a new organizational process such as quality. Hord summarizes the basic beliefs regarding change as follows:

- Change is a process, not an event;
- Change is accomplished by individuals;
- Change is a highly personalized experience;
- Change involves developmental growth;

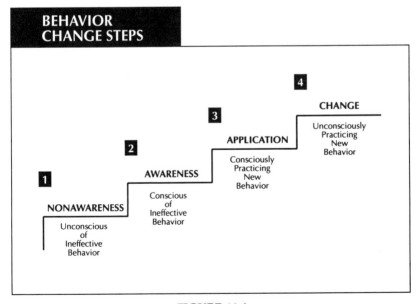

FIGURE 14.4

- Change is best understood in operational terms; and
- The focus of facilitation should be on individuals, innovations, and the context.

The fishbone diagram (see Figure 14.5) identifies major areas for consideration when deciding to implement a restructuring process within an educational organization.

COMMITMENT TO QUALITY STRATEGY

The business community defines quality as a process for operating internally. It is managing resources so that customers, both internal and external, have their requirements met and are satisfied with their products or services the first time they are presented.

There are several concepts upon which Quality is based:

- Customer satisfaction
- Continuous improvement
- Data driven decisions
- Teamwork
- Benchmarking

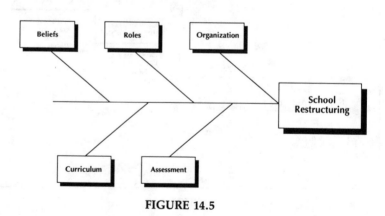

SCHOOL RESTRUCTURING ACTIONS

Beliefs   Roles   Organization

School Restructuring

Curriculum   Assessment

FIGURE 14.5

Quality can be advanced within an organization in many ways:

- Technical approach;
- Management-oriented approach; and
- Implementation approach.

The technical approach involves implementation through the use of the statistical tools. The management-oriented approach focuses on leadership, team-building, and interactive skills needed in an quality environment. The implementation approach focuses on the development concerns of individual groups within the organization and delivers training based on prioritized needs.

Figure 14.6 illustrates the leadership transition support strategies needed to implement successfully quality processes within an organization.

Leadership actions must include:

- Development of mission statement that sets a quality goal for each project
- Quality training
  - Quality Language
    Customer
    Cost of Quality
    Benchmarking

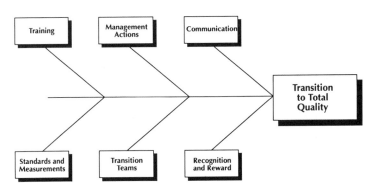

FIGURE 14.6

- Quality Improvement Process (QIP)

    Planning for Quality
    Organizing for Quality
    Monitoring for Quality

- Quality Tools

    Problem solving process (PSP)
    Interactive skills
    Meeting guidelines

- Choosing ways to implement Quality—either through site-based management or some other work unit, and by using existing efforts for "projects" (such as dropout prevention, school-business partnerships, development of a teacher center, development of a parent handbook, etc.)
- Selecting teams to manage various projects
- Supporting teams by providing process guides as needed and offering continued training to upgrade skills
- Recognizing and committing to a multiple-year effort to introduce and initiate Quality into a district

The identification of a transition team or implementation task force is imperative in order to involve all key stake holders from the beginning. Once this has been accomplished the flow chart shown in Figure 14.7 depicts the implementation planning for quality.

QUALITY TRAINING

The following topics are the basic areas of training needed in order to implement quality processes within schools and local school districts:

- QUALITY CONCEPTS
- COST OF QUALITY
    - Cost of Conformance
    - Cost of Non-conformance
    - Lost Opportunity

- BENCHMARKING

SUGGESTED PROCEDURE FOR THE QUALITY
IMPLEMENTATION TASK FORCE

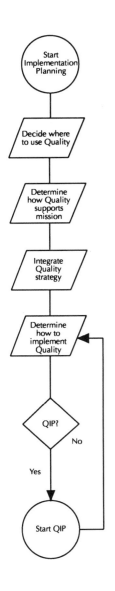

In what ever way the task force decides to use Quality, there must be a carefully thought-out implementation plan.

The task force should first decide how and/or where the division will implement Quality:
Option:
Throughout the division
In specified work units
As a strategy in support of specific initiatives

In whatever aspects of the school division the task force decides to implement quality, they must also:

• Determine the ways(s) in which Quality will support the mission of the division, work unit, or initiative.

• Integrate the Quality strategy with existing strategies.

• Having made the decision of how/where Quality is to be used, the task force then must decide what needs to be done to ensure a successful implementation of Quality.

A QIP effort to produce the division an implementation plan is one option

FIGURE 14.7

- ◆ QUALITY IMPROVEMENT PROCESS (QIP; see Figure 14.8)
  - • Planning for Quality
    1. Identify unit of work
    2. Identify customers for that work
    3. Identify the requirements for each customer

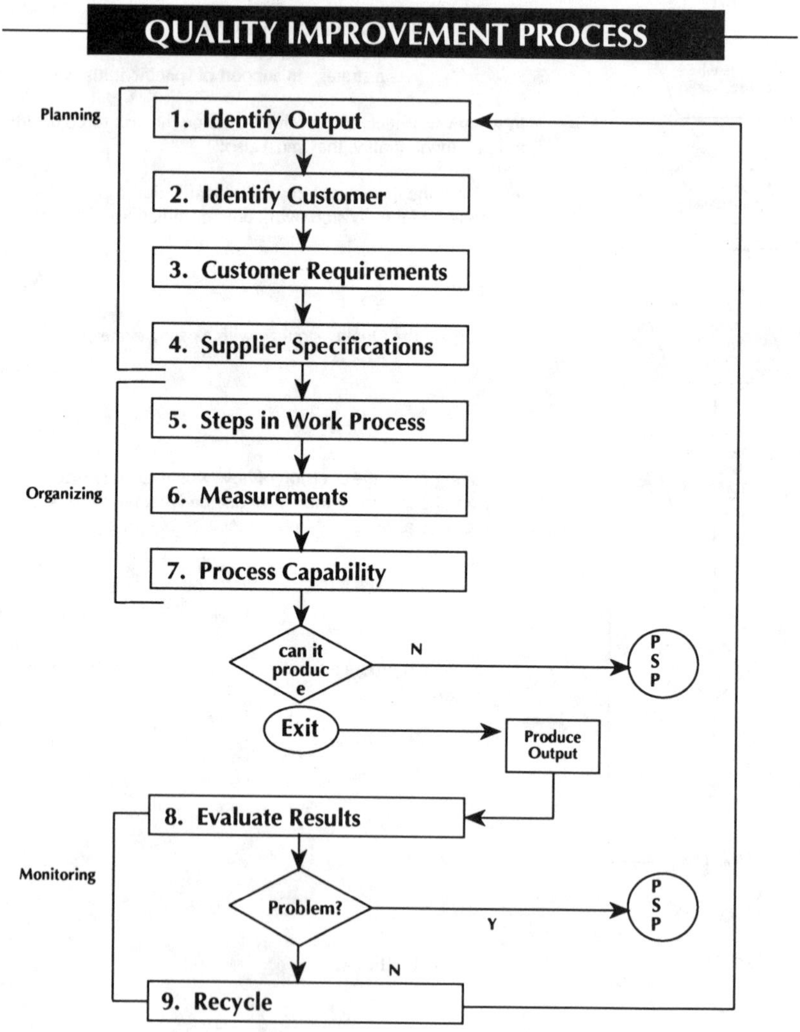

QUALITY IMPROVEMENT PROCESS

Planning
1. Identify Output
2. Identify Customer
3. Customer Requirements
4. Supplier Specifications

Organizing
5. Steps in Work Process
6. Measurements
7. Process Capability

can it produce — N → P S P

Exit → Produce Output

Monitoring
8. Evaluate Results

Problem? — Y → P S P

N

9. Recycle

FIGURE 14.8

4. Translate resolved customer requirements into objectives an specifications.

- Organizing for Quality

5. Identify steps in work process
6. Select measurements for critical process steps
7. Determine capability of process to meet requirements

- Monitoring for Quality

8. Evaluate process results and identify steps for improvement
9. Recycle the process from Step 1

• PROBLEM SOLVING PROCESS (PSP, see Figure 14.9)

The Problem Solving Process will ensure thorough analysis of the problem, determination of the true cause and careful planning of the optimum solution.
The 6 steps of the process are:

- Identify and select the problem
- Analyze the problem
- Generate potential solutions
- Select and plan the solution
- Implement the solution
- Evaluate the solution

  In context, the systematic and participative PSP promotes the application of statistical tools such as histograms, Pareto charts, cause-and-effect diagrams, and control charts in the decision making process.

• INTERACTIVE SKILLS

- Initiating Behaviors
  ◦ Proposing
  ◦ Building
- Reacting Behaviors
  ◦ Supporting
  ◦ Disagreeing
  ◦ Defending/Attacking
- Clarifying Behaviors
  ◦ Testing Understanding

PROBLEM-SOLVING PROCESS

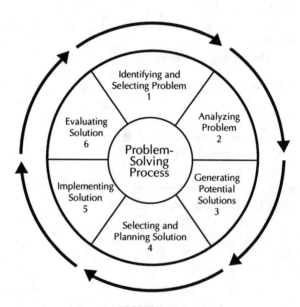

FIGURE 14.9

- ◦ Summarizing
- ◦ Seeking Information
- ◦ Giving Information
- • Process Behaviors
- ◦ Bringing In
- ◦ Shutting Out

- ♦ MEETING GUIDELINES
  - (1) Punctual attendance
  - (2) Meetings start on time
  - (3) Uninterrupted meetings

(4) Active listening
(5) No one-on-one or side meetings
(6) Active participation
(7) Willingness to reach consensus
(8) Shared responsibility for team's progress
(9) Freedom to check process and ground rules
(10) Respect agenda
(11) Timekeeping observed

Training optimizes organizational alignment within the system by providing common definitions, processes and procedures for all employees.

In *TQM: Leadership for the Quality Transformation*, Richard Johnson identifies 4 specific steps (see Figure 14.10) in the quality implementation process. Although the stages are identified as steps, progress is continuous with the steps overlapping as individuals and the organization advance.

FIGURE 14.10

QUALITY IN PUBLIC SCHOOLS

Is Quality really worth all the effort? Indications from participating local divisions reveal the following as related to the individuals within the system:

* Their ideas are heard.
* It gives them a sense of identity with the school system.
* It is fun.
* People are less resistant to change.
* Ideas under the Quality program carry more weight, people feel a sense of accomplishment, since they have really helped in the decision making process.
* People like to do a good job. It makes them feel good about themselves.

Division comments regarding quality implementation tend to reflect the following:

* The right people are making changes—these are the people who do the work.
* Helps pick up morale.
* Takes some of the burden off top management while a higher degree of accuracy is achieved in terms of "little things that make a big difference" by giving employees license to effect change.
* Top management is regarded with less negativity due to the fact that employees are trusted to formulate and implement their own recommendations.
* Return on assets. Teachers, principals, and all other workers in the school perform better, thus enabling students to perform better.
* Less time is spent dealing with the cost of nonconformance.

One important concept is the definition of Quality which states that Quality is satisfying the requirements of internal and external customers. Other concepts revolve around doing things right the first time and continuous improvement. Teamwork, collaborative decision making, benchmarking, and problem solving are at the heart of the Quality process.

During this period of school restructuring, school leaders need a process that offers them skills and a framework for which to operate. The National Center on Education and the Economy has identified 9 areas of concentration in order to restructure schools:

+ Decentralized decision making
+ High standards for all students
+ Challenging curriculum and instruction
+ Performance based accountability systems
+ High quality workforce
+ Public awareness, commitment and active support
+ Organizational change strategy
+ Improved infrastructure
+ Leadership and strategic management

Whether a school is moving to site-based management, collaborative decision making, strong community involvement, or team-based teaching, principals and teachers need a common language and a set of communication and team skills. Quality provides just that.

Quality is a process of change—cultural change—which is being used in schools to restructure for a different work place.

QUALITY IN FACT

+ Doing the right thing
+ Doing it the right way
+ Doing it right the first time
+ Doing it on time

In addition, Quality focuses on the needs of both internal and external customers. In order for schools to produce services to students which are of quality, internal customers must be considered and their requirements met. Not only must schools provide quality services to external customers (students and parents), it must attend to the quality of services to internal customers (*i.e.*, central office to principals; principals to teachers; principals to custodians; teachers to secretary; secretary to cafeteria staff).

QUALITY IN PERCEPTION

+ Delivering the right product
+ Satisfying our customer's needs
+ Meeting the customer's expectations
+ Treating every customer with integrity, courtesy, and respect

REFERENCES

Deming, W. Edwards, *Out of Crisis* (1986). Massachusetts Institute of Technology.

Hord, Shirley, et al., *Taking Charge of Change* (1987). Association for Supervision and Curriculum Development.

Johnson, Richard S., "TQM: Leadership for the Quality Transformation: Part 1." *Quality Progress*, Vol. 26 No. 1, 73-75 (January 1992).

Senge, Peter M., *The Fifth Discipline: The Art and Practice of the Learning Organization* (1990). New York: Doubleday.

Sheldon, James E., "Survival Code: A Willingness to Change." *The Quality Management Forum*, Vol. 18, No. 4, 2-5 (1992).

Xerox, "Leadership in School Restructuring Project Study Report to the Virginia Department of Education" (1989).

— 15 —

TEXAS GOVERNOR ANN RICHARDS' STATEWIDE INITIATIVE

Betty L. McCormick, *Former Education Policy Consultant to Texas Governor Ann W. Richards*

Introduction: *My first experience with TQM was in 1980, when I led a year long IBM Corporate research study on quality and productivity. In addition to using the principles of TQM in the rest of my IBM executive management career, I had an opportunity to see the implications for TQM in education when, in 1989, I joined IBM's Educational Systems Group. In 1991, when I was offered a position on Governor Richards' Education Policy staff, I jumped at the chance. I had heard of Governor Richards' commitment to quality and felt the time was right for a broader part of the education sector to really begin to understand the benefits of a quality management approach. This chapter presents the strategy and some of the resulting activities that have occurred over the past 2 years. To be involved in this effort, with the outstanding support and cooperation of the numerous professional education associations, state agencies, business, and education practitioners in the State, has been extremely rewarding. If any State can make TQM a way of life in schools, I think Texas can and we are well along on our journey.*

BACKGROUND

Early in her administration, Governor Ann Richards became convinced that quality management could be a key strategy to help jump start the Texas economy and, at the same time, check the uncontrolled growth of State government. Her *Blueprint for the New Texas* called for a "state government better organized, more efficient, and more responsive to the needs of the people." In a subsequent document, *Building from the Blueprint*, she called for all parts of the state to "reorganize with the customer in mind."

Two loaned executives were recruited from industry. W.C. Enmon, from Xerox, joined Governor Richards' staff to serve as her personal TQM adviser and to create a training and resource center for quality development in state government. Betty McCormick, from IBM, joined the education policy staff as an education consultant.

TEXAS QUALITY EDUCATION AWARD TASK FORCE

One of the first initiatives was to work on the development of a quality award for Texas. The Governor wanted to make it available to all sectors—public/private, for-profit, and not-for-profit. The challenges of including the education sector were not insignificant. Many insisted "education is different" and award criteria developed for industry could not be applied to education or understood by educators. A task force was formed under the leadership of the Governor's Education Policy Office and the University of Texas at Austin to provide advice on the quality award. The task force included representatives from

- Colleges of education
- Commission of Higher Education
- Corporate executives and quality/community affairs staffs
- Graduate business schools
- Junior/Community Colleges Association
- Principals associations
- Private School Association
- School Administrators Association
- State Education Agency
- State Senate Education Committee
- Teacher associations
- Technical colleges

Day-long meetings were held over several months where the task force members were trained on the U.S. Department of Commerce Malcolm Baldrige Quality Award criteria. Words and phrases were identified that would need to be clarified for educators. However, the number of actual criteria needing modification was minimal. As a result, it was determined that a glossary of terms for educators would be sufficient to support their interest in applying for the quality award and a separate award application for education would not be necessary.

TQM REVIEW TEAM

At this point a separate review team under the leadership of the Governor's Education Policy office and the Texas Association of School Administrators was established. Their charter was to develop an overall plan for TQM in Texas schools as well as support material for the Quality Award. It included representatives from

- Legislative Education Committees
- Principal's associations
- Regional Education Service Centers
- School administrators
- School Board Association
- State Education Agency
- State Employment Commission
- Superintendent's and principal's associations
- Texas Business and Education Coalition
- Texas LEAD Center

Two members of the review team traveled to NCEE headquarters in Rochester, New York, to evaluate the use of the Xerox quality curriculum in education. The curriculum was being provided at no charge from Xerox and it was determined it could be used for Texas educators with very little, if any, modification.

A *Resource Guide for TQM in Texas Schools* was quickly developed to introduce TQM concepts from the Xerox curriculum and to provide the glossary of terms for educators interested in the quality award. In providing the glossary, caution was given about being too prescriptive:

> An essential principle of quality is that it is user defined. While this glossary may be thought provoking, a more meaningful approach may be to get together a group of educators in your school or district and develop the definitions that best fit your environment. Are the students the customers or the workers? There are internal and external customers—does everyone involved in education relate to both? Answering these and other questions for yourselves as a work group provides the best possible education on the principles of TQM.

Another key element of the *Resource Guide* was the TQM Umbrella Chart (Figure 15.1). This chart depicts how some of the efforts already underway in Texas fit under the overall TQM umbrella. TQM is a total management system that ties together all these activities into a cohesive whole. It is not just another program to be added to the list. The 7 elements at the bottom of the umbrella are the examination categories of the Texas Quality Award.

The *Guide* was made available at the Texas Superintendents' Midwinter Conference in January, 1992, just 1 year after Governor

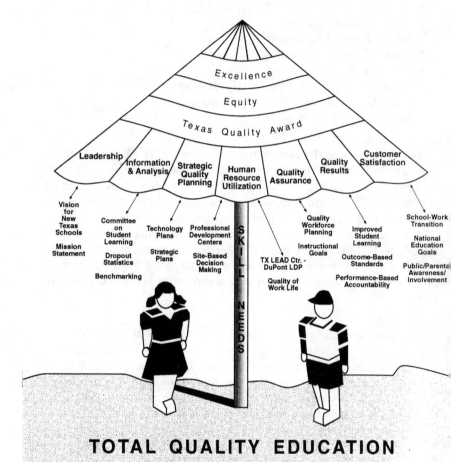

FIGURE 15.1

Richards' inauguration. In a cover letter to the *Resource Guide*, Governor Richards' described her vision of TQM for educators:

One of my highest priorities as Governor is to improve the quality of education for all Texas children and I believe TQM can help us get there. . . . As educators you have many customers to serve; however, attainment of our goals, to a great extent, will be determined by how well we can satisfy those customers' needs and wants. . . . The empowerment that is an essential part of TQM will assure the talents of all involved in the education process are brought to bear on the problems at hand.

Building a "Quality Texas" in all sectors of our economy will be essential to fulfilling the promise of a "New Texas." It is gratifying to know that educators are involved and willing to be valuable partners to government agencies and other organizations across the state as this initiative gains momentum. There are many businesses eager to share their expertise and the combination of all these resources will assure our ultimate success.

After completing the *Resource Guide,* attention was turned to developing the ongoing mission and plan of action for the Review Team.

TQM Review Team Mission

To develop a plan which will facilitate school restructuring (SBDM, improved student performance, etc.) by introducing, educating, implementing, and internalizing the principles of TQM for all Texas educators and other stakeholders.

The goal was to accomplish this *in a way that*:

+ Demonstrates a commitment by all stakeholders;
+ Provides for effective training and follow-up support;
+ Ensures awareness of TQM is widespread;
+ Supports continuous improvement through involvement;
+ Provides rewards and recognition for those that do it best;
+ Focuses on customer satisfaction;
+ Uses existing resources and vehicles for implementation;
+ Establishes a norm for quality;
+ Minimizes impact on financial resources.

So that: Texas public schools will maximize the potential of all students to excel in the global community of the 21st Century.

Payoffs anticipated were:

+ Achieve quality in schools
+ Meet legislative goals

* Have less prescriptive laws/rules
* Have less legislative oversight
* Increased customer satisfaction
* Solid base for continuing funding of schools
* Improved student achievement
* Success for students outside of school—in real world, work, family, community
* Stakeholders have better sense of control over future
* Increased self-esteem by all involved

Now the team knew what they wanted to accomplish, but they also knew it wouldn't be easy. There was great consensus that TQM should not become a prescription demanded by the legislature. There was already a legislative mandate for site-based decision making (SBDM) and TQM was an obvious way to help implement SBDM. The team approached their challenge as one of marketing TQM to a large prospect base. Therefore, a considerable amount of time was spent getting inside the head of the various constituencies (buyers) that would be involved in implementing any TQM initiative.

Buyer Characteristics: Mixture of satisfaction with progress/dissatisfaction with current level of student achievement. By segment:

* *Board members*—are willing to put in many volunteer hours in order to help kids; want understandable solutions that can be implemented quickly to get measurable results; deal with a community with diverse values and expectations of school and its methods; generally, lack in-depth training of school administrators; find day-to-day details sometimes take precedence over strategic policy issues; operate in a highly political environment; may be unsure of role under SBDM; many may not be familiar with new management systems and new culture required by TQM.
* *Superintendents*—are dedicated to career and hard-working; eager to find solutions to help kids learn; are under great pressure to perform; have many diverse constituents to please; have been conditioned by system to react to top-down mandates; are rewarded with bigger jobs when short-term results are achieved; are given little incentive for risk taking; have high need to maintain political harmony; sometimes skeptical of new solutions and outside help; may find new management role required by TQM foreign to past experience of what works.

- *Central office*—same as superintendents; may see jobs being threatened by decentralization and SBDM.
- *Campus*—same as above; mixed feelings about decentralization and SBDM; very concerned about student achievement; want increased authority to try new solutions, but concerned about accountability without control over variables.
- *State System for Public Schools*—is legally organized for top-down management; some legislators and State Board of Education members probably would find the principles of TQM inconsistent with what they see as their legal responsibility.
- *Teachers*—whole motivation is to help students learn; feel unrecognized and under rewarded for their efforts and dedication; often feel frustrated at being left out of decisions made at the top; sense lack of support for innovation and divergent methods; need greater preparation for teaching higher order thinking skills, analysis, synthesis, evaluation, problem solving, and decision making.

The team then wanted to identify all the factors that were driving schools toward a TQM decision as well as all the factors that would restrain such an initiative. The Force Field Analysis depicted in Figure 15.2 was developed.

Two major strategies were developed in this environment to accomplish the team's mission:

1. Communications Strategy

Objective: Provide consistent and widespread awareness of statewide TQM activities and success stories, reemphasizing TQM as a tool to help implement SBDM and improve student performance.

Actions included:

- Publish TQM *Resource Guide* for Educators
- Include educators in Department of Commerce "Quality Texas" awareness seminars around the state
- Include TQM workshops in state agency and education association conferences
- Include TQM success stories in education association publications
- Support regional TQM conferences
- Host national conference

FORCE FIELD ANALYSIS—TQM IN TEXAS SCHOOLS

RESTRAINING FORCES:
- Lack of educator awareness/understanding
- Competing "programs" (SBDM, etc.)—not seen as connected to TQM
- Could be seen as just another fad
- Anti-business sentiments—"won't work in education"
- To few role models
- Rural communities without business partners
- Lack of incentives for administrators/boards
- Preoccupation with school finance issue
- Lack of time and resources for staff development
- High tolerance for status quo
- Not taught in colleges, incoming staff unaware
- High turnover in leadership
- Some state laws inhibit—Career Ladder, teacher appraisal

TQM IN TEXAS SCHOOLS

DRIVING FORCES:
- Awareness of education problems growing
- Less tolerance for poor performing schools
- Level of business/parental involvement increasing
- TQM focus in other sectors of the State
- Strong business partnerships in place
- LEAD Center/DuPont training provides good model
- Local and national models exist
- Rallying point for communitywide TQM initiatives
- Provides umbrella to tie pieces of system together
- Legislated requirment for DBDM and strategic planning
- Way to empower teachers
- Incentive/innovative grants available
- State education association leadership supportive
- Economic development priority will add further incentive for educational improvement
- State agency waivers can support innovations required

FIGURE 15.2

2. *Training/Support Strategy*

Objective: Use existing vehicles/curriculum to minimize costs. Actions included:

- Evaluate Xerox TQM curriculum for education use
- Revise Texas LEAD Center curriculum to include TQM component
- Utilize AASA workshops
- Conduct TQM early bird seminars in conjunction with other education meetings
- Encourage pioneer districts to share expertise
- Encourage businesses to provide slots to educators in TQM training classes

GOVERNOR'S FORMAL TQM ANNOUNCEMENT

With much of the initial work completed, in March, 1992, the Governor was ready to make public the statewide TQM initiative. It included 4 elements:

- The State Government Initiative which was designed to assure "legendary customer service" by every state agency.
- The Department of Commerce was chartered to provide TQM awareness seminars for small businesses. state and local government employees, and educators. The sessions were delivered by volunteer corporate quality trainers.
- The Texas Quality Award.
- The Education Initiative for K-12 schools.

The following description of the education initiative was provided with the press release:

The TQM in education initiative is a collaborative effort for K-12 involving all the principle education players representatives. Their goal is to raise the TQM awareness level of educators across the state as a method to implement Site Based Decision Making and improve student performance. TQM helps educators identify their customers and respond to their needs and wants. It focuses school efforts on results and establishes continuous improvement as a way of life. It empowers students, teachers, and everyone involved in the education process to take the actions needed to improve educational performance. It provides a common language between educators and business people so they can work together as a community to solve mutual problems.

OTHER CONCURRENT INITIATIVES

Quality Work Force Planning Conference

There is a Quality Work Force Planning Committee under the tri-agency partnership of the Higher Education Coordinating Board, the Texas Education Agency and the Texas Department of Commerce and in cooperation with the Texas Employment Commission. The theme of their 1992 conference was TQM. The need to provide TQM skills to students at both the precollege and college levels was emphasized.

Regional TQM Conference

In April, 1992, 3 school districts in a suburban area south of Houston and the Regional Education Service Center decided to host an educators' conference on TQM as a way to get their own staffs trained at little or no cost. Over 600 people attended this 2-day forum and an additional 400 who applied could not be accommodated.

Focus Group on TQM Policy Barriers

During the conference a focus group of educators from all levels was convened to help identify policy barriers to statewide TQM implementation. Many of the items in the Force Field Analysis were validated, but the resounding issue involved staff development. Without sufficient time and resources for staff development and planning, successful TQM implementation would not be possible. Other major items were the need for informed and supportive leadership from school board members and less legislative direction in the "how" of school administration.

Statewide Network for TQM Educators

Another outcome of the conference was the establishment by Pasadena ISD of a Texas Quality Leadership network. The function of the organization is to:

* Facilitate informal study groups in difference geographical locations throughout the state
* Develop an annual conference on total quality leadership
* Support the abandonment of statutes and policies contrary to total quality philosophy
* Support the development of policies to foster total quality principles and processes, and
* Publish a newsletter on most current implementations of total quality in education

The intent is to establish a cadre of educators willing to share their implementation experiences and expertise. From this group, presenters and trainers would be developed to help others starting out on the TQM journey. Membership fees are $15 per individual and $25 for an organization. By year end (1992), 300 educators had enrolled. In early 1993, the network management was transferred to the Texas Association of School Administrators.

GOVERNOR RICHARDS' NATIONAL INVITATIONAL CONFERENCE

During 1991 and 1992, several Governors hosted conferences on the National Education Goals. Governor Richards decided, in early 1992, that she wanted to host a national conference on the goals, but to focus on TQM as a way to help accomplish the goals. Much of the work of the review team, plus additional representatives from industry, was dedicated to conference planning for most of 1992. The National Center for Manufacturing Sciences and Texas Instruments agreed to be conference co-hosts and provide substantial financial and additional fundraising support. The Regional Education Service Center in Houston agreed to provide conference logistics support. National organizations, such as the American Association of School Administrators, the National Alliance of Business, the National Governors Association, and the National Education Goals Panel, added their support to the concept. Additional state agencies and associations joined the effort to assure comprehensive coverage.

The conference was held at Houston's Convention Center on November 9-10, 1992. Over 1500 persons attended, representing 40 states and 5 countries. The conference consisted of 3 general sessions and 45 concurrent, elective sessions. The general sessions were:

- **Kick-off Session** with Governor Richards; W. Edwards Deming via a specially prepared taped message; Russell Ackoff, Chairman of INTERACT; and David Langford, President, Langford Quality Education.
- **Business/Education Panel** with Anthony Carnevale, Executive Director, Institute for Workplace Learning; John Helfrich, Superintendent, Tonawanda, New York; Carole Johnson, Chancellor, Minnesota Board of Technical Colleges; Robert M. Unterberger, ABS Director, IBM Corporation, Rochester, Minnesota; Shirley McBay, President, Quality Education for Minorities Network; and Donald P. Nielsen, President and CEO (retired), Hazleton Corporation.
- **Closing Session—TQM and the National Education Goals** with Shirley Malcom, Director of Education and Human Resources, American Association for the Advancement of Science; the Honorable William E. Brock, former Secretary of Labor; the Honorable Don Ritter, former Member of Congress, 15th District, Pennsylvania; the Honorable Roy Romer, Governor of Colorado; the Honorable Joseph Sensenbrenner, former Mayor of Madison, Wisconsin; Wilmer S. Cody, Executive Director, National Education Goals Panel.

Both of the panel sessions were moderated by Lloyd Dobyns, the famous journalist and author of *Quality or Else*. Videotapes of the general sessions are available from Mike Owens, Region IV Education Service Center, P.O. Box 863, Houston, TX 77001-0863, (713) 744-6514.

Forty-five concurrent, elective sessions were conducted with speakers from all over the country representing practitioners of TQM in schools, business/community partners to educators, and national and state level initiatives. Audiotapes were made of each concurrent session and can be obtained from Bill Fitch, AVW Audio Visual, Inc., (713) 853-8180.

Three other items made this conference unique:

* **Visual Synthesis**: Nusa Maal, a trained visual synthesizer from Great Falls, Maryland, drew pictures of the concepts presented during the general sessions on oversized flip charts. At the conference closing, reduced copies of these charts were distributed to all participants to take home as a visual record.
* **Outcomes Team**: A National Outcomes Committee was invited to meet before, during, and after the conference to establish, synthesize, and document the conference results. Copies of their report can be obtained from the Texas Governor's Office of Education Policy at (512) 463-1877.
* **IBM TEAMFOCUS**: a network of 14 personal computers were available to all participants to solicit conference comments or suggestions, questions for panelists, and provide input to the Outcomes Team.

As part of the conference handout package, the Educational Publishing Group, Boston, Massachusetts, provided a complimentary copy of their parental involvement newsletter, *Education Today*. The issue was customized to focus on TQM initiatives from around the country and included an interview with Governor Richards, from which comes the following:

TQM is the missing method to help achieve the national education goals. It is extremely helpful in freeing individuals to do out-of-the-box thinking. It teaches participants to clearly define a problem, then it allows them to use their creativity to solve the problem. This kind of process empowers any group, whether in business or education.

One thing parents can do to drive quality is to participate with teachers in identifying exactly what their children should know and be able to do as a result of instruction for a given time period. When everyone knows what it is they are striving toward, they can help children reach the educational goals and objectives. Everything at home and at school should support students reaching these academic goals. Parents will know that TQM is working if the lines of communication between home and school are significantly better, if student achievement is clearly defined, and if the morale of the teachers is heightened.

The Governors of Colorado, Minnesota, and New Mexico have announced their intention to host follow-on conferences on TQM and education in 1993, 1994, and 1995, respectively.

ONGOING ACTIVITIES

Texas Education Agency Site-Based Decision Making Strategy

With the legislated mandate for schools to implement site-based decision making, the state education agency has documented the high level of correlation between the principles of SBDM and TQM. Schools that have already implemented TQM are finding SBDM is implemented as well.

Texas Business and Education Coalition

Several major corporations in the coalition, including Texas Instruments, Hoescht Celanese, and Texas Eastman, have been including local educators in corporate TQM training sessions or conducting special sessions for educators. In addition, a series of regional TQM awareness sessions is being planned in conjunction with the Texas Association of School Administrators.

Texas A&M College of Education Initiative

Texas A&M University's College of Education, under Dean Jane Stallings, is taking the lead in restructuring their organization to facilitate TQM in schools. See Chapter 10 for a complete description of their approach.

Texas LEAD Center

In accordance with the objective to use existing resources and integrate TQM into the fabric of existing support structures, the Texas LEAD Center has made significant changes to its curriculum. In addition to incorporating TQM principles in existing Leadership seminars, a new section has been added that specifically addresses the philosophy of Deming and others in the quality movement. It also introduces some of the basic TQM tools. Funding has been provided from Southwest Bell Foundation grant.

The LEAD Center, co-sponsored by the 3 major administrator associations in the State (Texas Association of School Administrators, Texas Elementary Principals and Supervisors Association, Texas Association of Secondary School Principals), has been engaged in a statewide partnership with the E.I. DuPont Company since 1988. The resulting Leadership Development Process has been implemented across the State in all 20 education service center regions. Certified trainers, a total of 800 from service centers, universities, school districts, and corporations, have delivered this in-depth organizational effectiveness seminar to over 8000 school practitioners. The LEAD center has also become the base line resource for accomplishing the training needed to implement Site-Based Decision Making.

An important link is made in the TQM training to the tenets of SBDM. It clarifies for participants and places within a conceptual framework how the principles and skills of Quality can assist them in bringing about the systemic change that real restructuring necessitates.

The LEAD Center is also encouraging partnerships with the private sector to provide the necessary follow-up support to educators after their initial TQM training. The advanced statistical techniques and methods will have no value until they are used in the real world of the educator. Corporate partnerships can provide the "just-in-time" assistance when educators begin applying their new found skills and knowledge.

SUMMARY

There is a high level of interest and excitement about the possibilities of TQM in restructuring education in Texas. The journey is just beginning, but we have come far in raising the TQM awareness level of Texas educators. Much more will need to be accomplished and it will be difficult in light of the significant issues surrounding school finance in Texas. Even with those concerns, many schools in Texas are taking the plunge into TQM as portrayed in the directory in Appendix A. These leaders are to be complimented for starting on this journey long before Governor Richards was even elected. What the statewide initiative has accomplished is to provide a supportive framework to facilitate TQM efforts and to give encouragement to the brave pioneers in this endeavor.

— Part Five —

OTHER CRITICAL LINKS

— 16 —

THE TQM-TECHNOLOGY CRITICAL CONNECTION

Lewis A. Rhodes, *Associate Executive Director, American Association of School Administrators, Arlington, Virginia*

Clark Kirkpatrick, *Executive Director, Technology and Information Educational Services, Roseville, Minnesota*

Introduction: Lew Rhodes probably has a better understanding of the technological implications of TQM than anyone else in the country. He has long been a leader in educational technology circles, starting back in the 1960's when he directed a project on instructional television. His recent leadership in TQM has established AASA as the premier organization helping schools apply quality principles to their work. AASA's Total Quality Network now has over 700 members and their conferences and seminars continue to place greater emphasis on TQM. Clark Kirkpatrick, a former school teacher and superintendent, started his career in the computer industry. Together they have created a valuable chapter that will cause even current TQM educational practitioners to rethink the role of technology.

THE MYSTERY OF THE MISSING TOOLS

The renowned detective, Sherlock Holmes, used a *different lens*—both literally and figuratively—and in most cases his famous magnifying glass contributed less to his success than the different mental "lens" through which he viewed and made sense of the world around him. Using that perspective, he solved one of his most famous cases by noting the significance of a dog *not* barking—that is, an event not occurring that should have.

Today, as quality management principles and strategies have begun to be applied in schools, their most significant contribution has been the Holmes-like lens they are providing for making sense of what increasingly makes little sense. Among the most powerful consequences so far have been the questions they have forced us to ask about the ways we assumed schooling takes place.

Now, what if Sherlock Holmes used a *quality lens* to confront and make sense of the mystery of education's missing technologies? What might he ask, as he compared schools to other organizations in America, about what schools *do not do* with the tools that are available to them.

For example, in general, tools are *not* used:

* To increase their worker's productivity;
* To add value to their outcomes;
* Nor to ensure the equally distributed excellence that is the hallmark of quality results.
* Tools are not part of the *bottom-line* operating infrastructure. Their availability is largely dependent upon gifts and grants. (Can you imagine any business not understanding what tools are fundamental to its work and including them in the core budget as-the-way-they-do-business?)
* Tools are not made available *systemically*—e.g., they may be placed in one classroom or one building in a school district, with results similar to what might be expected were one to distribute wonder drugs randomly throughout a hospital. There are few examples, after more than 30 years, of appropriate applications when and where needed—and importantly, few opportunities to achieve any sustained effects.

Others who have tried to make sense of this strange anomaly traditionally end up blaming the educator. They imply that somehow educators are different—more fearful of change, not willing to learn how to do a more effective job, and ultimately not really caring enough to want the very best for children. The solution—these sense-makers conclude—is research, information dissemination, and training. Give them more information, prove to them that technology is effective, then teach everyone of them how to use it. It has not worked.

Holmes, on the other hand, as he looked at what had not and was not happening, might ask why these particular professionals would behave that way. They have as much, or more, education than peers in other public and private sector institutions; they are driven by a commitment to children that helps them endure conditions that would not be tolerated by other professionals; and many of them are technologically-literate outside the workplace. Why, he might ask as part of his sense making, wouldn't they welcome, if not seek out, ways to increase their impact on the children whose lives they touch?

Why indeed? Something doesn't make sense. If the educator isn't the problem, then

* Why aren't technologies used for more productive work?
* Why aren't they applied systemically?
* Why aren't educators demanding these tools?

Like Holmes, in this chapter we will look for the answers, not in the technology, but in the system. And in particular, in what the quality management lens is helping us learn about the nature of the work of schools, the system that supports it, and the needs of the practicing educator.

Through this lens we will see that American public education, information technology, and quality management are inextricably linked as partners in a learning venture upon which the future of America's schools, if not its society, will depend.

THE WORK DEFINES THE TOOL

The quality management principle that over 90% of any work problem lies in the system and not the workers comes up against a peculiar situation in education. What system?

It has become practically a cliche to talk about *systemic* change in education; yet there is no common understanding of just what that system is. Both noneducators and educators seem to have problems defining "the" system—and will spend hours validating their views of schooling as a political, or economic, or hierarchical system. With no common vision of the system to be improved, some even question whether or not there *is* a system.

While each may be correct within their perspective, they all miss the very important clue in what Deming provided the Japanese in his original "production as a system" flow chart. That is, we are looking for the *system of* **work**. The work of the people in the system—both adults and children—is the only thing that is manageable and is the primary arena to which technology can add value.

Understanding that work, therefore, becomes the prerequisite knowledge for any effort to improve it; as well as for any effort to add value to it technologically.

Ask most people what the work of schools is, and the answer generally will denote some form of delivery or transmission process—"*communicate* culture, *disseminate* knowledge, *transmit* information, etc." Yet the job of schools is no more the "delivery of information" than the job of hospitals is the delivery of medicine. True, medicine is "delivered" in hospitals, but only through a *managed work process* that tries to match it appropriately to need.

The work of hospitals, therefore, takes place in a setting structured and managed *to deliver appropriate service based upon continuing* **indi-**

vidual *diagnosis*. Most educators believe that is the nature of their work, also. But they attempt to accomplish that work in a setting that structured and managed around the concept of delivery. With this basic misunderstanding, is it any wonder that until now technologies have been seen as adding little value to the work of schooling, only cost. Productivity gain is impossible without understanding the work one is trying to make more productive.

Until recently, there has been little reason to question these fundamental assumptions about the nature of educators core work because we lacked ways to provide comprehensive, total organizational x-rays of school work processes. We could only take snapshots of its various component roles—here's what teachers do, or administrators, or curriculum developers, etc. In a supposedly loosely coupled organization of isolated practitioners, it has been practically impossible to envision how it all fit together.

Today however, quality management tools and processes provide organizational "x-rays" that allow us to view the nature of educators' actual work processes and to hold them up against what is known about the nature of work that produces quality results.

QUALITY-PRODUCING WORK

All world-class organizations are structured and managed around the same simple, common sense process regardless of whether they provide services or products. The process consists of 2 elements:

- A *core work process* involving those who "touch," or interact with, the product during its development; and
- An organization in which every function supports the *response-ability* of the core work.

The core work process itself is by nature a *response* process driven by needs and requirements of the client, customer, or product. The work, then, consists of *continuing informed interaction* between caring workers and the "outcome." Each cycle of interaction brings the outcome closer to the level of quality desired.

By nature, this quality producing work process is highly information dependent. Responses require continuing feedback that serves as the basis for determining the next act; and continuing exchange with the other organizational functions necessary to inform and support the interaction. In world class organizations, much of technology's value comes from the information it provides for this process. The work defines the tool.

It should not be difficult to see the parallels between this quality-producing work process and work of educators whose actions have produced quality results in form of growth and learning in others. Good teachers have always managed learning that way. And now, more importantly, cognitive research reveals that effective human learning requires just such a process. Each learner constructs personal meaning from these continuing interactions with the surrounding world.

Operating without this holistic perspective until now, it is obvious why technology has not become part of the ways schools do their business. Providing the connections, access, and new forms of information that make possible a continuing process of informed interaction are the very value-adding dimensions that, as in industry, can justify the cost of a districtwide information technology infrastructure.

One part of the missing technology mystery is clear. Over the years, technology's results and potentials have been clearly demonstrated, but seldom in ways that could be integrated into the ways the people within the system perform their daily tasks as part, or in support, of the core work process.

THE SYSTEM CONNECTS THE WORK

School practitioners increasingly claim "everything seems connected to everything else;" that their work settings are made up of parts that, intentionally or unintentionally, influence one another as they strive to impact the lives of children—their common organizational purpose. Unfortunately, most people do not directly perceive those seemingly ubiquitous influences on their work *as* a system. In education, recognizing that one is being impacted by a system—and understanding and perceiving that system—have been, until now, two wholly different issues.

The connections between the core teaching-learning interaction and the support functions of everyone else in the school system should become the blueprint for a school system structure that frames, aligns, and focuses on the common purpose of their work. Actually, for most outside the classroom, support of the core work is their *intention*. But accustomed roles and relationships developed around the misperception of the work process seldom allow fulfillment of these intentions. These deeply-set roles and relationships make up today's prevailing school structure—the target of the "restructuring" movement.

Today quality management provides us with a capability to view, understand, and then manage the actual interrelationships and interdependencies in a school district. Schools are learning that quality management processes can help them understand the fundamental nature and connectedness of their work as a system. They are discovering that:

- The manageable nature of their *system* lies in the white spaces between the boxes on the organization chart;
- Determining how to bridge those spaces with *functional relationships* is a primary role of organizational leadership;
- "Relationships" between and among functions in a work system are largely defined and maintained by the exchange of *information*--who gives it, gets it, how it's generated, and what types of decisions or choices it feeds; and that
- The fundamental challenge to transforming organizations is the ability *to link work processes together* in order to create and maintain a system.

As school personnel throughout a district engage in internal "customer-supplier" analyses, they begin to see their work in a flow of time and discover the already-present influences on each other's work. Using this type of total system x-ray, it is fairly easy to see the critical points where information technology could provide immediate value. These are the "disconnects"—the missing links separating dedicated professionals with something to contribute to each other's effectiveness. Also, we can see the points where critical information must be accessible as it is needed, and where new information must be generated from daily experience.

THE WORKPLACE OF THE MIND

Understanding school's core work and how to systemically support it will still leave our technology mystery unsolved. With a quality lens, we must look in greater depth at just what is being connected; the nature of what flows through those connections; and the cultural barriers that presently clog the open use of those connections.

As world class organizations have analyzed and prioritized their critical resources, a fundamental, and new, understanding has emerged. The workplace is no longer a physical space:

> "As a leader, your most precious possession is the people you have . . . and what they carry around in their heads."
>
> —*Robert Reich*

> "Today, as never before, the limit to innovation in business is not technology, but the managerial mindset."
>
> —*Richard Howard*

> " . . . 95% of American businesses are . . . stuck in a model that assumes that brains are needed at the top to manage, by remote control, the production line. And along that line, workers perform very limited, fragmented actions which render their thinking irrelevant. But earth has shifted its industrial axis. To compete globally, business needs to organize itself anew on a completely different basis: a belief in and the use of the brainpower of front-line workers."
>
> —*Ira Magaziner*

And *Shoshana Zuboff* notes, as she studies modern workplaces, that workers today must be learners, and managers must be teachers—that is, they must create environments where workers can learn from their work.

These ideas may not be unfamiliar to educational reformers advocating *site-based management* or *student-as-worker,* but the concept has yet to be accepted as a fundamental belief. The *sine qua non* of a quality work process is the understanding that the real core work process occurs in the workplace of the mind. Human beings are cognitive workers who, as they interact with their surroundings, continually process information to make sense of the world around them and their place in it; who integrate this information with what they have known before; and whose learnings represent the new information resulting from that integration.

Thus there is no difference between the work of teachers and administrators in the school. Each must manage environments where others can learn and grow from their work; and ultimately no difference between the work of adults and the children who must become self-managers of their own growth.

Because we are unaccustomed to looking at schools in this way, it may be hard to recognize the forms of already available information that feed this basic human process. For example:

Need	Types of Information
• To *orient* oneself and gain personal *meaning*; to understand how one personally "fits" or relates to the organization's purposes.	*Through vision, mission, goals, values*
• To know the *effects of one's own actions* in order to *self-correct*.	*Through coaching, access to formative feedback, and opportunities to reflect*
• To know what behaviors are *expected, ideal, successful*.	*By modeling, rewarding*
• To realize what *can* be done.	*Through opportunities for experience sharing with peers and access to research*
• To continually develop an *understanding* of the condition and situations to which one responds.	*Through opportunities to analyze scanning data, trend analyses, and student data*

"BARRIERS" IN THE WORKPLACE

With a common understanding of the mind as workplace—and perceiving information as the *nutrient* for growth, we now must recognize some other "information" already lying around that work area: Negative attitudes and perceptions formed from the ways information has been used in the past.

• From childhood on, data about one's actions are used to judge and blame, seldom for awareness and support. The con-

tinuum spreads from test scores and grades to politicians selectively taking numbers out of context to justify or blame.
* "Forms" are burdens; representing information to be collected for someone else's learning.
* "Reports" are information provided too late to be acted on.
* Even the concept of an information system is perceived as something that is separately managed, and which exists for those at the "top."

Fear and *lack of trust* run so deep in organizational settings such as schools, that the development of trust and the development of systemwide open exchange of information become intertwined issues in the effective management of schools as systems.

This is an area where quality management processes and tools are making major contributions. School staffs, working in groups apart from their traditional roles, find that trust emerges as a consequence of common problem solving experiences. Recognition of common purposes develops a base of mutual understanding on which future actions can be constructed.

Most significantly, identification and prioritization of schools' core and support processes, with the critical success factors vital to each, is beginning to fill in the vision of what an information system to support *response-ability* must look like. For example, consider how this exercise might identify the critical success factors in the core work process which could serve as a base for an information system that has the classroom, rather than the board room, as its core client.

Ask Teachers

(1) What do you need to know in order to be a little bit more effective tomorrow?
(2) Where is that data, information, or knowledge? Is it internal or external?
(3) How do you presently think you can get it?

Ask Principals

(1) What do you need to know in order to be a little bit more effective tomorrow?
(2) Where is that data, information, or knowledge? Is it internal or external?
(3) How do you presently think you can get it?

(4) To what extent is the data or information you need included in that which the teachers require first for their own use?
(5) To what extent do you have data or information needed by the teacher?

Ask Central Office

(1) What do you need to know in order to be a little bit more effective tomorrow?
(2) Where is that data, information, or knowledge? Is it internal or external?
(3) How do you presently think you can get it?
(4) To what extent is the data or information you need included in that which the teachers and/or principals require first for their own use?
(5) To what extent do you have, or have access to, the data or information needed by the building staffs?
(6) What do you need from the external environment in order for the system to continue to exist and grow?

THE CONNECTED LISTENING AND LEARNING ORGANIZATION

The nature of modern life requires that organizations be able to listen, learn, and respond holistically. To do this, a school system must provide an environment where people can trust the information they get. This means not only that they must trust each other enough to give open and honest information, but they must understand how everything "fits." They must have a vision that encompasses everyone's relationship to a common purpose, and the nature of what each person needs to know to be increasingly effective.

Policymakers believe they are addressing the major information needs of school reform when they focus on "standards" and "assessment." One provides indicators for direction, and the other indicators of where one is. But until now they have had no process for connecting them. As we have seen, because of a fundamental misunderstanding of the school's work process, there is no information driven process (comparable to what might be found in the modern hospital) that would allow continuing generation and analysis of "assessment" information to support daily diagnostic decisions, and to ensure their alignment with overall directions.

Now, the quality management movement is providing paradigm-shifting experiences that have uncovered new ways of looking at work in organizations. One "discovery:" a results driven management process requires a fundamentally different kind of information support. Required is a technology supported *information infrastructure* that goes beyond data, and traditional concepts of management information systems.

A system to support such *response-ability* would:

(1) **Provide continually updated background information about the conditions to which schools respond.** For example, teachers would have daily, up-to-date data about each student that would include not only quiz and test results, but information about learning styles, personal strengths, etc. Parents and students, as the other two decision makers who most influence learning, could access and use their own data.

(2) **Support self-correction.** Provide quick turnaround of information generated by student acts while something still can be done to take advantage of any unanticipated results, or to remedy any problems uncovered.

(3) **Provide analytic assistance at the classroom and school level.** Because teachers and principals have worked in such relative isolation, their analytic skills frequently have withered from lack of use. Software that supports local analysis can be an important tool. Technology can add value in analysis and understanding to ensure that "data" turns into institutionalized knowledge as the organization "learns."

(4) **Provide access regardless of setting.** In particular, information must be accessible at the professional's workspace—*the home*. One characteristic of professionals is that an important part of their work is done at times when they are not in direct contact with their clients. They reflect, research, strategize, and plan at times and in places where they will not be distracted. For teachers and administrators, this is most often at home.

(5) **Aggregate and analyze information at the building level**. Districts can provide scanning information, disaggregated data, and research that will support the principal's role as instructional leader.

(6) **Support, and increase the frequency of, organizational interactions.** These mostly informal exchanges serve to align and connect isolated actions of individuals and work groups as they fulfill the school system's aims.

(7) **Provide access to others' experiences through electronic "quality circles."** The problems faced by today's teachers and schools differ so much from the past that learning from each other's experience has become a fundamental requirement for effective schooling. Electronic conferencing can allow meaningful exchanges of experience and expertise that operationalizes interdependent roles.

CASE SOLVED

As he completed his investigation of the missing technologies, Holmes might have turned to his associate and concluded: "It's elementary, my dear Watson! . . . It wasn't the technology that was missing from the picture, . . . it was the people! When you look at schools as work settings, you'll see that in schools they ask, 'What can *technology* do?' In other work settings, they ask, 'What can *people* do . . . with the technology.'"

Holmes is right. But now educators, too, can ask that same question, and develop their own answers. The tools and processes of quality management—and the availability of information technologies—can allow educational leaders concerned with quality school outcomes to develop the understanding, experience, and the technology applications to *connect* personal and organizational productivity. The development of such a technology-facilitated quality support system can be the result of a new form of development process—**in-the-job learning.**

Enabled by information technology, this process can

+ Simultaneously develop trust;
+ Overcome a culture of information anxiety; and
+ Provide opportunities to learn how to apply unfamiliar technologies to daily work *as part of* that work.

Policymakers and practitioners, alike, can be empowered to:

+ Crack walls of professional isolation with networks of mutual support;

* Provide access to information and other resources at the places and times needed for timely responses;
* Establish and maintain new organizational relationships through supportive information flow; and, thereby,
* Contribute to what *schools can achieve* and at the same time, what *educators can do, and be!*

As Lawrence W. Lezotte notes as part of his Effective School approach:

The total quality effective school is probably unattainable (or even approachable) without a major commitment to the use of computers and other related information-processing technologies. The technology tool is critical if the quality school is going to be able to engage in the self-monitoring and adjustment processes that are a part of a dynamic and responsive organization. The first tools of technology being recommended should focus on how the adults in the school can develop and maintain information (a database) around each common place for each student, teacher, essential learning domain and classroom setting. Such information systems are essential if school leaders are going to be able to monitor the instructional system and make appropriate adjustments in a timely fashion. Most schools have only begun to realize the power of the computer as a tool of instructional delivery. Even fewer schools have recognized its potential as a management tool.

— Part Six —

APPENDICES

Appendix A

DIRECTORY OF TQM SCHOOLS BY STATE

Introduction: *This chapter provides information on 62 TQM schools in 28 states. It is organized by state to make it easy for readers to find sites near them. In the Fall of 1992, surveys were sent to 100 schools across the country that were believed to be implementing TQM. Responses were received from 40 schools which are summarized in this chapter. In addition, other schools appearing in recent periodicals or presenting at recent conferences have also been included. All of these schools can be used as reference or benchmark sites to find out more about their quality initiatives. If TQM is a new concept to the reader, it is suggested you try to visit one of these schools in order to get a firsthand idea of how to proceed.*

ALASKA

Larrae Rocheleau, Superintendent
Mt. Edgecumbe High School
1330 Seward Ave.
Sitka, AK 99835
Tel. (907) 966-2201

- ◆ 500 student, state-run boarding school, primarily Native Americans
- ◆ Began TQM journey in 1987
- ◆ *See Chapter 5 for further description*

ARIZONA

Arizona has a statewide strategy to integrate TQM into vocational/technical education and training. They have an annual TQM Vocational Student Organization Event and have provided TQM training in summer workshops. School boards are adopting quality management practices and industry is teaming up to facilitate TQM partnerships. For more information contact

Janet M. Gandy, State Supervisor, Business Education, Arizona Department of Education at (602) 542-5350.

J. Charles Santa Cruz, Principal
Delores Christiansen, Teacher
Gilbert High School
140 Gilbert Road
Gilbert, AZ 85234
Tel. (602) 497-0177, ext. 140

- 3300 student suburban high school
- Started TQM journey in 1988
- Classroom leadership initiatives from 9th to 12th grades

Carolyn J. Downey, Superintendent
Kyrene School District #28
8700 South Kyrene Rd.
Tempe, AZ 85284
Tel. (602) 496-4778

- 12,500 suburban school district
- Started TQM journey in 1990
- Used quality principles to look at curriculum management audit
- Mariposa Elementary School using TQM at classroom level. Contact is Sandra Smith, Principal

ARKANSAS

Emerson L. Hall, Superintendent
Florine Bingham, Quality Management Director
Forrest City School District
334 Graham
Forrest City, AR 72335
Tel. (501) 633-0804

- 5500 student rural school district
- Started TQM journey in 1989
- Districtwide initiative
- At classroom level—especially math classes

CALIFORNIA

Thomas A. Gemma, Principal
Will Roberts Middle School
4924 Dewey Drive
Fair Oaks, CA 95628
Tel. (916) 971-7889

- 850 student suburban school for 7th and 8th graders
- TQM journey started in 1988
- Mission is "quality education for lifelong learners"
- Education and business partnership in place called "Sacramento Total Quality Education Round Table"

Lee Jenkins, Superintendent
Enterprise School District
1155 Mistletoe Lane
Redding, CA 96002
Tel. (916) 224-4100

- 4000 student suburban school district
- Started TQM journey in 1991
- Using nonranking assessment for students developed with student participation
- Using alternative evaluation for teachers, satisfactory only, but teachers gather feedback from customers

Niel Malvetti, TQM Coordinator
Sacramento County Schools
9738 Lincoln Village Dr.
Sacramento, CA 95827
Tel. (916) 228-2223

- Covers 16 school districts supporting 200,000 students
- Started TQM journey in 1989

COLORADO

Beverly Ausfahl, Facilitator of Leadership Development
Public School District #60
315 West 11th Street
Pueblo, CO 81003
Tel. (719) 549-7177

* 18,000 student urban school district
* Started TQM journey in Fall, 1992
* Tying it with site-based decision making

CONNECTICUT

Kenneth R. Freeston, Assistant Superintendent
Newtown Board of Education
11 Queen Street
Newtown, CT 96470-2151
Tel. (203) 426-7616

* 3700 student suburban school district
* Began TQM journey in 1989
* First interest through business partnership with Union Carbide
* Used work of Glasser, Deming, Covey, and others to establish Newtown Success-Oriented School Model
* Mission is "all children can and will learn"
* Quality core groups in each school are shaping their own allotment of inservice time and resources to address quality issues

FLORIDA

J. Howard Hinesley, Superintendent
Pinellas County Schools
301 4th Street S.W.
P.O. Box 2942
Largo, FL 34649-2942
Tel. (813) 588-6295

* 96,000 student urban school district
* Began TQM journey in July, 1991
* First interest from attending business partners TQM training
* Established District Quality Council
* New elementary school opened with entire staff trained in quality
* Has TQ Schooling Union Bargaining Model

GEORGIA

Tom Upchurch, Superintendent
James E. "Mac" McCoy, Director of Quality Management
Carrollton City School District
P.O. Box 740
Carrollton, GA 30117
Tel. (404) 832-9633

 • 3500 students urban school district
 • Started TQM journey in 1989
 • Basing effort on effective schools research

ILLINOIS

Sam Spitalli, Assistant Principal
Palatine High School
206 Montana
Cary, IL 60013
Tel. (708) 516-8329

 • 1900 student suburban high school
 • Began TQM journey in December, 1990
 • Attended conference at community college
 • Speakers from area employers discussed Deming
 • Read Glasser's *Quality School* and implemented
 • Goals include (1) Focusing on what adds quality to students' work and lives, (2) Eliminate coercion, (3) Utilize self-evaluation
 • Training from Glasser's Institute of Reality Therapy
 • Funded by School District
 • Over 85% of teaching, counseling, support staff is involved
 • "There has never been more enthusiasm among students and teachers."
 • Lessons learned—Be patient
 • Results—teachers report students are working harder than before and not "leaning on their shovels"

D. Michael Risen, Superintendent
Midwest Central C.U. #191
1010 S. Washington
Manito, IL 61546
Tel. (309) 968-6868

- 1400 student rural school district
- Started TQM journey in 1991
- Three components to TQM initiative: An organizational structure called leadership teams, a team incentive policy, and school improvement project teams

KANSAS

Gary George, Superintendent
USD #231, Gardner-Edgerton-Antioch
P.O. Box 97
Gardner, KS 66030
Tel. (913) 884-7102

- Part of 16 district Quality Alliance started from original presentations from Xerox in 1989
- Support also received from AT&T, Sprint, and Kansas City Chamber of Commerce
- Alliance funded by fees from districts based on enrollment (total 120,000 students)
- Director hired and TQM curriculum developed
- Results have been a changing outlook, more use of data and tools, more customer sensitivity, more work with suppliers and much more emphasis being placed on continuous improvement

Mary Devin, Superintendent
Geary County School District 475
P.O. Box 370
Junction City, KS 66441
Tel. (913) 238-6184

- 7300 student suburban school district
- Started TQM journey in 1990
- Used TQM to implement technology that manages student performance data.
- As a result the majority of Chapter 1 teachers have returned to regular classroom, students' test scores now rank above the state average, and parent involvement has tripled

KENTUCKY

Terry Brooks, Special Assistant to the Superintendent
Jefferson Country Public Schools
3332 Newburg Road
P.O. Box 34020
Louisville, KY 40232-4020
Tel. (502) 473-3909

- 95,000 student urban/suburban district
- TQM journey began in 1988
- Result of partnership between Board of Education and Teachers Association which lead to contract providing for shared decision making
- Hope to guarantee increased educational achievement of all students and create local school and central office accountability systems
- Expect transition from a maintenance organization to a learning organization
- Training provided by district "academy"
- Some seed investment from local foundation and business partners
- All levels engaged in TQM effort from self-regulated work teams in central office to school level governing councils and task forces
- Lessons learned include resocialization required, training should provide specific skills, it takes time, superintendent and principal leadership is critical
- Preliminary results show gains in academic achievement, retention rates decreased, disciplinary actions lower and student and teacher attitudes improved.

LOUISIANA

The Louisiana State Department of Education has provided funding to 3 parish school districts to participate in the development of the design to adapt Deming's Quality Improvement principles, beliefs, and tools to the education environment.

F. Gary Brewer, Superintendent
Beauregard Parish Schools

P.O. Drawer 938
DeRidder, LA 70634
Tel. (318) 463-5551

- 6500 student rural school district
- Started TQM journey in 1991

MASSACHUSETTS

Karla Baehr DeLetis, Superintendent
Wellesley Public Schools
40 Kingsbury Street
Wellesley, MA 02181
Tel. (617) 446-6226

- 3000 student suburban school district
- TQM journey began in 1991
- Uses systems thinking as fundamental logic for TQM
- Feedback loop diagramming used to integrate special education into the classroom through co-teaching

MICHIGAN

Michigan has a statewide initiative under the Michigan Partnership for New Education in East Lansing. Chester A. Francke, Vice President of the Partnership, can be contacted for further information at (517) 336-2195. They believe the quality philosophy, combined with teaming and a scientific approach, offers schools an opportunity to develop a systemic approach to change. It provides a platform for introducing change, implementing site-based management, evaluating planned change efforts, and emphasizing customer delight.

Maurice L. Conn, Superintendent
Saline Area Schools
7190 Maple Road
Saline, MI 48176
Tel. (313) 429-5454

- 3500 Student suburban school district
- TQM journey began in 1985

- Labor strike demonstrated need for skill building in collaborative bargaining and ultimately decision making models were redefined
- Goal is to redesign entire K-12 school system
- Received counsel from Ford Motor Company and used their external consultants
- Training funded by school district
- All 400 employees have been trained
- Department/division and building level teams work on everything from food service to curriculum issues
- Lessons learned—Make haste slowly.

MINNESOTA

Minnesota has a statewide initiative under the Minnesota Academic Excellence Foundation in St. Paul and the Minnesota Council for Quality in Bloomington. Contacts are Zona Sharp-Burk and Jim Buckman, respectively. (Contact telephone number is 612-297-1875.) During the last 2 years, under a Partners for Quality Initiative, 16 K-12 and higher education institutions were matched with Baldrige Award pursuing businesses to test the relevance of TQM and the self-assessment process for education. Participants found the Baldrige criteria fit education without modification. The emphasis both sides of the partnerships placed on continuous improvement in their organizations resulted in new forms of collaboration and increased mutual respect. The shared "quality language" also enabled them to communicate more effectively.

Douglas Otto, Superintendent
Anoka-Hennepin School District 11
11299 Hanson Blvd.
Coon Rapids, MN 55433
Tel. (612) 422-5500

- 37,000 student suburban school district
- Started TQM journey in 1991
- Has joined Anoka County Quality Council to work with business leaders and local community college to use TQM to restructure education. Still in planning stage.
- Sees TQM as umbrella for all other initiatives—effective schools, outcome based education, site based management, etc.

Mary Bollinger
Eden Prairie Schools
8100 School Road
Eden Prairie, MN 55344
Tel. (612) 937-1650

- ✦ 7700 student suburban school district
- ✦ Started TQM journey in June 1990
- ✦ First interest from AASA seminar
- ✦ Influenced by Zytec Corp., 1991 Malcolm Baldrige winner
- ✦ Using outside consultants for training as well as AASA and university conferences
- ✦ Training has included teachers and school board members
- ✦ Lessons learned include "don't name it, just do it;" assign someone within the district who has a districtwide perspective to keep the fires lit; be sure top leadership supports it; it's a long process and there are no cookbooks

Nancy Martin, Director of Educational Services
Mahtomedi Public Schools
ISD 832 District Education Center
1520 Mahtomedi Avenue
Mahtomedi, MN 55115-1999
Tel. (612) 426-3224

- ✦ 2500 student suburban school district
- ✦ TQM journey began in 1989
- ✦ Developed clear vision of where district wanted to go and how quality principles would provide the framework to achieve vision
- ✦ Systemic change was central
- ✦ Partnership with 3M, Quality Management Services
- ✦ Intentional integration of many national reform initiatives (OBE, Whole Language, Effective Schools, Drug-Free Schools, and Elements of Instruction) within one cohesive framework for school improvement.

Lyle Koski, Director of Education
North Branch Area Public Schools
320 Main Street
North Branch, MN 55056
Tel. (612) 464-0425 or 674-5225

- 2650 student rural/suburban school district
- Began TQM journey in July, 1990
- Superintendent introduced concept and move toward customer satisfaction
- Goal is to restructure total district around quality concept — implementing site-based decision making and working toward quality/data based decision making process
- Training assistance received from local business partners like 3M, Honeywell, and Partners for Quality Initiative
- Lessons learned — it's easy to talk and believe in quality, but implementation is difficult because of lack of meaningful data and nonexistence of benchmarks

MISSISSIPPI

Mike Walters, Superintendent
Tupelo Public School District
201 South Green Street
Tupelo, MS 38801
Tel. (601) 841-8850

- 7200 student rural/small city school district
- Started TQM journey in January, 1992
- Encouraged by business/industry partners
- Goals are to raise expectations for all students and encourage all to do quality work
- Training provided by Dr. Julie Horine from University of Mississippi
- Classroom teachers being trained in Glasser *Quality School* techniques
- Lessons learned — takes time, does not happen overnight

NEW HAMPSHIRE

Henry E. LaBranche, Superintendent of Schools
Salem School District
206 Main Street
Salem, NH 03079
Tel. (603) 893-7040

* 3790 student suburban school district
* TQM journey began in July, 1990
* Superintendent turned to TQM to motivate staff and make strategic plan a living document
* Influenced by participation in a business-education collaborative and by Sitka, Alaska, story
* Goal is to infuse TQM tenets throughout organization—making the culture one of total interdependence and focused on mission
* Training from AASA, business partners, and US Chamber of Commerce and has focused mostly on administrators
* Jointly sponsoring training with local Chamber of Commerce for business and educational leaders
* Lessons learned—it's hard and requires a real passion by the CEO and a core team representing every functional element of the organization.

NEW JERSEY

Philip Esbrandt, Superintendent
Cherry Hill Public Schools
P.O. Box 5015
Cherry Hill, NJ 08034
Tel. (609) 429-5600

* 10,000 student suburban school district
* Started TQM journey in 1987
* Part of 10 district quality consortium
* Corporate support from AT&T, Xerox, Dupont, and Johnson and Johnson

NEW YORK

Lewis Rappaport, Principal
Franklin Schargel, Assistant Principal and Quality Coordinator
George Westinghouse Vo-Tech High School
105 Johnson Street
Brooklyn, NY 11201
Tel. (718) 625-6130

* 1700 student urban high school
* *See Chapter 4 for complete description*

Joan H. Wilson, Facilitator Trainer
South Huntington Union Free School District
60 Weston Street
Huntington Station, NY 11746
Tel. (516) 673-1749

- 5000 student suburban school district
- Began TQM journey in 1982
- Obtained support from local chapter of Association for Quality and Participation(AQP)
- Business partners included Hazeltine Corp., Grumman, and Estee Lauder

John E. Helfrich, Superintendent
Dorothy Vienne, Principal, Thomas Edison Elementary School
Kenmore-Town of Tonawanda School District
1500 Colvin Blvd.
Kenmore, NY 14223
Tel. (716) 874-8400

- 8800 student suburban school district
- *See Chapter 1 for full description*

George G. Hamaty, Superintendent
Corning-Painted Post Area School District
165 Charles St.
Painted Post, NY 14870
Tel. (607) 936-3704

- 5800 student urban school district
- Partnership with Corning Glass
- Started Koalaty Kid program (*see Chapter 7*)

Manuel Rivera, Superintendent
Patricia Hrankowski, Director, Organization Effectiveness
Rochester City School District
131 West Broad St.
Rochester, NY 14614
Tel. (716) 262-8271

* 33,000 student urban school district
* Started TQM journey in 1991
* Has developed Quality Award for High Performance Schools
* Recognizes continuous improvement
* Based on assessment matrix that incorporates the dimensions of systemic changes and provides a quantitative, data driven means of assessing progress
* Partnership with Eastman Kodak

NORTH CAROLINA

G. Thomas Houlihan, Superintendent
Johnston County Schools
P.O. Box 1336
Smithfield, NC 27577
Tel. (919) 934-6031

* 15,000 student rural school district
* TQM journey began in October, 1991
* Superintendent attended Deming seminars and realized need to view education from a system's perspective
* Working with business partners and Chamber of Commerce on community quality initiative
* First goal was to demonstrate "constancy of purpose" with new mission statement . . . to make continuous improvement in each and every area of education within our community for every student and for every staff member within the school community
* Training provided by outside consultant, Educational Services Institute, Cincinnati, Ohio, and mostly at leadership level at this point
* Funding from regular state and local education and training budget plus special grant from state to implement outcomes based education
* Lessons learned—TQM is not a program, but a belief system in how systems and organization should operate. It is not something that has a beginning and ending point, but a process that, once initiated, is a commitment for long-term implementation

OHIO

Ralph Waltman, Assistant Superintendent
Stark County School District
2100 38th Street NW
Canton, OH 44709
Tel. (216) 492-8136

- 34,000 student countywide school district
- Started TQM journey in June, 1991
- Influenced by readings and business/industry leader dis-
cussions
- Training provided by Education Services Institute, Cincin-
nati, Ohio
- Focus on cross-functional teaming
- Lessons learned – TQM takes time, but provides the pro-
cess, the tools needed to cope with change and to strive for
improvement.

Bob Bowers, Superintendent
South-Western City School District
2975 Kingston Avenue
Grove City, OH 43123
Tel. (614) 875-2318

- 16,600 rural/suburban school district
- Started TQM journey in February, 1991
- Interest stimulated from AASA annual conference – recog-
nized that TQM could help us do more with less
- Goals are to maximize efficiency of operation and provide
maximum learning opportunities for all students
- Training both in-house and using outside consultants
- Some business support from GM/Inland Fisher Guide,
Ohio Bell, Wal-Mart, and Xerox
- Lessons learned – must develop a critical mass of people
who see the value and can be the point persons for Quality
Integration

OREGON

Donald L. Tank, Superintendent
Clackamas County School District 62

Oregon City Public Schools
1417 Twelfth St.
P.O. Box 591
Oregon City, OR 97045
Tel. (503) 656-4283

 * 6400 student rural school district
 * TQM journey began in 1988
 * Mission—"Together, we are boldly committed to responsible lifelong learning."
 * Broad community involvement in strategic plan development and ongoing advisory councils
 * Quality circles in wide use, including K-12 classrooms
 * High School graduates receive warranty in event retraining needed
 * Broad involvement in hiring decisions, curriculum development, and textbook selection

PENNSYLVANIA

George J. Cardone
Altoona Area School District
1415 Sixth Avenue
Altoona, PA 16602
Tel. (814) 946-8350

 * 9400 student urban school district
 * Began TQM journey in 1984
 * Interest in solid staff development program involving teachers, administrators, and board members which would improve curriculum delivery
 * Goal is to empower each school to provide finest education possible for all students in our community
 * Training married TQM and school-based management
 * Funded by district, education association, and PA Milrite Council
 * Lessons learned—takes time, hard work, financial resources, and a willingness to experiment and take risks

Verel R. Salmon, Assistant Superintendent
Millcreek Township School District

3740 W. 26th Street
Erie, PA 16506
Tel. (814) 835-5329

- 7200 student suburban school district
- Began TQM journey in 1987
- Wanted to have common model with industry; Excellence Council was formed to encourage TQM in all parts of the community
- Training provided through Council and local Chamber of Commerce
- Teamwork practices used in most classrooms
- District highly computerized to support student teams
- TQM is a graduation requirement
- Lessons learned—it must be done systematically in all aspects of operations and instruction, it takes years
- Received the Erie Quality Award in Fall of 1992

Robert H. Bender, Superintendent of Schools
Crawford Central School District
RR 9, Box 462, Route 102
Meadville, PA 16335-9504
Tel. (814) 724-3960

- 4800 student rural/suburban school district
- Began TQM journey in September, 1989
- First exposure through Chamber of Commerce
- Goal to develop ongoing capability to establish and convene continuous improvement teams to address all parts of the district
- Training from Community Quality Coalition, Jackson, MI
- Additional support from local businesses
- Lessons learned—primary emphasis is on team building and interpersonal skills among cross-functional teams and multi-levels of employees

John Jenkins, Superintendent
Nazareth Area School District
8 Center Square
Nazareth, PA 18064
Tel. (215) 759-1170

- 3400 student suburban school district
- Began TQM journey in September, 1991

- Deming interest and support of Ben Franklin Center for Technology
- Goals include participatory decision making and continuous improvement through systems approach
- Koalaty Kids at school level
- Has resulted in a positive change in school culture and climate and increased personal commitment

Roger A. Place, Superintendent
Springfield School District
111 W. Leamy Ave.
Springfield, PA 19064
Tel. (215) 544-5800

- 3000 student suburban school district
- Began TQM journey Spring, 1991
- Attended introductory seminar at Delaware County Community College (DCCC)-*See Chapter 12 for more information about DCCC TQM Initiatives with local school districts*
- Training now down to teacher level
- Have selected narrowly focused problems with readily available data to obtain early successes
- School Board interest and support key to progress

Sheldon V. Whitaker, Jr., Superintendent
State College School District
131 West Nittany Ave.
University Park, PA 16801
Tel. (814) 231-1016

- 6400 student suburban/rural school district
- *See Chapter 13 for description of partnership with Penn State College of Education*

SOUTH CAROLINA

Joseph E. Gentry, Superintendent
John S. Taylor, Quality Contact
Rock Hill School District
P.O. Drawer 10072
Rock Hill, SC 29731
Tel. (803) 324-5360

- 13,000 student suburban school district
- Started TQM journey in 1991
- Originated from partnership with business/industry leaders in community

TEXAS

Texas has a statewide strategy. See Chapter 15.

Denny Dowd, Director of Personnel
Arlington Independent School District
1203 W. Pioneer Parkway
Arlington, TX 76013
Tel. (817) 459-7432

- 46,000 student suburban school district
- Started TQM journey Summer, 1991
- Influenced by partnership with Xerox
- Goals are improve learning and efficiency of tax dollars used to produce results
- Using internal trainers
- Most activity at campus planning team level
- Lessons learned—slow, never ending process, but does work and benefit the organization

Bonnie A. Lesley, Assistant Superintendent
Austin Independent School District
1111 West 6th Street
Austin, TX 78703
Tel. (512) 499-1700

- 70,000 student urban school district
- Began TQM journey in November, 1991
- TQM interest generated from William Glasser *Quality School* program
- Goals include increased sensitivity to internal and external customers, reduce costs, improve quality of staff and student work
- Institute of Reality Therapy has provided school training
- Business partners helping with administrator training
- Lessons learned—TQM without control theory doesn't make sense, need different training for different levels of staff, develop in-house training capability to keep affordable

Bill Borgers, Superintendent
Linda Hanson, Principal, McAdams Junior High School
Dickinson Independent School District
Drawer Z
Dickinson, TX 77539
Tel. (713) 337-1942

- 5800 student suburban school district
- *See Chapter 2 for complete description*

Gerald Anderson, Superintendent
Brazosport Independent School District
P.O. Box Z
Freeport, TX 77541
Tel. (409) 265-6981

- 12,500 student suburban school district
- Began TQM journey in April, 1989
- Board member was quality manager for Dow Chemical
- Initiative started with other school districts and community college at the same time
- Saw TQM as a way to eliminate waste and improve management system
- "Hope to see school district where we:
  - Are dedicated to customer success
  - Are making decisions based on data
  - Have driven fear out of the job
  - Have teachers that are facilitators of learning
  - Have students responsible for their own learning
  - Have high levels of communication
  - Focus on a common purpose
  - Share responsibility for the results
  - Have all stakeholders as active participants"
- Training from local businesses and community college
- Lessons learned—essential to have clear understanding of the process and how it will be implemented by all levels of top management and board

Mary Murphy, Executive Director
Administrative Staffing and Development
Houston ISD
3830 Richmond

Houston, TX 77027
Tel. (713) 892-6929

* 196,000 student urban school district
* Started TQM journey in 1991
* Received help from Houston Community College and Texaco to form quality partnership for education in Houston
* The partnership, Project Solve One (PS#1), is composed of numerous business partners and consultants who are members of Houston chapters of ASQC and AQP as well as the American Productivity and Quality Center
* Major focus is providing training assistance to educators in implementing quality through employee involvement using quality circles
* Educators have access to AQP's local "Quality Hot Line"
* An "Adopt a Quality School" program recruits quality professionals to assist school administrators and teachers

Mike Childress
Texas Eastman Company
P.O. Box 7444
Longview, TX 75607-7444
Tel. (903) 237-5082

* Texas Eastman is working with 5 Longview area school districts to implement Performance Management(PM) as part of their GLOBE program (Greater Longview Organization for Business and Education)
* PM is a systemic data oriented approach to improving student performance and having fun doing it
* It focuses on results, teamwork, continual improvement, and positive reinforcement for desired behaviors and results
* Documented results are showing that the program has a positive effect on a wide range of students from "at risk" to "gifted and talented"

Dawson Orr, Superintendent
Pampa ISD
321 W. Albert Street
Pampa, TX 79065
Tel. (806) 669-4700

* 4200 student rural district
* Began TQM journey in June, 1991
* School board election focused on quality movement
* Received assistance from Hoescht Celanese
* Objectives to lower failure rate, improve student performance measurements and close gap for minority students
* Principals and staff have received over 35 hours of training funded by grants, business partners, and district funds
* Greatest classroom use in high school math to reduce failure rates
* Lessons learned—train, retrain, and train some more and also need to educate community

Doris Fassino, Assistant Superintendent
Pasadena ISD
1515 Cherrybrook
Pasadena, TX 77502
Tel. (713) 920-6886

* 40,000 student urban school district
* TQM journey began Fall, 1990
* First interest generated by attending training provided by Texaco
* Purpose is to instill continuous quality improvement thinking in adults and children
* 50 person vertical team was trained and applied their learning to improvement projects. Now some of these are doing training of trainers
* Supplier provided some initial training as part of bid
* All administrators design and self-evaluate their own jobs
* 4 campuses moving to self assessment using portfolios
* Several campuses are using children on improvement teams
* Lessons learned—change for upper mid-management is difficult. Will not be fast process

Richard Clifford, Superintendent
Southwest ISD
Route 9, Box 205AF
San Antonio, TX 78227
Tel. (210) 622-3488

- 8300 student suburban school district
- *see Chapter 8 for complete description*

Jack Biggerstaff, Principal
Sanger High School
105 Berry
Sanger, TX 76266
Tel. (817) 458-7497

- 1600 student rural district, 400 in high school
- Began TQM journey in 1990
- Influenced by local business partners like TI, Boeing, and EDS
- New delivery system where teacher is facilitator and student is worker
- Students empowered and using cooperative learning to foster teamwork and creativity
- Much more aware of quality of work instead of grades
- Failure and drop-out rates are lower
- Absenteeism is down for both teachers and students

Kay Psencik, Assistant Superintendent
Temple Independent School District
200 North 23rd
Temple, TX 76503
Tel. (817) 778-6721

- 8400 student urban/suburban school district
- Began TQM journey in 1990
- Implementing through Glasser *Quality School* approach
- Now have a communitywide Quality Quorum where staff development activities are shared and learning from each other
- Major goals are that schools will become need satisfying places for all and students will be able to recognize quality in their own work
- Have seen some decrease in discipline problems

Leonard Merrell, Superintendent
Texas City Independent School District
1401 9th Avenue North
Texas City, TX 77590
Tel. (409) 942-2602

- 6100 student suburban school district
- Began TQM journey in December, 1991
- Influenced by other districts in area and local business partners like Union Carbide, Amoco Chemical, and Sterling Chemical
- Hope to accomplish total systems improvement by involving the total community
- Training on Glasser's *Quality School* for teachers, additional training from community colleges, business partners, AASA, and state conferences/seminars
- Have seen a more positive attitude from teachers
- Received innovation grant from state agency
- Lessons learned—TQM will not be accepted by everyone, takes time, paradigms hard to chance, essential to invest in employees through quality staff development, the more you learn about your customers, the more you recognize how much improvement can be made
- Have already seen a reduction in failures

Randee Reisinger, Director of Staff Development
Waco Independent School District
P.O. Drawer 27
Waco, TX 76703-0027
Tel. (817) 752-8341

- 15000 urban school district
- Began TQM journey in 1992
- Had been implementing Glasser *Quality School* and wanted to include TQM at upper levels
- Attended Deming Conference
- Each campus has team being trained in TQM and they will train faculty
- McLennan Community College is providing training
- Lessons learned—tremendous amount of time to be invested to fully understand concepts

Leslie V. Carnine, Superintendent
Wichita Falls ISD
P.O. Box 2570
Wichita Falls, TX 76307-2570
Tel. (817) 720-3100

- 14,500 student urban school district
- Started TQM journey in 1988
- Business partner support from Howmet, Xerox, GM, and Exxon
- Sees TQM as umbrella for school improvement initiatives, participatory decision making, and SBDM

VIRGINIA

Virginia has a statewide strategy. See Chapter 14.

Claude C. Parent, Quality Mgr. &
Dir. of Communications Development
Portsmouth City Public Schools
3651 Hartford St.
Portsmouth, VA
Tel. (804) 393-8555

- 18,000 student urban school district
- Began TQM journey in 1989
- Has tied TQL with Effective Schools Research
- Joint TQL resolution between Superintendent and School Board signed October, 1992

David M. Gangel, Superintendent
Robert T. Chappell, Assistant Superintendent/Quality Trainer
Rappahannock County Schools
P.O. Box 273
Sperryville, VA 22740
Tel. (703) 987-8773

- 1029 students in rural school district
- Began TQM journey in October, 1990
- Introduced by Xerox Corporation training
- Four school associates received 80 hours of training from Xerox to become trainers of the rest of the staff
- Training was voluntary to increase buy-in, but 65% signed up
- To date nearly 90% of all school associates have received the 30-hour training
- Quality Steering Committee formed

- Customer surveys of parents used to identify problems to work on
- Cross-functional Quality Problem Solving Project Teams established
- Quality processes used in all departments and grade levels to improve instruction
- Lessons learned—quality problem solving procedures initially take more time than bureaucratic methods, but be patient

WASHINGTON

Dewayne Gower, Superintendent
South Kitsap School District
1962 Hoover Ave. SE
Port Orchard, WA 98366
Tel. (206) 876-7344

- 11,000 student suburban school district
- Began TQM journey in 1991
- Superintendent had been interested for several years and followed the process in the literature
- Attended AASA seminars
- Networking with Puget Sound Navel Shipyard for additional support
- Training provided by Chamber of Commerce workshops and also Glasser *Quality School*
- Has interfaced to Outcomes Based Education
- Lessons learned—take plenty of time and sample the wide diversity of materials and presentations available; Synthesize these materials and design a process that is appropriate for your institution
- TQM is a long, time consuming process without shortcuts; The key is information, in-service and commitment from the top

WISCONSIN

Charles A. Melvin, III, Superintendent
School District of Beloit Turner
1231 Inman Parkway
Beloit, WI 53511
Tel. (608) 362-0771

- 994 student suburban school district
- Began TQM journey in 1989
- Read professional article tying TQM and Effective Schools
- Part of 5-district consortium
- Using control charts as student improvement tools—students charting their own achievement

Steven M. Ashmore
Brodhead School District
2100 W. 9th Avenue
Brodhead, WI 53520-0258
Tel. (608) 897-2141

- 1400 student rural/small town district
- Began TQM journey in August, 1989
- Looking for way to energize middle management to take proactive role in systemic change
- Part of 5-local school district consortium on TQM
- Goal—every student, parent, employee will become a manager of their quality world
- Training from consultant, funded by grants and reorganization of existing dollars
- Lessons learned—not cookbook, but philosophy, need top level commitment, takes time
- Students pursuing higher education has increased from 64% in 1989 to 90% in 1992

David Romstad, Superintendent
Michael Jamison, Elementary Principal
Parkview School District
719 St. Lawrence Avenue
Jamesville, WI 53545
Tel. (608) 879-2352

- 1100 student rural school district
- *See Chapter 3 for full description*

— Appendix B —

SELECTED REFERENCES, K-12 FOCUS

Mel Silberberg, *Silberberg Associates, Salem, Massachusetts*

Introduction: *Mel Silberberg is a founding board member of the National Educational Quality Initiative, Inc. (NEQI) and chairs its task force on educational quality management. He is also a founding member of the National Quality Alliance and the Massachusetts Municipal Quality Network. For the past several years he has maintained a comprehensive list of texts, articles and other references on TQM in education. We are printing here a subset of that list specifically focused on K-12 schools.*

TEXTS

AASA. *Introduction to Total Quality for Schools: A Compilation of Articles on the Concepts of Total Quality Management and W. Edwards Deming.* American Association of School Administrators, 1991.

Aguayo, Rafael. *Dr. Deming: The Man Who Taught The Japanese About Quality.* Simon & Schuster, 1990.

Backaitis, Nida and Rosen, Harold H. *Managing for Organizational Quality— Theory and Implementation: An Annotated Bibliography.* AASA, 1991.

Bonstingl, John J. *Schools of Quality: An Introduction to TQM in Education.* The Association Society for Supervision & Curriculum Development (ASCD), 1992.

Byrnes, Margaret A., Cornesky, Robert and Byrnes, Lawrence B. *The Quality Teacher: Implementing TQM in the Classroom.* Cornesky & Associates Press (P.O. Box 2139, Bunnell, FL 32110), 1992.

Covey, Stephen R. *The Seven Habits of Highly Successful People.* Simon & Schuster, 1989.

Covey, Stephen R. *Principle-Centered Leadership.* Simon & Schuster, 1991.

Crawford-Mason, Clare and Dobyns, Lloyd. *Quality . . . OR ELSE: The Revolution in World Business.* Houghton-Mifflin, 1991.

Fiske, Edward B. *Smart Schools, Smart Kids.* Simon & Schuster, 1991.

Gabor, Andrea. *The Man Who Discovered Quality.* Times Books, 1990.

Gardner, Howard. *The Unschooled Mind: How Children Think and How Schools Should Teach.* Basic Books Div., Harper Collins, Publishers, 1991.

Glasser, William. *Control Theory in the Classroom.* Harper & Row, 1986.

Glasser, William. *The Quality School.* Harper & Row, 1990.

GOAL/QPC. *The Memory Jogger for Education: A Pocket Guide for Continuous Improvement in Schools.* GOAL/QPC, Methuen, MA, 1992.

Goldman, Gary. *Quality Student Leadership: Strategy for School Improvement.* (Student Manual/Teacher's Guide.) Quality Improvement Associates, Inc. (645 N. Michigan Avenue, Chicago, IL 60611), 1992.

Goldratt, Elihu M. and Cox, Jeff. *The Goal.* North River Press (Croton-On-Hudson, NY 10520), Second revised edition, 1992.

Goodlad, John I. *Teachers For Our Nation's Schools.* Jossey-Bass, 1990.

Hunt, V. Daniel. *Quality in America.* Business One-Irwin, 1992.

Juska, Jane. "The Unteachables: A Case Study on Improving Writing via TQM in the Schools." *The Quarterly* (National Writing Project and the Center for the Study of Writing), January 1989. (Also available from AASA.)

Kline, Peter. *The Everyday Genius: Restoring Children's Natural Joy of Learning—And Yours, Too.* Great Ocean Publishers, 1990.

Levine, Daniel U. and Lezotte, Lawrence W. *Unusually Effective Schools.* National Center for Effective Schools Research & Development, University of Wisconsin (1025 West Johnson Street, Madison, WI 53706), 1990.

Lewis, James, Jr. *Achieving Excellence in Our Schools by Taking Lessons from America's Best-Run Companies.* J.L. Wilkerson Publishing Co. (731 Franklin Street, Westbury, NY), 1986.

Lockwood, Anne Turnbull, *et al.* "Total Quality Management." *Focus in Change,* Fall 1992. (A publication of the National Center for Effective Schools Research & Development.)

Neuroth, Joann, Plastrik, Peter and Cleveland, John. *The Total Quality Management Handbook.* On-Purpose Associates (109 Allen Street, Lansing, MI), 1992. (Also available from AASA.)

Rinehart, Gray. *Quality Education.* Quality Press (ASQC), 1992.

Sarason, Seymour B. *The Predictable Failure of Educational Reform: Can We Change It Before It's Too Late?* Jossey-Bass, 1990.

Savery, Louis M. *Creating Quality Schools.* AASA, 1992.

Schenkat, Randolph. *Quality Connections: Transforming Schools to Total Quality Management:* The Association for Supervision & Curriculum Development (ASCD), available Spring 1993.

Senge, Peter M. *The Fifth Discipline: the Art and Practice of the Learning Organization.* Doubleday, 1990.

Schmoker, Michael J. and Wilson, Richard B. *Total Quality Education: Profiles of Schools Demonstrating the Power of Deming's Management Principles.* Phi Delta Kappa, Publishers (P.O. Box 789, Bloomington, IN 47402).

Scholtes, Peter R. *The Team Handbook.* Joiner Associates, Inc. (Madison, WI), 1989.

Sergiovanni, Thomas J. and Moore, John H., Editors. *Schooling for Tomorrow: Directing Reforms to Issues That Count.* Allyn and Bacon, 1989.

Toch, Thomas. *In the Name of Excellence: The Struggle to Reform the Nation's Schools,* Oxford University Press, 1991.

Walton, Mary. *The Deming Management Method*. Putnam, 1986.
Walton, Mary. *Deming Management At Work*. Putnam, 1990.

ARTICLES

Ashmore, Steven M. "A New Management Philosophy: Moving From 'Boss' Management to 'Shared' Leadership." Available from the author, c/o the School District of Brodhead, WI 53520.

Ashmore, Steven, M. "Total Quality Leadership." *Loc. cit.*, April, 1991.

Axland, Suzanne. "Congressional Forum on Quality Education: Legislators Learn About Quality." *Quality Progress*, October 1992.

Bailey, Elizabeth, Bayless, David L., *et al*. "The Quality Improvement Management Approach As Implemented in a Middle School." *Center for Research on Educational Accountability and Teacher Evaluation (CREATE)*, Western Michigan University (Kalamazoo, MI 49008), 1992.

Barkley, Robert, Jr. "Teaching Schools A Lesson." *Management Review* (an AMA publication), October 1991.

Barrows, Linda K., Melvin, Charles A., *et al*. "Interdistrict Collaboration for School-Focused Quality Improvement." *Proceedings Fourth Annual Hunter Conference on Quality* (Madison, WI), April 1991.

Basom, Richard E., Jr., and Crandall, David C. "Implementing A Redesign Strategy: Lessons from Educational Change." Regional Laboratory for Educational Improvement of Northeast & the Islands (Andover, MA), July 1989.

Bayless, David L., *et al*. "Quality Improvement in Education Today and the Future: Adapting W. Edwards Deming's Quality Improvement Principles and Methods to Education." *Center for Research on Educational Accountability and Teacher Evaluation (CREATE)*, Western Michigan University (Kalamazoo, MI 49008), 1992.

Bayless, David L., *et al*., "The Need and Prospects for Developing a New Quality Improvement Model of Student Performance and Self-Evaluation of Teacher Performance: Adapting W. Edwards Deming's SPC Model." *Ibid.* (An expanded version of paper presented at the 4/91 AERA Meeting, Chicago.)

Bayless, David L., Massaro, Gabriel A., Legum, Stanley, *et al*., "A Plan to Adapt W. Edwards Deming's Quality Management Theory to an Educational Environment." *WESTAT, Inc.* (Rockville, MD), April 1992.

Bell, Barbara M. "Tales and Travails from the Cutting Edge." *Quality Network News* (AASA), Vol. 2, No. 3, May 1992.

Bender, Robert H., "If You Can Count It, You Can Improve It: Total Quality Transformation Tools Sculpt Better Handle on System." *The School Administrator*, November 1991.

Blankenstein, Alan M., "Lessons From Enlightened Corporations." *Educational Leadership*, March 1992.

Boe, Erling E., "The Entrepreneurial Restructuring of Public Education: School Incentives and the Merit School Component." *Loc. cit.*

Bonstingl, John J., "Total Quality in Education: A Prescription for Improving Our Schools." *The Early Adolescence Magazine*, Vol.V, No. 6, July-August, 1991.

Bonstingl, John J., "Deming's Fourteen Points Applied to Companies and Schools." (Available from the author, PO Box 810, Columbia, MD 21044).

Branson, Robert K., and Johnson, F. Craig, "Total Quality Management: The New Look At Accountability, School Improvement Programs and Site-Based Management." Center for Educational Technology (Florida State University), July 1991.

Caplan, Frank, "The National Educational Quality Initiative: Its History and Status." *Quality Progress*, October 1992.

Castle, Shari and Watts, Gary D., "Temporal Tensions:The Tyranny of Time." *Doubts & Certainties: A Forum on School Transformation* (National Education Association, Center for Innovation, Washington, DC), Vol. VII, No. 2, October 1992.

Cho, Fujio, "Today's Educated Workforce." Presented at 1992 Convention, the Association of School Administrators, San Diego, CA, February 20, 1992. (Copies available from AASA, Arlington, VA.) (Mr. Cho is President/CEO, Toyota Manufacturing USA, Inc., Georgetown, KY.)

Christensen, Delores, "Total Quality in the High School Classroom: Applying the Continuous Improvement Process In Education." (Available from Janet M. Gandy, Arizona Department of Education, 1535 W. Jefferson, Phoenix, AZ 85007.)

Clark, Sandra, "Links Between Strategic Planning and Quality." *Quality Network News* (AASA), Vol. 2, No. 5, September 1992.

Covey, Stephen R., "Basic Principles of Total Quality." *Executive Excellence,* May 1990.

DePalma, Anthony, "Principals of Success: Should the Model be the Corporate Manager or the Curriculum Leader?" *New York Times,* "Quarterly Education Supplement," November 3, 1991.

Downey, Carolyn, "Can the Lone Ranger Join the Dream Team?" *Quality Network News* (AASA), Vol. 2, No. 5, September 1992.

Freeston, Kenneth R., "Other People's Theories." *Education Week,* January 22, 1992.

Freeston, Kenneth R., "Getting Started with TQM." *Educational Leadership,* November 1992.

Freeston, Kenneth R., "Anticipate Obstacles To Change." *Quality Network News* (AASA), Vol.2, No. 4, July 1992.

Fusco, Armand A., "Beyond TQM to TQMS." *Ibid,* Vol. 2, No. 6, November 1992.

Gagne, James, "America's Quality Coaches." (Available from Dow-America, Quality Performance Department, Midland, MI.)

Galagan, Patricia A., "Joining Forces: Business and Education Take On Competitiveness." *Training & Development Journal,* July 1988.

Galagan, Patricia A., "Beyond Hierarchy: The Search for High Performance." *Training & Development*, August 1992.

Gangel, David M., "Translate Quality Into 'Educationese'." *Quality Network News* (AASA), Vol. 1, No. 2, November 1991.

Gangel, David M., "Pick the Low Fruit First." *Ibid.*, Vol. 2, No. 3, May 1992.

George, Gary, and Trigg, Tom, "A Look Inside A District's Quality Toolbox." *Ibid.*, Vol. 2, No. 4, July 1992.

Glasser, William, "The Quality School." *Phi Delta Kappan*, February 1990.

Glasser, William, "The Quality School Curriculum." *Ibid.*, May 1992.

Greenhouse, Steven, "The Coming Crisis of the American Workforce: Are Urban Youth Prepared for Rigors of Work in the 21st Century?" *New York Times*, June 7, 1992.

Halder, Robert, "Arm Yourself for the Battle of the Bureaucracy." *Quality Network News* (AASA), Vol. 2, No. 4, July 1992.

Hammond, Jane, "'Barrier Bashers' Welcome Here." *Ibid.*, Vol. 1, No. 1, September 1991.

Heilmann, Ronald L., "Education's Critical Role in America's Competitiveness." *Actionline* (The Automotive Industry Action Group, 26200 Lahser Road, Suite 200, Smithfield, MI 48034), September 1989.

Heilmann, Ronald L., "Quality in the Schools: A Power Education." *Ibid.*, September 1990.

Helfrich, John E., "New York District Wins Quality Award." *Quality Network News* (AASA), Vol. 2, No. 5, September 1992.

Herman, Jerry J., "Total Quality Management Basics: TQM Comes To School." *School Business Affairs*, Vol. 58, No. 4, April 1, 1992.

Holcomb, Edie L., McIsaac, Donald M., *et al.*, "The Use of Technology in School Improvement: Building and Implementing Effective Management Information Systems." *Proceedings AASA Annual Meeting*, New Orleans, LA, February 1991.

Holly, Peter, "Catching the Wave of the Future: Moving Beyond School Effectiveness by Redesigning Schools." *School Organization* (Carfax Publishing Co., Hopkinton, MA), Vol. 10, No. 32-3, 1990.

Horine, Julie E., "Public School Districts Implementing Total Quality Management." National Survey: Final Report:NASA/ASEE Summer Faculty, *Fellowship, University of Mississippi*, October 1991.

Horine, Julie E., "Reading, Writing and Quality Tools." *Quality Progress*, October, 1992.

Houlihan, G. Thomas, "Planning a Total Quality School District in Johnston County, North Carolina." *Proceedings, Fourth Annual Hunter Conference on Quality*, April 10-12, 1991.

Houlihan, G. Thomas, "Patience, Focus Needed for District Transformation." *Quality Network News* (AASA), Vol. 1, No. 1, September 1991.

Hunter, Bruce, "What Does TQM Mean for Policy?" *Quality Network News* (AASA), *loc. cit.*

Jenkins, Kenneth D.,Ward, Michael E., and Phillips, Judy, "Brokers,

Barriers and Bridges: A Study In Central Office Restructuring." *Annual Conference* (AASA), San Diego, CA, February 1992.

Johnston, Denise A. and Neal, Sue, "Understanding Variation: Creating Learning Partnerships with Public Schools." *Proceedings, Fourth Annual Hunter Conference on Quality*, April 10-12, 1991.

Joiner, Brian L., "Goals: Use With Caution." *Quality Network News* (AASA), Vol. 2, No. 1, January 1992.

Kelly, Tricia, "Elementary Quality". *Quality Progress* (ASQC), October 1991.

Kimple, James A., Jr., Murray, Dennis, *et al.*, "Applying Quality Principles in Public Education." *Transactions 1991 ASQC Quality Congress*, Milwaukee, WI, May 1991.

Leonard, James F., "How to Use Data in the Total Quality School." *Quality Network News* (AASA), Vol. 1, No. 2, November 1991.

Levinson, Eliot, "Will Technology Transform Education or Will the Schools Co-opt Technology?." *Phi Delta Kappan*, Vol. 72, No. 2, October 1990.

Lezotte, Lawrence W., "Base School Improvement on What We Know About Effective Schools." *American School Board Journal*, Vol. 176, No. 8, August 1989.

McCleod, Willis B., Spencer, Brenda A., and Hairston, Leon T., "Towards A System of Quality Management Applying the Deming Approach to the Educational Setting." *Spectrum: Journal of Educational Research & Information*, Vol. 10, No. 2, Spring 1992.

Melvin, Charles A., III, "School Restructuring the Deming Way." *Proceedings Fourth Annual Hunter Conference on Quality*, Madison, WI, April 10-12, 1991.

Melvin, Charles A., III, "Restructuring Schools by Applying Deming's Management Theories." *Journal of Staff Development*, Volume 12, No. 3, Summer 1991.

Melvin, Charles A., III, "Translating Deming's 14 Points for Education: A Wisconsin Consortium Turns to Total Quality System Improvements." *The School Administrator*, November 1991.

Melvin, Charles A., III, "Quality Improvement the Deming Way." *Wisconsin School News*, October 1991.

Miller, Richard D., "Quality Management, You're No Silver Bullet." *Quality Network News* (AASA), Vol. 2, No. 3, May 1992.

Moen, Ronald D., "The Deming Philosophy for Improving the Educational Process." Presented at the Third Annual International Deming Users Group Conference, Cincinnati, OH, August 22, 1989; revised May 25, 1991.

Mt. Edgecumbe High School, *Continuous Improvement Process: Information Packet*. (Available from Mt. Edgecumbe High School, 1330 Seward Ave., Sitka, AK 99835.)

Munro, Roderick A., "Using Quality Improvement to Improve Quality Training." *Journal of Quality & Participation*, Vol. 14, No. 6, December 1991.

Negron, Edith, "Working to Make Learning Job 1." *New York Newsday*, March 1, 1991.

Nyland, Larry, "One District's Journey to Success With Outcomes-Based Education." *The School Administrator,* November 1991.

Olson, Lynn, "Schools Getting Swept Up In Current of Business's 'Quality' Movement." *Education Week,* Vol. XI, No. 25, March, 1992.

Reed, John R., "Partners in Quality: Business and Education." *Quality Network News* (AASA), Vol. 2, No. 1, January 1992.

Rhodes, Lewis A., "Why Quality Is Within Our Grasp . . . If We Reach." *The School Administrator,* November 1990.

Rhodes, Lewis A., "Beyond Your Beliefs: Quantum Leaps Toward Quality Schools." *Ibid.,* December 1990.

Rhodes, Lewis A., "Barriers on the Road to Quality." *Quality Network News* (AASA), Vol. 1, No. 1, September 1991.

Rhodes, Lewis A., "On the Road to Quality." *Educational Leadership,* March 1992.

Rhodes, Lewis A., "Stop and Smell the Blooms of Critics." *Quality Network News* (AASA) Vol. 2, No. 4, July 1992.

Rocheleau, Larrae, "One Hundred Days of TQM Training at the Alaska State Department of Education." Presentation at the October, 1991, *Alliance '91 Conference* sponsored by the Galileo Quality Institute and Franklin Pierce College at Bretton Woods, NH. (Available from Mt. Edgecumbe High School, 1330 Seward Ave., Sitka, AK 99835.)

Rocheleau, Larrae, "Mt. Edgecumbe's Venture in Quality: How One Superintendent Learned the Difference Between Managing and Leading." *The School Administrator,* November 1991.

Rossmiller, Richard A., and Holcomb, Edie L., "The Effective Schools Process for Continuous School Improvement." *Proceedings, 17th Annual Professional Development Conference, the National Council of States,* San Diego, CA, November 1992. (Available from Dr. Rossmiller, NCES R&D, University of Wisconsin, Suite 685, 1025 W. Johnson Street, Madison, WI 53706.)

Salvia, Anthony A., "QC Education: Some Questions (The Academic Community has Some Responsibility to Respond to Societal Need and U.S. Society Needs Quality Majors)." *Quality Progress,* August 1987.

Sarazen, J. Stephen, "Schools Build In Quality." *Quality Progress,* January 1989.

Sarazen, J. Stephen, "Continuous Improvement and Innovation." *Journal of Quality & Participation,* Vol.14, No. 5, September 1991.

Schargel, Franklin P., "Promoting Quality in Education." *Vocational Education J.,* November 1991.

Schargel, Franklin P., "School Changes Way of Doing Business." *WORK AMERICA* (National Alliance of Business), Vol. 9, No. 1, March 1992.

Senge, Peter M., "The Fifth Discipline: The Art and Practice of the Learning Organization: A Conversation with Peter Senge." 1990. (Available from Innovation Associates, Framingham, MA 01701.)

Sharp-Burk, Zona, "Partners in Action!" *Quality Network News* (AASA), Vol. 1, No. 2, November 1991.

Siu-Runyan, Yvonne and Heart, Sally Joy, "Management Manifesto:

Deming's 14 Principles Have Revitalized Japanese Industry and They Can Form the Basis for Restructuring the Education Workplace As Well." *The Executive Educator*, January 1992.

Stampen, Jacob O., "Improving the Quality of Education: W. Edwards Deming and Effective Schools." *Contemporary Education Review*, Vol. 3, No. 3, Winter 1987.

Stephens, Gail M., "Link Up For Total Quality Schooling." *Quality Network News* (AASA), Vol. 1, No. 2, November 1991.

Suro, Robert, "Teachers to the Front: Local School Districts, Not Education Schools, Train Staff In Curriculum and Class Management." *New York Times*, "Quarterly Education Supplement," November 3, 1991.

Tribus, Myron, "TQM at the Grass Roots." (Available from Dr. Tribus c/o Exergy, Inc., Hayward, CA 94541.)

Tribus, Myron, "Quality Management In Education." *Prepared for the Third Annual Symposium on the Role of Academia In National Competitiveness & TQM*, Lehigh University, July 1992. (Available from Dr. Tribus c/o Exergy, Inc., Hayward, CA 94541.)

Tribus, Myron, "The Application of Quality Management Principles in Education at Mt. Edgecumbe High School, Sitka, Alaska." November 1990. (Available from Dr. Tribus c/o Exergy, Inc., Hayward, CA 94541.)

Tribus, Myron, "Above All, Culture Change Is An Education Process; Creating the Competitive Organization." *Journal for Quality & Participation*, Vol. 15, No. 3, June 1992.

Tsuda, Yoshikazu, and DeBie, R.K., "Education in Vocational School." *Proceedings 35th EOQ Conference*, Prague, June 1991.

Tucker, Sue, "Why Total Quality Management Can Help Transform America's Schools." 1992. (Available from GOAL/QPC, Methuen, MA 01844.)

MISCELLANEOUS

National Alliance of Business, "Quality in Education: Creating High Performance Schools." *Proceedings, 6th Annual Business/Education Forum*, Cincinnati, OH, March 25-27, 1992. Sponsor: The Center for Excellence in Education, National Alliance of Business, 1201 New York Avenue, NW, Washington, DC 20005-3917.

Leaders' Workshop on Total Quality Learning. Co-sponsors: The National Learning Foundation and the National Education Association, Washington, DC, April 13-14, 1992. Information from the Learning Laboratories Initiative, NEA, 1201 16th Street, NW, Washington, DC 20036-3290.

"K-12 Track." *Proceedings, Third Annual Symposium on the Role of Academia in National Competitiveness & TQM: Quality in Action in Academe*, July 28-31, 1992. Sponsor: The Quality in Education Consortium (QIEC). Proceedings available from the Iacocca Institute, Mountaintop Campus, Lehigh University, Bethlehem, PA 18015.

"Benchmarking and Improvement Strategies for Education in Kindergarten through Grade 12." *Conference on TQM in K-12*, Chicago, IL, November 12-13, 1992. Sponsor: The International Quality & Productivity Center, Penton Publications, International Quality & Productivity Center, P.O. Box 43115, Upper Montclair, NJ 07043-7155.

Governor Ann Richards' National Invitational Conference on Total Quality Management and the National Education Goals, Quality and Education: Critical Linkages, November 9-10, 1992. *Outcomes Report* available from State of Texas, Governor's Office of Education Policy, P.O. Box 12428, Austin, TX 78701, Attn: Robin Roberts.

Proceedings, First International Conference on Standards & Quality in Education and Training, December 13-16, 1992. Co-sponsors: The University of Oklahoma and the National Educational Quality Initiative, Inc. (NEQI). Proceedings available from the Center for Standards and Quality in Education, University of Oklahoma, 555 East Constitution, Norman, Oklahoma 73037-0005.

"Total Quality & Systemic Change Track." *Proceedings, 125th Annual Convention*, the American Association of School Administrators (AASA), Orlando, FL, February 12-15, 1993. For information contact AASA, 1801 N. Moore Street, Arlington, VA 22209-9988.

The Total Quality and Site-Based Management Journal. Fall 1992. (Publisher: The National Center to Save Our Schools, P.O. Box 948, Westbury, NY 11590.)

The Journal for Quality and Participation, Vol. 16, No. 1, Jan/Feb 1993. (AQP, 801-B West 8th Street, Cincinnati, OH 45203-1607.)

— Appendix C —
AUTHOR
DIRECTORY

Mr. Paul Bailey
Business Planning Manager
Sterling Chemical Company
1200 Smith Street, Suite 1900
Houston, TX 77002-4312
713-654-9537

Mr. Keith Byrom
Manager, Quality Process
H. B. Zachry Company
PRO. Box 21130
San Antonio, TX 78221
210-922-1213

Dr. Richard D. DeCosmo, President
Ms. Susanna Staas, Quality Coordinator
Delaware County Community College
Media, PA 19063
215-359-5325

Dr. William T. Hartman, Director
Center for Total Quality Schools

Penn State University
308 Rackley Building
University Park, PA 16802
814-865-2318

Dr. John E. Helfrich, Superintendent
Mrs. Dorothy Vienne, Principal
Kenmore-Town of Tonawanda Schools
Union Free School District
1500 Clovin Blvd.
Tonawanda, NY 14223
716-874-8400

Ms. Linda Hanson
Principal
McAdams Junior High
4007 Video Street
Dickinson, TX 77539
713-534-6886

Mr. David P. Langford
President
Langford Quality Education
P.O. Box 80133
Billings, MT 59108-0133
406-652-7502

Dr. Susan Leddick
President
Profound Knowledge Resources, Inc.
16775 Addison Road, L.B. 11
Suite 110
Dallas, TX 75248
214-407-0020

Ms. Betty L. McCormick
President
Critical Linkages Consulting
802 Terrace Mountain Dr.
Austin, TX 78746
512-329-0919

Mr. Lewis A. Rappaport, Principal
Mr. Franklin P. Schargel, Quality Coordinator
George Westinghouse Vo-Tech High School
105 Johnson Street
Brooklyn, NY 11201
718-625-6130

Mr. Lewis A. Rhodes
Associate Executive Director
American Association of School Administrators
1801 North Moore Street
Arlington, VA 22209
703-875-0733

Dr. David Romstad, Superintendent
Mr. Michael Jamison, Elementary Principal
Parkview School District
719 St. Lawrence Avenue
Jamesville, WI 53545
608-879-2352

Mr. Mel Silberberg
Principal
Silberberg Associates
17 Front Street
P.O. Box 4551
Salem, MA 01970-4551
508-740-9132

Dr. Joseph A. Spagnolo, Jr.
Superintendent of Public Instruction
Mr. James C. Chancey, Jr.
Lead Specialist Teacher Education
Virginia Department of Education
P.O. Box 2120
Richmond, VA 23216-2120
804-225-2737

Dr. Jane A. Stallings, Dean
Dr. Bryan R. Cole, Associate Professor
College of Education
Texas A & M University

College Station, TX 77843-4226
409-845-2716

Ms. Betsy Van Dorn, Editor-in-Chief
Ms. Jesseca Timmons, Editor
The Educational Publishing Group, Inc.
The Statler Building, Suite 1215
20 Park Plaza
Boston, MA 02116
617-542-6500